Springer Series on Comparative Treatments for Psychological Disorders

Arthur Freeman, EdD, ABPP, Series Editor

Arthur Freeman, EdD, ABPP, received his doctorate from Teachers College-Columbia University. He is board certified in clinical, family, and behavioral psychology by the American Board of Professional Psychology. Dr. Freeman has published more than 40 books and over 60 chapters and journal articles on various aspects of cognitive behavior therapy. He has lectured extensively in the United States and in 20 other countries in recent years. He is past president of the Association for Advancement of Behavior Therapy. Dr. Freeman is currently Dean of the School of Professional Studies and Professor of Psychology at the University of St. Francis in Fort Wayne, Indiana. His work has been translated into German, Dutch, Swedish, Japanese, Spanish, Italian, Bulgarian, Portuguese, and Chinese.

Donna M. Martin, PsyD, is an instructor and director of the academic support program at the Philadelphia College of Osteopathic Medicine, where she received her doctorate in clinical psychology. In her present position she works closely with medical students and graduate students to enhance both their successful performance and to remediate problems that arise in the graduate student population. She is currently involved with institutional outcome research to measure the effectiveness of this program's, and the school's other various interventions, on success in the first year of medical school. Dr. Martin is also manager of the Center for Brief Therapy, the PCOM training clinic, and is involved in the supervision and training of psychology practicum students and interns. She has sat on the board of the American Foundation for Suicide Prevention. Dr. Martin has published several articles and chapters, and has recently edited and co-authored a chapter in the second edition of Cognition and Psychotherapy with Arthur Freeman, EdD, Michael Mahoney, PhD, and Paul DeVito, PhD. (Springer Publishing 2004).

Mark H. Stone, PsyD, is a member of the Doctoral Care Faculty and a Distinguished Service Professor. Dr. Stone earned his BA and BM at North Park University, in Chicago, Illinois, his MM at the Chicago Musical College, and his Diplomate in Clinical Psychology at Forest Institute of Professional Psychology, Springfield, Missouri. He is a Diplomate and Fellow of the American Board of Professional Psychology and School Psychology and of the American Board of Medical Psychotherapists. Dr. Stone is a Certified Supervisor and Alcohol and Other Drug Abuse (AODA) counselor for Community Services for Drug and Alcohol Abuse (CSADC). He teaches courses in research methods, statistics, and psychometrics, assessment of dementia, and other neuropsychological topics. His additional interests include Rasch measurement, data analysis, attention and memory, treatment of sex offenders, psychotherapy supervision, and organizational consulting.

Comparative Treatments for Borderline Personality Disorder

Arthur Freeman, EdD, ABPP
Mark H. Stone, PsyD
Donna Martin, PsyD
Editors

Springer Series on
Comparative Treatments for
Psychological Disorders

Springer Publishing Company, Inc.
11 West 42nd Street, 15th Floor
New York, NY 10036

Acquisitions Editor: Sheri W. Sussman
Production Editor: Betsy Day
Cover design by Joanne Honigman

04 05 06 07 08 / 5 4 3 2 1

Library of Congress Cataloging-in-Publication Data

Comparative treatments for borderline personality disorder / edited by Arthur Freeman, Mark H. Stone, Donna Martin.
    p. cm. — (Springer series on comparative treatments for psychological disorders)
    Includes bibliographical references and index.
    ISBN 0-8261-4835-2
    1. Borderline personality disorder. 2. Borderline personality disorder—Treatment. I. Freeman, Arthur, 1942– II. Stone, Mark H. III. Martin, Donna M. (Donna Marie), 1954– IV. Series.
RC569.5.B67C655 2005
616.85'85206—dc22   2004025029

Printed in the United States of America by Integrated Book Technology.

Contents

Contributors

David M. Allen, MD, is Associate Professor of Psychiatry and Director of Psychiatric Residency Training at the University of Tennessee Center for Health Sciences, Memphis, Tennessee.

Jack Apsche, EdD, is Professor of Psychology at Regent University, Virginia Beach, Virginia.

Andrea Bloomgarden, PhD, is Adjunct Assistant Professor of Clinical Psychology and Practicum Coordinator at the Philadelphia College of Osteopathic Medicine, Philadelphia, Pennsylvania.

Anne Boos, PhD, is Professor in the Department of Psychology of the Technische Universität, Dresden, Germany

Windy Dryden, PhD, is Professor of Counseling at Goldsmiths College, London, England, and a consultant at the Albert Ellis Institute in New York City.

Jill Ehrenreich, PhD, is Research Assistant Professor and Director of the Child and Adolescent Fear and Anxiety Treatment Program at Boston University's Center for Anxiety and Related Disorders, Boston, Massachusetts.

Arthur Freeman, EdD, is Professor of Psychology and Dean of the School of Professional Studies at the University of Saint Francis, Fort Wayne, Indiana.

Gina M. Fusco, PsyD, is Adjunct Assistant Professor of Clinical Psychology at the Philadelphia College of Osteopathic Medicine, Philadelphia, Pennsylvania, Adjunct Professor at Chestnut Hill College, also in Philadelphia, and Clinical Director of The Pines Treatment Center, Northeast, Pennsylvania.

Nicole M. Hoffman, PsyD, is a core faculty member at the Adler School of Professional Psychology, Chicago, Illinois.

M. David Liberman, PhD, is in private practice in Chicago, Illinois, and an Assistant Professor at Chicago Medical School.

Donna M. Martin, PsyD, is Assistant Professor of Clinical Psychology at the Philadelphia College of Osteopathic Medicine, Philadelphia, Pennsylvania.

Mark A. Reinecke, PhD, is Professor of Psychology and Director of the Department of Psychology in the Department of Psychiatry at the School of Medicine of Northwestern University, Evanston, Illinois.

Liliana Rusansky-Drob, PsyD, is a child clinical psychologist on the staff of Woodhull Hospital, Brooklyn, New York.

Mervin R. Smucker, PhD, is Professor in the Department of Psychiatry at the Medical College of Wisconsin, Milwaukee, Wisconsin.

Mark H. Stone, EdD, is Provost-emeritus and a core faculty member at the Adler School of Professional Psychology, Chicago, Illinois.

Acknowledgments

This volume emerged as part of the Springer Series on Comparative Treatments of Psychological Disorders. As the editors of this volume we are indebted to the staff of Springer Publishing for their help, direction, encouragement, and forbearance. This is especially true of Sheri W. Sussman, Senior Vice President, Editorial. It was Bill Tucker's vision that helped to develop the series generally and Sheri's on this volume specifically.

We wish to thank the contributors who gave of their valuable time and clinical acumen. Their contributions have resulted in what we believe to be a comprehensive comparison of some of the most widely practiced interventions for the treatment of Borderline Personality Disorder. Our contributors have carefully examined the case of Linda and applied their theoretical and therapeutic skills toward developing a conceptual framework, a treatment direction, and a set of interventions that are designed to help the patient to better cope.

You, the reader, must be acknowledged for your interest and investment in treating this often maligned and underserved patient group. You are part of the front-line troops who will ultimately be in the consulting room with the patient. Virtually all of our contributors serve both as clinicians and as teachers. Our students are to be thanked because it is by their questions that our clinical insights have grown.

Our patients have trusted us to help them. Some we have helped more than others, but we wish to acknowledge their contribution to this volume. We have grown as clinicians by our work as therapists.

Finally, we wish to thank our teachers, mentors, and supervisors, who have offered to us the distillation of their training, knowledge, and experience that we now offer as a synthesis in this volume.

Arthur Freeman
Mark H. Stone
Donna M. Martin

1

A Review of Borderline Personality Disorder

Arthur Freeman, Mark Stone, Donna Martin, and Mark Reinecke

INTRODUCTION

Words and phrases sometimes acquire an emotional charge or associated meaning and therefore come to represent something different than their original or intended meaning. For example, the terms *idiot, imbecile,* and *moron* were not originally pejorative terms but were legitimate clinical diagnostic terms for levels of intellectual ability.

Clinical psychology has been a fertile breeding ground for such terms. *Personality disorder* has come to have a pejorative meaning, and within that broad rubric, few categories seem to strike as much fear into the hearts of clinicians as does the term *borderline personality disorder.* Merely mentioning to a fellow clinician that your new patient is a *borderline* virtually guarantees a sigh of knowing sympathy, even absent any additional details. Yet because *borderline* is an emotionally charged term, it may lead to a less-than-accurate view of the situation. Clinicians will most likely picture a patient, probably a woman, who is erratic, unreasonably demanding, impulsive, self-injurious, relationship-needy, yet relationship-aversive. Beyond its meaning in diagnosis, the term *borderline* implies a syndrome, a level of functioning, a dynamic constellation, a prognostic statement, and an insult and accusation. When a patient is difficult to treat, sometimes psychotic, resistant, unstable, or insulting to the therapist, the term *borderline,* accurate or not, comes to mind.

1

Borderline personality disorder (BPD) has become one of the most researched of the personality disorders (Trull, 2001). The term *borderline* was originally coined by Stern in 1938 in an effort to describe a group of patients who usually appeared neurotic but were prone to brief psychotic experiences. Stern conceptualized these individuals as existing between neurosis and psychosis—literally on the borderline, and sometimes finding themselves "south of the border." These patients often have a long psychiatric history, suggesting previous therapeutic failure and an interpersonal style portending difficulty in establishing the working alliance. It is estimated that 2–3% of the general population may suffer from this disorder, making it the most commonly diagnosed personality disorder (Trull, 2001). Individuals with this diagnosis account for about one-half of patients with personality disorders seen in clinical settings. BPD is diagnosed in 11% of psychiatric outpatients and 19% of psychiatric inpatients (Rathbun, 2002). These patients often have a history of sexual and/or physical abuse or have suffered significant early losses. There is an above-chance level that there are mood disorders and substance abuse among family members, and BPD patients often have an erratic and depressed mother and a father who was absent or who had a major character problem (Rathbun, 2002; Soloff, Lynch, & Kelly, 2002; Trull, 2001). In clinical settings, 40–76% of adults with BPD report childhood sexual abuse, and 25–73% report childhood physical abuse (Zanarini, Roser, Frankenburg, & Hennen, 2000). A history of childhood abuse discriminates adult, adolescent, and child patients with BPD from patients with other Axis II disorders (Paris, Zweig-Frank, Bond, & Guzder, 1994). This disorder is five times more common in the first-degree relatives of affected persons (Rathbun, 2002).

The accumulating research has shed some light on the etiology and prevalence of BPD, but, as with most research and statistics, these facts and figures are not universally accepted or supported. For example, the often-quoted gender difference has come under recent scrutiny. According to Zlotnick, Rothschild, and Zimmerman (2002), the literature in the last decade on the relationship between gender and borderline personality disorder had caused more controversy than clarity, and published studies thus far have reported contradictory findings. These researchers cite Becker's (2000) characterization of borderline personality disorder as the "bad girl" of psychiatric labels because the diagnosis is presumed to be significantly higher in women. According to Becker, this amounts to sex bias in the diagnosis of BPD.

Treatment of BPD is challenging, and these patients account for a substantial proportion of mental health care consumption (Rinne, van den Brink, Wouters, & van Dyck, 2002). Patients suffering from BPD exhibit a broad range of symptoms and problems, and with the intensity of patients' reactions, anger, and impulse control problems and their rapidly changing moods, BPD may be the most challenging and complex personality disorder to treat (Layden, Newman, Freeman, & Byers Morse, 1993; Freeman, Pretzer, Fleming, & Simon, 1990, 2004; Beck, Freeman, Davis, & Associates, 2003; Freeman & Fusco, 2004). These patients represent a large segment of the mental health population and consume a substantial proportion of mental health services (Rinne, et al., 2002).

DEVELOPMENT OF BORDERLINE PERSONALITY DISORDER

Although the causes of BPD are not known, a number of biological and psychosocial variables have been associated with risk for developing this disorder (Paris, 1993, 1994, 1999; Trull, Sher, Minks-Brown, Durbin, & Bur, 2000; Zanarini & Frankenberg, 1997). Many individuals with BPD report histories of neglect, trauma, and loss as children, and a significant percentage have been sexually abused. Studies also suggest that neural systems implicated in the regulation of arousal in response to threat may be affected in individuals with BPD. The authors agree with Paris (1999) that BPD can best be understood as stemming from the interaction of genetic, biological, social, and psychological factors. The cognitive-developmental model attempts to incorporate findings from each of these domains. It is, as such, a biopsychosocial, diathesis-stress model. Each of these domains is examined below.

Although research is limited, studies suggest that genetic and biological factors may be associated with risk for BPD. For example, a number of emotional characteristics associated with BPD (e.g., affective lability, neuroticism, and behavioral impulsivity) appear to be heritable, at least in part (Jang, Livesley, Vernon, & Jackson, 1996; Lively, Jang, Schroeder, & Jackson, 1993; Paris, 2000; Plomin, Defries, McClearn, & Rutter, 1997; Silk, 2000). It is worth acknowledging, however, that linkage and adoption studies have not, to date, identified specific genetic vulnerabilities for BPD. Rather, it appears that genetic factors may contribute to the development of personality dimensions associated with BPD.

There is evidence, as well, that neurological factors may be associated with BPD. Positron-emission tomography (PET) studies, for example, suggest that individuals with BPD may manifest decreased metabolism in the prefrontal cortex (for reviews, see Adams, Bernat, & Luscher, 2001; Paris, 1999), an area of the brain implicated in executive function, affect regulation, and behavioral inhibition. Whether these metabolic differences are specific to BPD or are characteristic of other conditions is not yet known. Moreover, their role in the etiology of BPD also is not clear. That said, it is possible that individuals with BPD manifest deficits in the development of neurocognitive systems associated with emotional and behavioral regulation (Silk, 1994). Factors associated with vulnerability to BPD are summarized below:

- Behavioral impulsivity
- Neuroticism/negative affectivity
- Emotional lability
- Familial history of depression, impulse control disorder, substance abuse
- Chaotic home environment
- Disorganized attachment
- Severe or chronic abuse/neglect
- Separation/early loss

DEVELOPMENT OF AFFECT REGULATION

The cognitive-developmental model posits that change processes in psychotherapy are essentially similar to those in normative development. The cognitive developmental therapist, as such, serves as a scaffold, guiding and supporting the development of affect regulation skills. This is accomplished by providing support, serving as a resource to buffer the patient from the effects of potentially traumatic life events, and guiding the development of more sophisticated emotion regulation skills through modeling and guided practice.

The unstable, intense, and volatile emotions that characterize individuals with BPD contribute to risk for impulsive behavior (Eisenberg & Fabes, 1998) and may lead them to view themselves as flawed, damaged, or unlovable. A reciprocal relationship may exist, as such, between deficits in affect regulation and the development of negative beliefs about the self. Strategic cognitive-behavioral techniques, such as rational responding and a developmental review of evidence, are used to counter negative views about the self. It can be helpful as well to use experiences within the therapeutic relationship to challenge negative beliefs about the self.

As noted, *borderline* was originally used to refer to clients who presented both neurotic and psychotic types of symptoms and who were thus seen as falling on the border between neurotic and psychotic disorders. In common usage, the term often meant "nearly psychotic" or "somewhat psychotic." In fact, these patients might be more appropriately diagnosed at times as experiencing a brief reactive psychosis.

BORDERLINE AS A SYNDROME

The borderline syndrome generally implies a diminished capacity for work. Patients may have work-related difficulties or low energy levels that preclude them from successfully working. There is a high degree of impulsivity and patients may act-out or act-in without considering the consequences to themselves or to others. There may even be mild or brief psychotic-appearing episodes in which patients act in ways contrary to reality, such as believing a relationship is more intimate than it is or demanding behaviors from others that will likely not be offered. Patients' behavior may be (or appear to be) manipulative. There may be self-injurious threats or actions that have the effect of being demanding of attention or reaction from others. There will often be a rapidly shifting identification or self-percept in the presence of a love object. This shift may be from wanting/demanding the attention and affection of the love-object to denial and rejection of that individual.

The disturbances in relationships can often be traced back to the family of origin. These experiences are usually played out throughout life, as well as in multiple successive therapeutic experiences.

The patient with BPD can be viewed as hyperreactive. Stone (1993) offered the following conceptual diagram (see figure 1.1) as a way of explaining the hyperresponsiveness, hyperreactivity, and exquisite sensitivity of the patient with BPD.

A graphic metaphor for the sensitivity of the patient with BPD is the following (see figure 1.2).

Patients with BPD see themselves as perched precipitously on the peak of a mountain. They are vulnerable to every wisp of air and may, at any moment, be sent crashing to their destruction. All of their energy

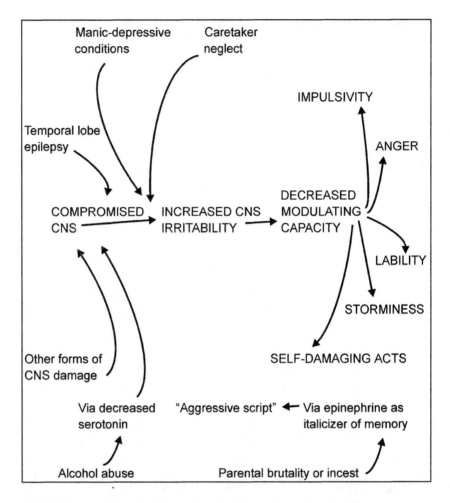

FIGURE 1.1   The etiology of borderline personality disorder.

is expended on maintaining their balance, with little left over for the niceties of reasonable social conventions. They may, therefore, appear rude, curt, or overly demanding because all of their behavior is focused on the single intent of survival against what they perceive as powerful and almost continuous adverse situational pressures. They lack a stable base from which to operate.

The hyperreactivity and hypersensitivity often revolve around the issue of abandonment. In fact, the patient with BPD may become en-

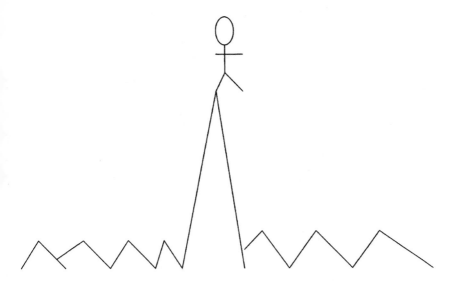

FIGURE 1.2   Graphic metaphor for the BPD patient.

raged or suicidal when threatened with real or perceived abandonment. It is often at this point when the patient may appear to be out of touch with reality.

Patients' relationship with reality will sometimes differ from the norm, though patients with BPD usually have adequate reality testing and therefore do not meet the criteria for psychotic reactions. This is often seen as their holding overvalued ideas without delusions but with disturbances in internalized images of self and others. Patients' sense of self may appear quite diffuse, and they are likely to have significant boundary issues. These boundary issues are bidirectional in that patients are hyperreactive to violations of their own boundaries but often unaware of when they cross into the personal space of others. If patients are aware of these boundary crossings, they often explain them as "necessary," for example, "How was I to get your attention unless I called you at 3:00 A.M.?" Patients appear to have poor controls for limiting or tolerating internal (or internalized) stressors, leading to a decrease in adaptive behavior. Their energy is focused on survival, against all odds.

Because patients see their own behavior as reasonable, they tend to externalize their difficulties in effective functioning and may blame others. This other-blaming position makes taking responsibility that much more difficult for patients. Their problems in separation and individuation continually impact their thoughts, feelings, and actions, and these are generally seen as negative or maladaptive.

From a therapeutic perspective, the diagnosis of BPD can also be used as a technique to avoid therapist responsibility and as an explanation for therapeutic failure: "After all, what can one do with a borderline?"

Borderline personality disorder typically emerges in adolescence and becomes most severe in the 20s. About half of patients with BPD spontaneously improve in their 30s and 40s. Failure in education, employment, and relationships is common. Suicide claims 8–10% of patients with borderline personality disorder. These patients present with a wide range of problems and symptoms and are a heterogeneous group of patients with which to work. Even the same patient will present with a wide variety of problems at different times.

ETIOLOGY

When this diagnostic category was first described, the etiology of borderline personality disorder was explained in intrapsychic terms and based on therapists' experiences with individual patients. Expectedly, attention was given primarily to family relationships, primarily to the relationship between the patient and her or his mother. This was based on the dominant psychodynamic theoretical model of human development of the time and the fact that the biological mother or female caretaker most often provided child care. From this perspective, and also from personal experience with these patients, according to Koengsberg, Kernberg, Stone, Appelibaum, Yeoman, and Diamond (2000), clinicians came to certain conclusions: The patient had experienced insufficient mirroring from the mother (Kohut, 1971); had introjected negative aspects of the mother (Kernberg, 1975); and/or had had an ambivalent relationship with a mother that blocked age-appropriate detachment but did not provide age appropriate caring during the "rapprochement-separation" phase of development (Masterson & Rinsley, 1975).

The recent attempts to explain the intense behaviors of BPD through patients' physiology have some early precursors. Kernberg alluded to the biological constitution of the patient as a possible factor that contributed to difficulties, that is, the patient's tendency to have strong needs that were not always well controlled (Koensberg, et al., 2000). Only recently have the possible biological concomitants of this condition received more attention (Coccaro, Silverman, & Klar, 1994; Golomb, Ludolph, Westen, Block, Maurer, & Wiss, 1994).

DIAGNOSTIC ISSUES

The term *borderline* was created to fulfill the need for a diagnostic category, other than psychosis or neurosis, in which to place a group of particularly difficult and complex patients. Based on clinical observation, these patients seemed to display some characteristics of each of these conditions but did not belong in either category. While the patients sometimes had transient breaks with reality, they did not have any of the other characteristics of other well-known psychotic syndromes. In addition, these patients, mostly female, had long-standing characterological difficulties, largely in the areas of impulsivity, interpersonal relationships, identity stability, and depression (Guttman, 2002). Borderline personality disorder was first recognized as a diagnostic category in the third edition of the American Psychiatric Association's *Diagnostic and Statistical Manual of Mental Disorders* in 1980 and was further defined in the revised version in 1987 (American Psychiatric Association, 1987). According to the *Diagnostic and Statistical Manual*, fourth edition, text revision (*DSM-IV-TR*), the most recent edition of this manual (American Psychiatric Association, 2000), its distinguishing characteristics are as follows:

1. Frantic efforts to avoid real or imagined abandonment. *Note:* Do not include suicidal or self-mutilating behavior covered in Criterion 5.
2. A pattern of unstable and intense interpersonal relationships characterized by alternating between extremes of idealization and devaluation.
3. Identity disturbance: markedly and persistently unstable self-image or sense of self.
4. Impulsivity in at least two areas that are potentially self-damaging (e.g., spending, sex, substance abuse, reckless driving, binge eating). *Note:* Do not include suicidal or self-mutilating behavior covered in Criterion 5.
5. Recurrent suicidal behavior, gestures, or threats, or self-mutilating behavior.

6. Affective instability due to a marked reactivity of mood (e.g., intense episodic dysphoria, irritability, or anxiety usually lasting a few hours and only rarely more than a few days).
7. Chronic feelings of emptiness.
8. Inappropriate intense anger or difficulty controlling anger (e.g., frequent displays of temper, constant anger, recurrent physical fights).
9. Transient, stress-related paranoid ideation or severe dissociative symptoms.

Definition of Terms

The development of the *Diagnostic and Statistical Manual* over the last 50 years has allowed professionals to share a language. The criteria sets and the multiaxial diagnostic system starting in 1987 have attempted to add clarity to diagnosis. Part of the difficulty in understanding and using *DSM-IV-TR* has been the lack of clear and specific definitions. Despite what appear to be clear statements, there is still significant room for clinicians to interpret and project their own meanings onto the criteria sets. To try to offer some clarity to the diagnostic scheme of BPD, Freeman and Fusco (2004) added more-specific definitions. The diagnosis of Susan exemplifies the problem. Her two-year relationship ended precipitously. She is depressed, and each day she calls her former boyfriend at 6:00 P.M. and leaves a message on his voicemail. This has gone on for six months. Does this behavior qualify for criterion 1, "Frantic efforts to avoid real or imagined abandonment"? She has made 180 phone calls that have garnered no response, but is that behavior frantic? By definition, the answer is no. Susan's behavior is predictable, annoying, and obsessive, but it is not frantic. Multiple calls to many persons, with clear threats of dangerous actions, such as "If you don't call me, I will kill myself and it will be your fault" would be more in keeping with the criterion.

Criterion 1—Frantic Efforts to Avoid Real or Imagined Abandonment

Definitions

Frantic: Marked by extreme excitement, confusion, and agitation. Synonyms would include *behavior that is frenetic, feverous, or frenzied.*

Abandonment: Having been given up and left alone; the act of forsaking. Synonyms include being deserted or left destitute.

Synthesis

Patients with BPD exhibit behaviors that are frenetic, and intense, powerful, and extreme emotions accompany their perception of real or imagined abandonment. In patients with BPD, the feeling of abandonment is perceived as complete, total, and irreversible. Thus, the desperation associated with the feeling is related to the belief of the finality of the experience as well as the perception of the abandonment.

Criterion 2—A Pattern of Unstable and Intense Interpersonal Relationships Characterized by Alternating Between Extremes of Idealization and Extremes of Devaluation

Definitions

Pattern: A configuration.

Unstable: Not physically or emotionally steady or firm; also, the quality or condition of being erratic and undependable. Synonyms would include *capricious, changeable,* and *insecure.*

Intense: Extreme in degree, strength, or effect; exceptionally great in concentration, power, or force. Synonyms would include *fierce* and *vehement.*

Extreme: Going to great lengths beyond normal limits; severe or radical.

Idealization or *Ideal:* Showing a tendency to envision things in a perfect but unrealistic form; not necessarily in line with reality. Synonyms would include *quixotic, romantic,* and *unrealistic.*

Devaluation: To make less or become less in value. Synonyms would include *to deprecate.*

Synthesis

The BPD patient's emotions and behaviors in relationships are characterized by extremes. There is a concentrated or forceful effect, particularly within the emotional realm of relationships, which impacts both interpersonal and intrapersonal reactions.

The definition of instability captures the capricious and changeable nature of how a patient with BPD vacillates within a relationship. The style of the patient with BPD creates relationships that are erratic in nature. The basic rules that guide such relationships become undependable and vague, and the relationships are continually vulnerable to the erratic shifts associated with instability.

Patients with BPD often experience others in idealized or perfect form. The BPD patient schematically perceives idyllic qualities in the other despite disconfirming evidence that may be obvious and apparent. Others may demonstrate that they are mere mortals, which directly contradicts the idyllic version that the BPD patient perceives. The idealization is unrealistic and inflated, and appears almost superficial.

In interpersonal relationships, the fundamental aspects of this criterion combine such that the patient with BPD experiences erratic, changeable, and forceful perceptions and emotions that vacillate between extremes of idyllic images of the other and a rapid shift to devaluation of the other. This shift can occur very quickly.

Criterion 3—Identity Disturbance: Markedly and Persistently Unstable Self-Image or Sense of Self

Definitions

Identity: Being the same person as one claims to be. Synonyms would include *self.*

Markedly: Noticeable.

Persistent: Unremitting.

Disturbance: Disruption of the establishment of a sense of self that will cause emotional or cognitive disturbance.

Self: An individual's awareness of what contributes to his/her essential nature and distinguishes him/her from all others. Synonyms would include *identity.*

Synthesis

The set of behaviors or personal characteristics of the individual with BPD seem to continue in spite of the difficulty by which an individual is recognizable. BPD patients are at times unable to recognize or distinguish the attributes or idiosyncratic traits particular to their own identity or sense of self. And because they do not always immediately or easily recognize their own sense of self, those with BPD will, at times, assume the traits of those around them as a grounding mechanism. This is largely due to their lack of cohesiveness.

Those with BPD do not have the regular or predictable sense of self or of the emotions that they experience. They may truly not be able to gauge how they feel about a situation or experience or to predict their response in a given situation due to this precarious sense of self. This lack of knowing or experiencing the self often is troubling enough to cause distress. The disturbance often occurs when the patient experiences a stressor or pressure (internal or external); at such times, the patient's lack of cohesion provides few coping resources.

Patients with BPD experience a dramatic and, at times, painful sense of not knowing what constitutes the basic differences that separate them from others. The question of what makes one person similar to or different from another often goes unanswered. This lack of knowing who they are relative to others is experienced as powerful psychic pain or distress.

Criterion 4—Impulsivity in at Least Two Areas That Are Potentially Self-Damaging

Definitions

Impulsivity: Rash; acting without apparent forethought, prompting, or planning and characterized by unthinking boldness and haste. Synonyms would include *spontaneous, rash, unpremeditated, reflex.*

Potentially: Possibility, can be unthinking or unemotional; nonconsequential thinking sometimes unplanned but not necessarily self-damaging.

Self-damaging actions: Actions that are clearly and imminently dangerous. This would exclude smoking, sexual activity, casual drinking, or other activities that, while ultimately damaging, do not carry imminent risk, such as with driving at high speed while intoxicated or unprotected sexual behavior.

Synthesis

Impulsivity involves actions or behaviors that happen without forethought. Patients do not comprehensively process stimuli perceived from the internal and external environments. It is as if the BPD patients' information processors lack a key component to mediate and modulate the message perceived from sensation to actual action. Impulsive behaviors are basic gut responses made in haste without the benefit of applying and associating prior experience, knowledge, and common sense to incoming and ongoing stimuli. These behaviors can be very damaging physically, emotionally, and interpersonally, as well as to patients' self-esteem.

Criterion 5—Recurrent Suicidal Behaviors, Gestures, or Threats, or Self-Mutilating Behavior

Recurrent suicidal behaviors, recurrent suicidal gestures, recurrent suicidal threats, and recurrent self-mutilating are expanded to include self-injurious behaviors.

Definitions

Recurrent: Happening or appearing at regular intervals; cyclical. Synonyms would include *periodic.*

Suicidal: Any act that has the intent to cause death.

Gesture: A token or symbol performed for its effect on the actions or attitudes of others: or an expressive, meaningful body movement. Synonyms would include *indication, motion, signal, sign.*

Self-injurious behavior: Serious damage to oneself through cutting, burning, or use of drugs or other harmful substances, that has a clear and significant impact on physical well-being.

Synthesis

The criterion uses the term *recurrent,* and the definition states that such behaviors are cyclical or occur at regular intervals, spaced one from another. However, for those with BPD, these recurrent episodes are not necessarily sequential or cyclical. What makes treatment very difficult is that there is very little predictability as to when an episode may occur. At certain times, the patient with BPD may experience an increased likelihood of resorting to self-mutilating or suicidal behaviors; however, the episodes are unpredictable. This often thwarts self-monitoring or other therapeutic interventions that might be implemented by the therapist and patient to deter an escalation of symptoms.

The patient with BPD can engage in two types of suicidal behaviors. The first is self-injurious behaviors (SIBs), which are defined as severe and sometimes life-threatening acts that cause damage to the subject's own body. Examples include scratching, cutting, burning, or ingesting medications in larger quantities than prescribed. The intent may not be to actually kill oneself but to receive some type of relief obtained through the gesture. The second type of suicidal behavior is a gesture actually intended as an attempt to end one's life. A characteristic of patients with BPD is impulsivity. If patients with BPD become overwhelmed or unable to regulate their emotional state, they may make impulsive suicidal gestures or injure themselves.

An SIB or a suicidal gesture by a patient with BPD is usually an expression related to some type of emotional state or dysregulation. And as the synonyms imply, some type of signal or sign is underlying the actual action. Potentially, the gesture may indicate an eruption or disruption of mood that escalates into a need for some type of relief that is fulfilled by making a gesture. Again, the gesture may be made as an attempt to decrease subjective distress, or the act may be an actual attempt to end one's life. This type of behavior involves persistent and ruminative suicidal ideation and a plan to harm oneself that may escalate into an attempt.

Criterion 6—Affective Instability Due to a Marked Reactivity of Mood (e.g., Intense Episodic Dysphoria, Irritability, or Anxiety Usually Lasting a Few Hours and Only Rarely More Than a Few Days)

Definitions

Affective: Emotional; evoking a usually strong mental or emotional response or impact.

Reactivity: Vehemently, often fanatically opposing progress or reform; behavioral responses.

Synthesis

Patients with BPD experience emotional and affective dysregulation. Emotions rapidly shift, are intense, and are not easily identified. Fully emotional, BPD patients are also intrapersonally distressed, which inevitably leads to interpersonal distress. Intrapersonally, BPD patients experience episodes of shifting moods consisting of anxiety, depression, and severe dysphoria. Riding a roller coaster of emotional states, BPD patients become frustrated at their lack of self-determined emotional direction. This lack of direction can result in patients living in a state of apprehension and anticipation of their next mood and affective shift. Interpersonally, the patients' affective instability causes very strong emotional and mental responses in others. Circular in nature, BPD patients' mood is often erratic and unpredictable. This causes strong reactions from those around them. In turn, these reactions from others contribute to the frustration of the patients, further impairing their ability to regulate their emotional state.

Including fanatical oppositional forces in the definition of *reactivity* captures the essence of the nature of patients with BPD. The consistent vacillation between opposing forces and the reactivity of those with BPD causes additional vulnerability to both internal and external stressors. As patients struggle to manage a stressor, their usual coping mechanisms are blocked by their own idiosyncratic tendency to oppose and go against adaptive problem solving.

Criterion 7—Chronic Feelings of Emptiness

Definitions

Chronic: Of long duration. Synonyms would include *consistent, lingering, persistent.*
Emptiness: Total absence of matter; total lack of ideas, meaning, or substance; desperate sense of loss; lacking a desirable element. Synonyms would include *barrenness, hollow, destitute, devoid, blankness.*

Synthesis

For those with BPD, all of the different definitions offer insight into the chronic and persistent feelings they experience. Patients with BPD experience an overall absence of direction or meaning. This absence is experienced within the intrapersonal and extrapersonal realms. People's direction and meaning in life are driven both internally and externally. Internally, goals are defined and identified by individuals' internal reference points of cognition and emotion. Because of their extreme vacillation and reactivity, BPD patients often experience the sensation of drifting without a solid and cohesive sense of self-identity (see criterion 3). This lack of any internal reference points encompasses a sense of emptiness that becomes a painful reminder to patients of their vacant or hollow existence. Externally, the drifting identity of BPD patients causes dysfunction and distress within interpersonal relations because no sense of internal cohesion exists, resulting in unpredictability of the self's place in relation to others.

Criterion 8—Inappropriate Intense Anger or Difficulty Controlling Anger

Definitions

Inappropriate: Improper or unfit.
Intense: Extreme in degree, strength, or effect.

Synthesis

For those with BPD, inappropriate displays of anger are often characterized by anger that is expressed at times when it is not necessarily warranted for the situation. It may also be an extreme reaction of anger when anger is potentially appropriate, but in a more limited sense.

Those with BPD often exhibit unwarranted displays of anger that are not only inappropriate but are also intense—of great extreme or disproportionate to the situation. The degree of expressed anger is great and, combined with impulsivity (see criterion 4), can result in an outburst or expression of feelings that can damage self or others. Patients may experience great difficulty in controlling the anger and may subsequently regret their actions.

Criterion 9—Transient, Stress-Related Paranoid Ideation or Severe Dissociative Symptoms

Definitions

Transient: Transitory; lasting or existing only for a short time. Synonyms would include *fleeting* or *temporary*.
Paranoid ideation: Beliefs about potential danger coming from persons, situations, or objects with the intent of damaging the individual.
Stress: Pressure; the act, condition, or effect of exerting force on someone or something.
Dissociative: Break; detachment, separation, disengagement.

Synthesis

A transient state is one in which symptoms are short lasting, from either a few minutes to a few hours. If these states last longer, additional Axis I diagnoses should be considered.

For those with BPD, stress can be identified as any force creating tension or pressure. Tension or pressure can include both internal and external forces. Often stress-related states are the result of perceived abandonment (see criterion 1) that results in an increased internal tension state. Additionally, if external stressors such as an argument or any shift in a relationship occurs, enough tension may be triggered to result in a brief and transitory change in mental status.

Dissociative states for patients with BPD are short lasting and involve feelings of depersonalization or feeling outside or not part of oneself. Patients may describe themselves as numb or floating. These symptoms are usually the result of a perceived loss or abandonment and will ordinarily remit upon the real or perceived return of the caregiver.

SUMMARY

The difficult reputation BPD patients have acquired and the pejorative connotation the diagnosis has taken on are unfortunate because these patients can often be helped enormously. In studies investigating therapy lasting a year or more, the results are encouraging. However, borderline patients are difficult to treat and to keep in therapy, often fail to respond to therapeutic efforts, and make considerable demands on the therapist's resources (Linehan, 1993).

REFERENCES

Adams, E., Bernat, J., & Luscher, K. (2001). Borderline personality disorder: An overview. In P. Sutkers & H. Adams (Eds.), *Comprehensive handbook of psychopathology* (4th ed.). New York: Free Press.

American Psychiatric Association. (1980). *Diagnostic and statistical manual of mental disorders* (3rd ed.). Washington, DC: Author.

American Psychiatric Association. (1987). *Diagnostic and statistical manual of mental disorders* (3rd ed., revised). Washington, DC: Author.

American Psychiatric Association. (2000). *Diagnostic and statistical manual of mental disorders* (4th ed., text revision). Washington, DC: Author.

Beck, A., Freeman, A., & Associates. (1990). *Cognitive therapy of personality disorders.* New York: Guilford.

Beck, A., Freeman, A., Davis, D, & Associates. (2003). Cognitive therapy of personalities (2nd ed.). New York: Guilford.

Becker, D. (2000). When she was bad: Borderline personality disorder in a posttraumatic age. *American Journal of Orthopsychiatry, 70,* 422–432.

Coccaro, E., Silverman, J., & Klar, H. (1994). Familial correlates of reduced central serotonagic system function in patients with personality disorder. *Archives of General Psychiatry, 51(4),* 318–324.

Eisenberg, N., & Fabes, R. (1998). Contemporaneous and longitudinal prediction of children's sympathy from dispositional regulation. *Developmental Psychology, 34(5),* 910–925.

Freeman. A., & Fusco, G. (2004). *Treating borderline personality disorder: Therapist's manual.* New York: W.W. Norton.

Freeman, A., Pretzer, J., Fleming, B., & Simon, K. (1990). *Clinical applications of cognitive therapy.* New York: Kluwer.

Freeman, A., Pretzer, J., Fleming, B., & Simon, K. (2004). *Clinical applications of cognitive therapy* (2nd ed.). New York: Kluwer.

Golomb, A., Ludolph, P., Westen, D., Block, M. J., Maurer, P., & Wiss, F. C. (1994). Maternal empathy, family chaos, and the etiology of borderline personality disorder. *Journal of the American Psychoanalytic Association, 42,* 525—548.

Guttman, H. & Laporte, L. (2002). Family members' retrospective perceptions of intrafamilial relationships. *Contemporary Family Therapy: An International Journal, 24*(3), 505–522.

Jang, K., Livesley, W., Vernon, P., & Jackson, D. (1996). The genetic basis of personality at different ages: A cross-sectional twin study. *Personality and Individual Differences, 21*(2), 299–301.

Kernberg, O. (1975). *Borderline conditions and pathological narcissism.* New York: James Aronson.

Kohut, H. (1971). *The analysis of the self.* New York: International Universities Press.

Layden, M., Newman, C., Freeman, A., & Byers-Morse, S. (1993). *Cognitive therapy of borderline personality disorder.* New York: Allyn & Bacon.

Linehan, M. (1993). *CBT for borderline personality disorder.* New York: Guilford.

Lively, W., Jang, K., Schroeder, M., & Jackson, D. (1993). Genetic and environmental factors in personality dimension. *American Journal of Psychiatry, 150,* 1826–1831.

Masterson, J., & Rinsley, D. (1975). The borderline syndrome: The role of the mother in the genesis and psychic structure of the borderline personality. *International Journal of Psychoanalysis, 56,* 163.

Paris, J. (1993). *Borderline personality disorder: Etiology and treatment.* Washington, DC: American Psychiatric Press.

Paris, J. (1994). *Borderline personality disorder: A multidimensional approach.* Washington, DC: American Psychiatric Press.

Paris, J. (1999). Borderline personality disorder. In T. Millon, P. Blaney, & R. David (Eds.), *Oxford textbook of psychopathology* (pp. 625–652). New York: Oxford University Press.

Paris, J. (2000). Childhood precursors of borderline personality disorder. *Psychiatric Clinics of North America, 23,* 77–88.

Paris, J., & Zweig-Frank, H. (1992). A critical review of the role of childhood sexual abuse in the etiology of borderline personality disorder. *Canadian Journal of Psychiatry, 37*(2), 125–128.

Paris, J., Zweig-Frank, H., Bond, M., & Guzder, J. (1996). Defense styles, hostility, and psychological risk factors in male patients with personality disorders. *Journal of Nervous Mental Disorders, 184,* 153–158.

Plomin, R., DeFries, J. C., McClearn, G. E., & Rutter, M. (1997). *Behavioral genetics* (3rd ed.). New York: Freeman.

Rathbun, J. (2002). *Borderline personality disorder.* Retrieved March 2, 2003, from http://psychdef.com/bpd.htm

Rinne, T., van den Brink, W., Wouters, L., & van Dyck, R. (2002). SSRI treatment of borderline personality disorder: A randomized, placebo-controlled clinical trial for female patients with borderline personality disorder. *American Journal of Psychiatry, 59*(12), 2048–2054.

Silk, K. R. (1994). *Biological and neurobehavioral studies of borderline personality disorder.* Washington, DC: American Psychiatric Press.

Silk, K. R. (2000). Borderline personality disorder. Overview of biologic factors. *Psychiatric Clinics of North America, 23*(1), 61–75.

Soloff, P. H., Lynch, K. G., & Kelly, T. M. (2002). Childhood abuse as a risk factor for suicidal behavior in borderline personality disorder. *Journal of Personality Disorders, 16*(3), 201–209.

Stern, A. (1938). Psychoanalytic investigation of therapy in the borderline group of neuroses. *Psychoanalytic Quarterly, 7,* 467–489.

Stone, M. (1993). *Abnormalities of personality: Within and beyond the realm of treatment.* New York: W. W. Norton.

Trull, T. (2001). Structural relations between borderline personality disorder features and putative etiological correlates. *Journal of Abnormal Psychology, 110*(3), 471–481.

Trull, T., Sher, K., Minks-Brown, C., Durbin, J., & Burr, R. (2000). Borderline personality disorder and substance use disorders: A review and integration. *Clinical Psychology Review, 10,* 235–253.

Zanarini, M. C., Skodol, A., Bender, D., Dolan, R., Sanislow, C., Schaefer, E., Morey, L., Grilo, C., Shea, M., McGlasham, T., & Gunderson, J. (2000). Risk factors associated with the dissociative experiences of borderline patients. *Journal of Nervous Mental Disorders, 188,* 26–30.

Zanarini, M., & Frankenberg, F. (1997). Pathways to the development of borderline personality disorder. *Journal of Personality Disorders, 11,* 93–104.

Zlotnick, C., Rothschild, L., & Zimmerman, M. (2002). The role of gender in the clinical presentation of patients with borderline personality disorder. *Journal of Personality Disorders, 16*(3), 277–284.

2

Case History of a Borderline Personality: Linda P.

In the creation of this book, contributors were all given a copy of the following case study and asked to respond to the following questions:

1. Please describe your treatment model.
2. What would you consider to be the clinical skills or attributes most essential to successful therapy in your approach?
3. What would be your therapeutic goals for this patient? What are the primary and secondary goals of therapy?
4. What further information would you want to have to assist in structuring this patient's treatment? Are there specific assessment tools you would use? What would be the rationale for the use for the use of those tools?
5. What is your conceptualization of this patient's personality, behavior, affective state, and cognitions?
6. What potential pitfalls would you envision in this therapy? What would the difficulties be, and what would you envision to be the source(s) of the difficulties?
7. What level of coping, adaptation, or function would you see this patient reaching as an immediate result of therapy? What result would be long term at the end of therapy?
8. What would be your timeline (duration) for therapy? What would be the frequency and duration of the sessions?
9. Are there specific or special techniques that you would implement in the therapy? What would they be?
10. Are there special cautions to be observed in working with this patient (e.g., danger to self or others, transference, counter-

transference)? Are there any particular resistances you would expect, and how would you deal with them?

11. Are there any areas that you would choose to avoid or not address with this patient? Why?

12. Is medication warranted for this patient? What effect would you hope/expect the medication to have?

13. What are the strengths of the patient that can be used in therapy?

14. How would you address limits, boundaries, and limit-setting with this patient?

15. Would you want to involve significant others in the treatment? Would you use out-of-session work (homework) with this patient? What homework would you use?

16. What would be the issues to be addressed in termination? How would termination and relapse prevention be structured?

17. What do you see as the hoped-for mechanisms of change for this patient, in order of relative importance?

CASE STUDY

Linda P. is a 31-year-old white woman who came to therapy at the referral of her lawyer. Although she initially stated that she came because of her depression and anxiety, the legal referral was related to an auto accident in which she was accused of ramming another car on a city street. Her lawyer wanted a "psychological report" that might be used on her behalf in the legal proceedings.

When questioned about the auto incident, Linda reported that she was late for an appointment and had been in a hurry. She was driving on a crowded city street. The car in front of her was going slowly, so she flashed her lights and honked her horn several times to get the driver to speed up or get out of her way. The other driver neither pulled over and let her go by nor did he speed up. At a traffic light, she claimed she "lightly bumped" his car to "give him the message." From the consequences, it seems that she hit the other car rather hard. There was significant damage to both her car and the car in front of her. The elderly couple in the car were taken away in an ambulance with claimed whiplash injuries.

Linda reported being both depressed and anxious "for years, on and off." At this point, in addition to the legal proceedings, she reported that the anxiety is the major symptom. She reported being "jumpy" and easily angered, stating, "little things just bug me and I just react." While this has been a pattern for a long time, it seems to be more prominent at this point.

She is a college graduate who reported having had problems in relationships for the past eight or nine years. She was married for a year and a half, and the marriage ended in divorce. She has no children. She is presently unmarried and is not presently dating.

She was raised in a strict family in an evangelical Lutheran tradition. Her family were regular churchgoers. She was born and brought up in the same ethnic German neighborhood in Chicago where her parents were born and raised. She had several aunts and uncles, and most lived with their families in the same neighborhood.

She is presently employed as an elementary school (fourth grade) teacher in an upper-middle-class suburb of Chicago. The school district is racially mixed. The job pays well ($52,000 per year), with good benefits. She has been working in that school system since college graduation. She has generally functioned well in her work, given the structure of the job. She has far more trouble when given more independence, such as when asked to take charge of some group or committee. At those times, work is more difficult and problematic for her. "I get overwhelmed by a lot of the things that I do." She has had a history of difficulty in dealing with some children and some parents. As a result of the interpersonal difficulties with some parents, she has been reported by the parents to school administrators. As a result, she has been called in for several "counseling" sessions with school administrators. The difficulty generally came when Linda sent notes home to parents commenting on the parental need to do more for the children, to help with homework, or to not help with homework. The letters were often seen by the parents as angry, aggressive, or even inflammatory.

To ease the situation with parents, Linda was being required to submit any letters or notes for parents to an assistant principal before being sent. Linda has chosen not to send any notes home. "They are just loading me with this garbage, so I have just stopped sending notes home. The kids will suffer, but that's their choice."

She lives close to the school in a condominium garden apartment complex for single adults. She chose this setting to be away from children: "I see kids all day long. I don't want to have to see them when I'm at home." She has a two-bedroom apartment with one and a half baths.

When she was an undergraduate, she went to school and then either went home or to work. All through her undergraduate years, she worked as a clerk at a convenience store.

She has a master's degree in education. She completed her degree while teaching. She met her ex-husband while they were both in graduate school.

FAMILY CONSTELLATION

Her parents have retired to Florida. She is the eldest child of three. Her sister is four years younger, and her brother is seven years younger. Her mother was 29 years old and her father was 31 years old when they were married.

Her mother was a practical nurse who went back to work full time when Linda was 12. Linda reported that her mother was a perfectionist, for example, with how the house was kept, how the children should behave, and how to act at the dinner table. She reported that her mother would inspect the children's rooms. All underwear was expected to be folded a certain way. Her mother found a pair of panties "incorrectly" folded and dumped the entire drawer onto the floor in the middle of the room with the demand that it all be properly folded.

After her mother went back to work, Linda was expected to take care of her siblings. Because she was the first child, her parents did not have a lot of experience parenting, so they expected her to be a perfect child. As an oldest (and for a brief time an only child) she was expected to be "super-responsible."

Her father was a Chicago police officer. He worked different shifts, and therefore was not always home with the children. Both parents regularly went to church (except when working). She grew up in what might be termed a "high arousal environment" that was often explosive. When her father came home from work, he liked to have two or three beers. On some evenings (two or four times a week), he went to a neighborhood bar after dinner to have a few more beers "with the boys."

Linda believed that he was not a womanizer and was probably faithful to his wife throughout the marriage. The mother and father would fight because he often worked overtime and would come home and want to be by himself in front of the TV or be "out with the guys." He demanded that dinner be ready when he came home, and he wanted the children fed and quiet. After a night of drinking, he would come home and loudly demand to have sex with his wife. This often led to arguments between her parents that involved her father demanding sex and her mother commenting on his smelling bad, being drunk, or that he was an "animal." This was a source of ongoing friction in the home. Linda's impression of her parents' sex life was that her father wanted sex after coming home from the bar and that her mother "submitted" infrequently. She did not think that her mother ever enjoyed sex but did her "wifely duty." On several occasions, her father would tell Linda that she had better learn how to accept sex with her husband and not be a "frigid bitch" like her mother.

Linda and her siblings went to a Lutheran parochial school to be "with their own kind." They later went to a Lutheran high school.

Linda's brother is age 24, single, and presently serving in the army in Germany as a military police officer.

Her sister is age 27, married, has one child, and works as a nurse, having graduated and passed the nurse registry examination.

EDUCATION

Linda went to Chicago State University with a major in Elementary Education. She commuted to school by public transportation. She always did well in school and saw education as a way out. She did not join any clubs or sororities in college. She felt very much out of place, in that the majority of the students at Chicago State (70%) were Black. She paid for her school by working evenings. Her school district paid for her master's degree at Northern Illinois University.

DATING

She described herself as an attractive adolescent. She was not allowed to go out alone. Her father "knew" what boys wanted. Her dating was restricted to groups and to school events. Her father told her that were she to go out on her own, one of two things would happen. Either she would attack the man or the man would attack her. She did not date much as an adolescent. When she was in college, she violated her father's rule and went out on a single date. The man became very insistent and sexually demanding, and she came home with a ripped blouse. Her parents' response to her upset was to say "I told you so" and then totally restrict her dating.

In graduate school she met a fellow graduate student, a psychology major, and began dating him. They dated for three months, but after a certain point, Linda believed that his interest in her waned, and she thought that he was dating other women. She reported that they had many "real arguments." She reported that she had several rage attacks directed at him when he told her that he did not like her anger, insults, and her temper tantrums. He finally stated that he wanted to break up with her. The reason was her insistent refusal of physical contact. She would allow him to kiss her but not to touch her. When he said that other women would be interested in him, she first cried and begged, "Please don't leave me," and then began screaming and threatening to kill herself if he left. After several episodes, she then allowed sexual intercourse. She now believes that he saw her as a patient, in effect, a therapeutic project. Despite what he said or did, she saw him as kind and protective, no matter what she asked or did. After six more months of a very stormy relationship, they married. Her parents were against the marriage because he was Catholic.

After one year of a very stormy marriage, she found out via a phone call that he was "cheating" on her. When confronted, he told her that he was tired of her rage, anger, unpredictability, and jealousy. For example, if he came home at 6:15 instead of the agreed upon 6:00, she would throw his dinner in the garbage because she would think that he was late because he was leaving her. She states that all she wanted was to have him close. After the confrontation, he admitted the affair, packed his bags, and left. She went through his remaining belongings and destroyed many things with a knife (e.g., clothing, his college diploma).

The evening that he left she engaged in impulsive behavior. She went to a club at a local hotel, picked up a man, and had sex with him. This "made her feel better." She felt as if she was getting even with her husband and also "felt loved" by the stranger. This filled the void, though briefly. Afterward she was angry that this man didn't call. He gave her a phone number, and when she called it she found that it was a wrong number. She then kept calling the hotel in which he stayed, demanding his name and address. The hotel staff, of course, refused to give her any information. She became more and more upset and then threatened them. At this point, they said that they would call both the telephone company and the police if she continued to call.

Throughout the next six years, she had a number of episodes of going to bars and putting herself in danger by having impulsive, often unprotected, sex. When asked about her dating patterns, she replied that she was, at that point, "dating a lot of strange men." What this actually meant was that she did not go out on dates but met men in bars and clubs and had brief sexual encounters. This was often done in a "bingeing" manner. She would go to several bars in a week, and then not go for several weeks. She also reported occasions of binge eating when she was angry or upset.

She reported an affair with a married colleague who taught at her school. He was attentive to her and told her how beautiful she was. Seeing him at school was not sufficient. She would "need to have contact" and she would call him at home. After about three months, he wanted to end the relationship, which Linda refused. She cried and finally threatened to tell everyone at school and to call his wife and tell her about the affair if he ended it. His wife finally called her at home and said, "Don't annoy or call my husband ever again or I'll kill you."

BACKGROUND

Linda's hobby was to cultivate and raise bonsai. She has filled her apartment with dozens of miniature plants.

Her complaints for therapy were, "I need to deal with this legal thing and get it off my back," "my life is empty," "there's nothing in my life," "my sister has no interest in me because of her having a baby," "my parents in Florida want nothing to do with me," "my neighbors dislike me."

She reported that her neighbors in her condominium development avoid her because she has had difficulty with them. For example, she reported that several of her neighbors did not clean up after walking their dogs. She followed them, took names and house numbers, time of offense, and on some occasions, pictures. She would then follow the "offenders" and berate them loudly. She then had gone to homeowner meetings with her "evidence." She could not understand why the homeowners association did not stop the wrongdoers and instead criticized her for being "paranoid and intrusive."

An example of her behavior near her home involved a woman moving into Linda's apartment complex. Linda greeted her and tried to be friends with her. At first the woman welcomed Linda's attention, but Linda was quickly rebuffed when she wanted to spend several nights a week with her. Linda later saw the woman with "others." The new neighbor even had a party and did not invite Linda. Linda could not understand that this woman had friends before moving in.

Linda is also an overspender. She has run up very large bills for clothing at expensive stores. The clothes are for "going out." Linda has not worn them.

She spent her time alone with her plants. She watched TV, read, and cried.

She reported a suicide attempt by taking a dozen aspirin after the phone call from the fellow-teacher's wife.

She has also had angry outbursts with colleagues. The principal has spoken with Linda about them and is now tired of dealing with her.

Linda reported that there are times that she gets very angry and then "spaces out." She may lose several hours. For example, on several occasions she came home from school at 3:00 p.m. and took a phone call filled with tales of her sister and the sister's new baby from her mother. She remembered the call coming at 4:00 p.m. because she had just started watching a TV show. Linda reported that the next thing she knew it was 1:00 a.m. and she was sitting in her living room smoking a cigarette. Linda does not presently smoke. She had stopped smoking ten years ago, so she knew that she had to have gone out to buy the cigarettes. When she became aware of her surroundings, she looked down at the ashtray and saw ten cigarette butts. She did not remember going out to buy the cigarettes or smoking several of them. She also reported having been told of phone conversations with her mother or sister that Linda does not remember having.

Linda reports no remorse regarding the auto accident. She believes that the "old people are just trying to get away with making money from my insurance company. Kind of like the lottery."

3

Self-Psychological Treatment

M. David Liberman

This chapter discusses Linda's case from the perspective of a psychoanalyst with a strong commitment to the self-psychological position of Heinz Kohut.

DESCRIPTION OF THE TREATMENT MODEL

The self-psychological model, based in large part on the work of Heinz Kohut, focuses on the vitality and the sense of cohesion of the self. Procedurally, the self-psychologist functions within the same framework as does the classical psychoanalyst: The analyst listens and interprets the patient's associations while paying particular attention to the kinds of transferences that arise during the course of treatment. While self-psychology retains the emphasis on both interpretation and transference, the goal of the self-psychologist is to understand the patient through empathic immersion in the patient's subjective world. As the patient works through the feelings and transferences generated by the analytic setting, the sense of understanding that is communicated by the analyst to the patient is an important component of the curative aspect of the self-psychological treatment.

The self-psychological position holds that the vitality, cohesiveness, and resilience of the self are dependent upon the development and transformation of narcissism. Following classical theory, Kohut (1971) originally envisioned the infant as existing initially in a state of objectless "bliss." Due to the inevitable failures in mothering, this state of bliss is ruptured. In order to reestablish this primary narcissistic state, the infant develops the image of a perfect parent (i.e., the idealized parent imago) and of a perfect self (i.e., the grandiose self). In order for growth to take place, the developing child needs to experience a series of manageable disappointments in both the idealized parental imago and in the grandiose self. As Kohut (1971) originally theorized, this series of manageable disappointments allows the child to internalize or draw back into himself the narcissistic libido or energy that the child has attached to the idealized parental imago. If these disappointments are too intense, then the developing individual will be traumatized. The development of mature narcissism (i.e., realistic and resilient self-esteem) starts to occur as the child begins to realize that neither the idealized other nor the grandiose self is quite as perfect or as powerful as the child had imagined. These manageable disappointments lead to a more realistic sense of both self and self-esteem.

In addition to their restitutive functions, the development of both the idealized parental imago and the grandiose self leads to the development of significant sources of motivation for the growing self. The development of an idealized parental imago allows the child to develop an image of how he or she wants to see the self; in other words, it allows for the development of ideals. The development of the grandiose self provides the individual with the direction and underpinnings for what he or she may hope to achieve, that is, for the development of ambitions. As Kohut said, "The individual is led by ideals and pushed by ambitions" (Siegal, 1996). Kohut (1977) talked about this motivational tension between ambitions and ideals as the "bipolar self" with an arc of talents existing between the twin poles of ambition and ideals.

It is believed that patients who suffer from disorders of the self have either been traumatized by or simply denied these needed relationships and experiences. As a consequence of this, the patients have developed distortions and defenses that impair their developmental processes. In order for development of the self to resume, these patients need to work through the defenses and distortions that have arisen so that they can establish the kinds of relationships that were appropriate to the phase in which their development was stopped. These relationships are recreated clinically in the transferences that power the self-psychological treatment. Self-psychology recognizes the development of unrealistic perceptions or expectations of the analyst or therapist as important recreations of the patient's interrupted development. The kinds of transferences that are established with the therapist are crucial to the resumption of the patient's development. Diagnostically, the kinds of transferences that arise in the course of therapy indicate not only what initially went wrong in the patient's developmental process but also where and with whom. Kohut (1971) described a number of different kinds of transferences; however, only the two main categories are described here: the mirroring and the idealizing transferences. If the therapist is seen merely as someone who is there to reflect the "wonderfulness" of the patient, then we have the development of the mirroring transference. The mirroring transference is crucial to the development of the grandiose self. The self-psychological position recognizes that the reestablishment of the grandiose self is a crucial step in growth. While the patient's grandiosity may be interpreted, the self-psychologist recognizes it as an important stepping-stone to mature self-esteem. If, on the other hand, the analyst is seen as being "perfect," then the patient is in an idealizing transference. Idealizing transferences are critical in the reestablishment of the idealized parental imago.

The forward movement of the therapeutic process is dependent upon the therapist's ability to reestablish an empathic atmosphere in which the patient feels deeply understood by the clinician. The therapist, operating from a position of empathic immersion, is able to both understand and empathically—not traumatically—interpret to the patient what is transpiring between them. The self-psychologist undertakes two tasks in this kind of treatment. The first is to understand and interpret the patient's resistances to the awakening and reawakening of the patient's frustrated narcissistic needs. Once the process is underway, the second task is to empathize with and interpret the vicissitudes of the patient's idealizations and denigrations of the analyst and/or the patient. If this process is successfully negotiated, the self-development of the patient will resume.

Failures in the empathic connection between the therapist and patient are recognized as being not only inevitable but also necessary. These failures can bring about anger and rage in the patient. The self-psychological analyst sees the patient's anger and rage as a breakdown product that results from a rupture or failure of the empathic bond between the therapist and patient. Further, the self-psychological position holds that it is the successful repair of these empathic failures that moves the individual's development forward. Empathic breaks between the therapist and the patient are not viewed as unfortunate setbacks but as new opportunities for growth and progress. The successful understanding and interpretation of the patient's frustration with and disappointment in the therapist are a crucial component to the development of the self. Those things that were initially admired in the idealized parent are made part of the self through the manageable disappointments in the idealized parental imago. Kohut (1971) described this as the process of "transmuting internalization." Through this ongoing process of transmuting internalizations, the individual builds up the psychological structures that allow that individual to regulate internal tension and self-soothing. The developing individual becomes more and more capable of taking over the functions of emotional homeostasis that were originally managed—or mismanaged—for the patient by others.

Kohut (1971) saw that interference at different stages of development would give rise to different impairments in the development of either the idealizing process or the grandiose self. One of the consequences of this interference is the development of what Kohut referred to as the "vertical" split. The vertical split was distinguished from the "horizontal" split of classical analysis because it was a split in or, perhaps more correctly said, within consciousness. Unlike the horizontal split, the individual is aware that he or she is holding two opposing views, but the contradiction does not appear to cause conflict in the mind of the patient. One or the other views is disavowed. The synthesizing function of the ego does not appear to be operating. Through the healing of these vertical splits, the developing individual is able to reclaim a sense of cohesion and wholeness.

ESSENTIAL CLINICAL SKILLS AND ATTRIBUTES

The process of self-psychological treatment depends heavily upon the ability of the analyst to empathize with the patient. A core requirement for the self-psychological approach is the ability of the therapist to genuinely feel, understand, and accept the meaning of an experience for the other person. This requires that the therapist is both willing and able to recognize the countertransferences and counter-resistances of the therapist to the therapeutic process. It also requires that the therapist be able to accept a genuine recognition of the limitations we all have in understanding another person. This is particularly important in a self-psychological treatment, as the self-psychologist becomes the self-object onto which the patient's early narcissistic needs and disappointments are transferred. The analyst must continuously strive to be comfortable with the patient's idealizations and denigrations and to maintain his or her empathic stance. Sometimes this can be quite trying as patients react with rage when their narcissistic needs are disappointed or frustrated. The therapist must also concurrently recognize his or her own discomfort with the process and then work through it. In order to continue the empathic immersion in the patient's world, the analyst has to be able to stay in emotional contact with the patient through the ups and the downs of the therapeutic process. Empathy is, then, not only the ability to understand the feelings of another but also the result of a continuous struggle on the part of the therapist to stay in touch with the patient, to remain emotionally steady, and to sensitively interpret what the patient is recreating between the two of them. It is crucial that the therapist be able to work through the countertransferences and the counter-resistances that are the fabric of the self-psychological exchange. If the therapist is able to handle these multiple demands, he or she can function as an effective self-object who is able to tolerate both the idealizations and the de-idealizations of the different idealizing transferences as well as being able to accept and understand the intense demands and deadening impact of the various mirroring transferences. A successful therapeutic process requires that the therapist continuously work through his or her counter-resistances and countertransferences even as the patient is dealing with his or her own. I have found that therapy often stalls as I struggle to catch up in my own self-analysis with the analysis of the patient.

Kohut (1977) discussed some of the major countertransference problems that are encountered by the therapist in a self-psychological treatment. A therapist who has not sufficiently worked through his or her own deficits in the grandiose self will be made uncomfortable with the patient's idealization and unable to accept the patient's regard in the idealizing transferences. Conversely, a therapist whose grandiose self was not sufficiently nurtured may become caught up in the patient's idealizations and lose sight of the transference nature of the patient's feelings. The demands on the therapist can be equally intense when the patient's grandiose self is the focus of the work. The self-object nature of the transference can become quite difficult to tolerate. The patient's treatment of the therapist may range from a mild condescension to a demand for perfect attunement and mirroring. In the mirroring transferences, the patient's treatment of the therapist can evoke feelings in the therapist that range from frustration to rage or from boredom to a feeling of "deadness" in the presence of the patient.

Again, it is critical that the therapist be able to tolerate these feelings, understand them, and work them through to the point where the therapist can again reestablish emotional contact with the patient.

THERAPEUTIC GOALS

The general goal of treatment for the self-psychologist is always the same: To help the patient to restart the development of the self became blocked. Kohut (1984) believed that the real goal of treatment was to help the individual to feel that he or she could live a satisfying and fulfilling life and to be able to appreciate and make use of his or her talents and abilities. Linda has done some things of which she should be proud. It is my impression, however, that she is getting no sense of gratification from any of them. I would hope that by the end of her therapy she would be able to feel vitalized and gratified by her achievements.

A second goal of therapy would be to help Linda develop the ability to soothe herself. It is clear that when Linda is upset, she is unable to calm herself. She is given to rages like those she described with her ex-husband and with some of the other men with whom she has been involved. Perhaps the incident that initially brought her into therapy was another. Linda tries to calm herself with cigarettes, through sexual bingeing, or through purchasing expensive clothing that she does not wear. There appears to have been very little soothing or understanding available to the patient as she was growing up. Linda gave graphic descriptions of a number of empathic failures in the kind of soothing that is needed by the developing child: her parents "I told you so" attitude to Linda's being assaulted, her mother's rages during her clothing inspections, the parents rages with one another, and the descriptions of the home environment as "high arousal."

Another crucial aspect of this woman's treatment would be the establishment of an empathic environment in which she would be able to settle down and begin a process of self-exploration. The job of the therapist would be to create a situation in which Linda can begin to feel safe and secure enough to expose and explore her childhood needs for admiration and understanding. In order to facilitate this process, in the early phases of treatment, the therapist does not interfere in the development of transferences by the patient. It is the task of the therapist to accept the developing transference and to be careful to interpret only the patient's resistances to this unfolding of these needs.

FURTHER INFORMATION AND ASSESSMENT

The question of assessment and of the structuring of the treatment touches on a central question about this patient having to do with her diagnosis with borderline personality disorder. In terms of the self-psychological perspective on these kinds of patients, Kohut (1977) considered the "true" borderline patient to be essentially psychotic but with an adaptive defensive covering that allowed the patient to protect him- or herself from becoming openly psychotic. Kohut viewed the "truly" borderline patient as either not having a self or having a self that had been seriously damaged or distorted. He did not believe that such patients were appropriate for psychoanalytic treatment. However, I'm not certain that Linda would fall within the self-psychological conception of borderline personality disorder. Kohut (1977) actually described two kinds of narcissistic patients: the narcissistic personality disorder and the narcissistic behavior disorder. The description provided of Linda would fit very well into the latter category. If we are defining Linda as a borderline personality disorder based on the behavioral criteria used in the *Diagnostic and Statistical Manual of Mental Disorders 4th edition, text revision* (American Psychiatric Association, 2000), we need to remain aware that those diagnoses are based on behavioral descriptions, not intrapsychic phenomenon. In considering a patient for self-psychological treatment, or any form of psychoanalysis, we need to make an intrapsychic evaluation of the patient.

The critical factor for the self-psychological psychoanalyst or therapist in discriminating the borderline personality from the narcissistic personality in the self-psychological sense is in the determination of the essential state of the patient's self. The self-psychological clinician who is uncertain about the self state of the patient must make that determination through patient and careful observation of the patient. In fact, it is often the patient's response to treatment that allows the clinician to arrive at a definite appraisal of the patient's self state. If there is sufficient concern about the patient's self state at the beginning of treatment, a referral should be made for psychological testing that includes a comprehensive workup with projective testing. (Silverstein [1999] addressed the issues of projective testing and self-psychology.) In my clinical experience, I have seen a number of severely narcissistic patients who appeared to behave in a manner that was almost indistinguishable from the *DSM-IV-TR* descriptions of borderline personality disorders. Based on the case material presented here, I don't think that I would exclude Linda from a self-psychologically oriented treatment. However, due to Linda's propensity for acting out, her suicidal gesture, and her lapses in consciousness, I would want to spend considerable time evaluating her. I would also refer Linda for psychological testing and would ask the examiner to pay particular attention to the patient's ability to tolerate an emotionally taxing therapy. If the results of the patient's testing and initial interviews did not show basic defects in the self, I would proceed with a self-psychological treatment.

CONCEPTUALIZATION OF THE PATIENT

It is my impression that Linda is a reasonably intelligent and hard-working individual who is looking for an intense mirroring relationship. It appears that her self-development was interrupted at a very early level and that she has been looking for the kind of relationship—probably at the level of the merger experience—that she missed out on quite early in life. In merger relationships, patients hope to have the total interest of the other person. They long to feel completely understood, perfectly responded to, and unreservedly admired by the other person. Linda's demanding behavior and her attacks of narcissistic rage appear to be the result of the disappointments and failures that she keeps experiencing as she attempts to establish this kind of intense mirroring relationship. She cannot tolerate being disappointed by her self-objects when they do not value her as deeply and intensively as she needs. Individuals who are stuck at this early stage of development and on this particular track of narcissistic development are often prone to outbreaks of intense and inappropriate rage. Their expectations, demands, and outbursts usually seem completely outrageous to those around them. Linda's history exemplifies this: She demands the kind of attention a two-year-old would expect, is quite easily upset when she doesn't receive it, and is almost completely unable to quiet herself when she has again been disappointed. She has almost no understanding of the feelings or needs of those around her, and this is particularly true when she has begun to view the other person, such as her husband or her new neighbor, as an essential self-object. Linda appears to be reasonably bright and certainly well motivated—as witnessed by her ability to put herself through college—but her emotional neediness overrides her cognitive capacities. This is particularly true when she begins to sense that she will not get the kind of unconditional and intense approbation for which she is so desperate. Everything else is swept away before her emotional neediness. Linda's use of denial and projection as her defenses also speaks to the early age of the damage.

Linda's lapses in consciousness are more concerning. Such lapses can occur in extremely narcissistic individuals who are feeling overwhelmed and overstimulated. I have seen narcissistically damaged patients suffer lapses in consciousness when their meager ability to self soothe is overtaxed. Such individuals have no way to incorporate overstimulating experiences, and they may become split off from consciousness. Linda's lapses in consciousness appear to be getting to that point and, possibly, beyond.

POTENTIAL PITFALLS AND DIFFICULTIES

The most concerning elements in the treatment of a patient such as Linda is the possibility that the patient is actually suffering from a concealed psychosis that could become fully active in a psychoanalytic treatment. This issue, however, was previously addressed.

Psychoanalytic therapy involves a very intense relationship. While Linda appears to be desperately hungry for such a relationship, she also may be unable to maintain a therapeutic alliance when she encounters the frustrations and disappointments that are inevitable. As the therapist allows the unfolding of an intense mirroring transference, patients like Linda can begin to misinterpret the understanding stance of the therapist. Individuals like this are sometimes unable to accept the limitations of the therapeutic relationship. They begin to view the therapist as a "real" object and start to demand that the therapist actually meet their needs for praise and approval. Patients who need intense mirroring and have poor impulse control and unclear senses of social boundaries are more prone to try to convert the therapist from a transference object to an object of reality. If the therapist interprets rather than acts upon such patients' wishes to change the nature of the relationship, the patients may experience this as yet another injury to their self-esteem and either terminate treatment or begin acting out.

Acting out would be a potential problem for Linda in her therapy. Acting out has been an ongoing problem for Linda, and we see numerous examples of this in her history. As patients begin to drop their old defenses and begin to recognize their feelings and their narcissistic needs, they will also start to experience these feelings and needs more intensely. These heightened experiences can result in patients making more urgent and overt attempts to assuage old hurts or to satisfy these needs. Given Linda's proclivity for reacting to her feelings, acting out could be a real source of difficulty as she got more deeply involved in her treatment.

COPING LEVEL AND PROGNOSIS

It is possible that Linda might gain an immediate sense of relief from her treatment. Self-psychologists believe that a crucial part of individuals' ability to function and to grow is their experience of feeling understood. A patient like Linda is in desperate need of a continuing experience of feeling understood. The intensity and regularity of psychoanalytic treatment could meet that need and offer her an immediate sense of relief. If Linda and her therapist were able to develop a therapeutic framework for their relationship so that Linda would have some sense of what she could and could not expect from her treatment, it is possible that Linda might settle down and experience a feeling of stability, understanding, and hope that have not been part of her life. Linda has antagonized many people with her acting out of her emotional neediness. The availability of an understanding therapist several times a week could provide Linda with some relief from her desperate daily search to find a continuing source of understanding, acceptance, and soothing.

With someone like Linda, it is really difficult to evaluate prognosis. Despite the host of difficulties that she presents with, Linda has also shown some definite ego strengths: She has shown determination and tenacity both in getting her education and in maintaining herself in the emotionally taxing school environment. She has maintained her job commitments despite the frustrations and difficulties she has experienced with her students, their parents, and the administration. If the initial difficulties of establishing a good therapeutic frame could be negotiated, I think the prognosis could be good.

The goal of self-psychological treatment is the development of an ability to appreciate oneself and maintain a sense of self-esteem in the face of disappointment and frustration and also to develop the ability to calm oneself in the face of upset. In long-term therapy, such as analysis, I would also hope to see Linda develop an effective level of insight that would allow her to recognize, understand, and accept not only her own needs but also those of other people. We engage in an intense therapeutic process over an extended period of time so that the individual can develop and maintain these kinds of capacities and abilities even after he or she has completed treatment. With the information available, I think that it might be possible for this woman to achieve that level of self-development.

TIMELINE OF THERAPY

I would recommend that Linda go into psychoanalysis. Psychoanalytic treatment normally has four to five sessions per week, with each session normally lasting 45–50 minutes. I would estimate that it would take at least four to five years for Linda to complete her analysis. If formal psychoanalysis were not possible, I would recommend that Linda be seen for psychoanalytic therapy at least three times per week.

SPECIFIC TECHNIQUES

At this point, I would not recommend any modifications for treatment outside of the therapist making him- or herself as available as possible to this patient.

SPECIAL CAUTIONS AND RESISTANCES

There are several cautions that the psychoanalytic clinician would want to take with this patient. While Linda appears to be desperately hungry for an intense relationship, she may be unable to maintain the therapeutic alliance when she encounters frustration and disappointment. As the therapist allows the unfolding of an intense mirroring transference, Linda could begin to misinterpret the understanding stance of the therapist and begin to believe that the therapist was there to gratify Linda's unmet need for a "real" relationship. Linda would become unable or unwilling to accept the limitations of the therapeutic relationship and might begin to demand that the therapist meet her needs for praise and approval. Patients with an intense need for mirroring, poor impulse control, and an unclear sense of social boundaries are more prone to try to convert the therapist from a transference object to an object of reality. As the patient's wishes are interpreted rather than acted upon, the patient may experience this as another injury to self-esteem and either terminate treatment or begin acting out.

This same kind of reaction can be used as a resistance. Patients who are unwilling to either accept the pain of their past or the emptiness of their current living situation may also attempt to change the parameters of the therapeutic relationship. Their efforts are not due to an inability to tolerate their psychic distress but rather are an effort to escape facing their inner pain and its consequences. The acting-in becomes a manifestation of resistance. However, this acting-in can also become a path of realization if the analyst is able to understand what the patient is reenacting in the therapy session. While understanding the patient's actions is difficult enough, in order to be truly effective, the analyst needs to be able to achieve this understanding while maintaining his or her empathic stance and emotional connection with the patient. Work with this kind of patient requires the therapist to constantly engage in a process of self-analysis. The therapist continuously needs to work at resolving the counter-resistance that he or she will set up against empathizing with the patient's actions. These counter-resistances prevent the therapist from being able to maintain a genuinely empathic connection with the patient as the patient works his or her way through these feelings. As can be imagined, this is an ongoing and emotionally taxing process. It is particularly difficult to maintain this stance with a patient like Linda. It is tempting for the therapist to write off the breakdowns in therapist-patient empathy as more of the patient's "foolishness" or "insatiability." Sometimes it is so much easier for the therapist to avoid self-examination to see what is going on inside. Too often, patients like this remind us of things about ourselves of which we would rather remain unaware. The result of this is that we deny any understanding of the actions of the patient and our empathic understanding becomes hollow.

With patients like Linda, acting out is always a potential form of resistance. As the patients begin to drop their old defenses against the recognition of their feelings and needs, they will often experience these old feelings and needs more intensely. This heightened awareness can result in patients making more overt attempts to assuage old hurts or to satisfy the needs that they are now experiencing more intensely. Linda has acted out on a number of occasions. The clinician would have to be very alert to the possibility of Linda's acting out in response to both situational elements as well as to the ups and downs of her therapy. I would try to enlist Linda's cooperation as much as possible in understanding this as a potential impediment to our work and urge her to try to bring her feelings into therapy instead of acting on them. I have also made myself as available as possible to patients with this problem and asked them to contact me whenever they felt that they were going to act out on their feelings. Given the circumstances, I would want to have a psychiatrist ready to initiate a hospitalization if Linda wound up in severe crisis.

AREAS TO AVOID

This is also another very interesting question for the self-psychologist. Kohut (1977) described what others came to criticize as the "incomplete" analysis of Mr. M. The goal of a classical analysis has been the "complete" reworking of the trauma that initially affected the patient. Kohut's perspective on mental health was that no individual is ever completely free from the effects of failed self-object experiences. For Kohut (1977), what constituted a mentally healthy individual is the ability to utilize and appreciate one's own talents and abilities so that one can live a fulfilled life. This is a significant departure from the more classical perspective. It means that when self-psychological patients successfully complete their analysis, they have reached a point where they are able to discover and use the prized aspects of themselves and to engage in relationships that are satisfying and rewarding to them.

In the older classical models of therapy, it was considered crucial that the patient "relive" all of the pain and suffering with the therapist. If the patient failed to do so, the analysis was considered to be incomplete. Many well-intentioned therapists would push the patient to deal with the undoubtedly repressed rage and anger and, in so doing, undermine both the patient's gains and the relationship itself. In self-psychological treatment, Linda might come to a successful resolution of her therapy without having to transfer all of the painful and negative experiences of her life onto the person of the analyst. She could finish her therapy without having to go through the rages and anguish that she had left unfinished with her parents. In self-psychology, we recognize that much of the rage and anger is because of the failure of significant others to understand and appreciate the real person of the patient. If the self-psychological therapist does not repeat these missteps, there is a reasonable chance that the patient will not have to repeat all of these feelings again in her treatment.

MEDICATION

Linda should be evaluated at the outset of treatment for antidepressants and mood stabilizers. Psychoanalytic therapy can be emotionally demanding, and Linda might need medical assistance, at least in the early stages of treatment, in handling her feelings.

PATIENT STRENGTHS

Linda has shown tenacity and determination both in putting herself through school and in holding onto a very stressful job. She has done this while receiving little emotional support from her family. She has been able to hold on to a teaching position in the public school system, to stay with her students, and to finish each year. She has done this despite the pressure she appears to have gotten from her parents and the lack of support that she seems to have received from her administration. It appears that Linda has shown the ability to make commitments, to stay with them, and to finish what she has started. If these strengths could be recognized and mobilized in her therapy, I think that she could commit to and finish a course of psychoanalytic treatment.

LIMITS AND BOUNDARIES

This is an extremely important consideration. At the start of psychoanalytic therapy, it is very important to explain to the patient the process of psychoanalytic treatment and the limits within which the analyst or therapist works. In the past, too often, this was not done. Instead, the patient's ignorance of what could and could not be expected was often interpreted as "resistance" rather than as a reasonable ignorance of the process of psychoanalysis. As a rule—and particularly in a case like this—I explain to my patients that we sometimes have to forgo the normal social conventions such as my answering personal questions or saying the things that one would normally expect another person to say. I explain that this is not meant as a discourtesy but rather to allow for a relationship in which the patient has the opportunity of developing a deeper understanding of her self. I think that it is also a good policy to acknowledge that these limitations can be frustrating and upsetting but that ultimately they do have a use and a purpose.

Given the current circumstances, I would also urge Linda to try to not act on her feelings of frustration and anger. Rather, I would encourage her to try to note her feelings, contain herself, and then try to bring these feelings into her sessions. When she understands her feelings, she may find that they are less disruptive and upsetting than in the past.

HOMEWORK AND THE INVOLVEMENT OF OTHERS

Generally, psychoanalysts don't involve others in the treatment of an adult patient. The only out-of-session work that I normally encourage patients to do is to try to remember their dreams. Again, with Linda, I would also encourage her to try to pay attention to her feelings and then to bring them into her sessions rather than acting on them.

TERMINATION ISSUES AND RELAPSE PREVENTION

The termination process would be a critical part of Linda's therapy. Linda has had difficulty in managing separations from significant others in her life. When she has been on her own, Linda has shown lapses in good judgment and an inability to handle herself in relationships. This may indicate that Linda is reenacting her initial traumatic separations by continuing to mishandle relationships with both men and women. Mahler, Pine, and Bergman (1975) have written of the problems that people have when their separation/individuation experiences have been improperly negotiated. According to Mahler et al. (1975), the child initially experiences a kind of psychological birth that extends from the child's physical birth to the age of about three years. A significant part of this "birth process" is the child achieving a psychological separateness from the mother. This process goes through stages. In one stage, the practicing subphase, the child has physically separated from the mother because the child is now capable of locomotion. This necessitates that the child be able to move away from and back to the mother as the child's psychological needs might dictate. It is important that the mother is able to understand the child's need for separateness and to stay in empathic contact with the child as the child negotiates this phase of emotional and cognitive development. After the practicing subphase has been traversed, the child will again try to emotionally reattach to the mother but at times in a very confusing fashion. During this period, the child's needs are often confusing, if not contradictory. The success with which the parents respond to this process can set the pattern for all future interactions. Again, all of this depends upon the ability of the parents to maintain an empathic connection with the child.

Given the case study information about the parent's interactions and responses in Linda's later years, it appears that this phase of Linda's development was largely unsuccessful. Linda may not have successfully negotiated either the later practicing subphase or the rapprochement phase of the separation/individuation process. The dramatic lack of understanding that Linda's parents have at times shown toward her would make it even more likely that they were equally unempathic to Linda's needs in this early process of learning to be on her own. This would make Linda's process of separating from the therapist even more crucial. Given Linda's self-state, it is conceivable that she would reenact and act out with her therapist the trauma of separation that she initially suffered. It could be quite important to be able to be in touch with Linda as she alternated between her wishes to be on her own and to be with the therapist at the same time. These feelings are confusing to the patient, so it is very important to relate them to the possibility of her approaching and appropriate termination.

Another aspect of the process of termination that complicates this period of treatment is the reemergence of all the old issues that initially brought the patient into treatment. When a patient is terminating an intense analytic therapy, it is quite common for all the old issues to flare up again. It can be quite discouraging when all the issues that had already been worked through appear again in therapy. Both patients and therapists sometimes do not understand that this recrudescence of old material in the last stages of treatment is very much part of the patient's termination process. It is, in a sense, a last desperate attempt on the part of the patient to stave off the healthy separation toward which the patient is moving. This flare-up of symptoms needs to be understood and interpreted with compassion. It is easy to misunderstand these events and, because of this misunderstanding, to not stay in touch with the patient's simultaneous needs for closeness and separation. (This is the dilemma often faced by parents of teenagers who are preparing to leave home. The teens' regressive, angry, and contradictory behavior can drive the parents to distraction, and even the best child's behavior ranges from the difficult to the impossible.) For some patients—and Linda may fall into this group—the understanding manner of the therapist is critical to the patients' ability to separate from the treatment. Therapies can be completely undone because of the therapist's unempathic handling of this aspect of the termination process. It is therefore critical that the therapist keep the issue of approaching termination clearly in the foreground with the patient at all times.

In terms of interpreting and structuring the termination phase, analytic therapists take their lead from the patient. As issues of separation and termination show up more frequently in the patient's associations and dreams, the therapist will begin to point out that leaving seems to be on the patient's mind. At some point, the patient will generally discuss with the therapist how this should be accomplished. Often, this is actually a question that the patient cannot quite bring him- or herself to ask the therapist, such as "Are you going to support my wish to stop seeing you?" or, even more poignantly, "Will you miss me as much as I'm going to miss you?" Again, this is part of the separation process. If the parents did not sensitively handle separation when the patient was small, this can be a second chance for a previously unhappy experience to be reworked.

In analytic therapy, some kind of timeline is usually established for the ending of treatment. As the therapy proceeds, patients become more confident about their ability to take care of themselves and about their therapist's ability to handle the loss. Usually I follow the patient's lead in setting a definite termination date. To avoid retraumatizing the patient and precipitating a regression during the termination process, I would not hold Linda to the termination date. It is important to allow patients to decide if they can manage to actually stop on the termination date that they have set for themselves. It is also important to make it clear to patients that they can always return to therapy if they feel it is necessary. Again, the therapist needs to be very empathic to the contradictory needs that patients are again working through with the analyst.

The question of relapse is also quite complex. Everyone stumbles and falls. That is part of life. To look at a patient's stumbling or falling as a "relapse" is destructive to the patient and to the work that has been done. Some people never need to return to therapy, and some people never want to leave therapy or simply can't leave. If patients experience a resurgence of symptoms, it is critical that they feel they can return to see the therapist without feeling that they have failed. One of the best ways to help patients make the transition out of treatment is to ensure that they know they are always welcome to come back. I try to make it clear that I do not see their need for more time with me as a failure in their treatment. The therapist's failure to understand and express this can be a further blow to the patient's already weakened self-state.

MECHANISMS OF CHANGE

The mechanism of change in self-psychological treatment is the remobilization of the self-object needs in the transferences. The remobilization of these needs may be expressed in the idealizing, mirroring or twinship transferences. Through the reemergence and expression of these needs (to be idealized or to have someone to idealize) in the transferences, the patient is able to revitalize the thwarted self. As these needs are expressed and worked through in the self-object transferences, there is a restructuring of the defective or stunted aspects of the self. Kohut described this remobilization and working through of the self-object needs and the complementary self-object configuration as the process of transmuting internalization. In the process of transmuting internalization, the old, thwarted, and defective self-object structures are reworked again in the transference. In a successful working through, patients are able to recognize their needs, reexperience these needs differently, and find new resolutions to these failed relationships or develop new structures to compensate for them. Compensatory structures work to satisfy individuals' needs in a healthy way. Kohut viewed the development of compensatory structures as a replacement for the needed but unsatisfying defensive structures that were being replaced. The development of these new and healthier compensatory structures was viewed as a successful outcome to treatment.

The case study has examples of Linda's attempts to meet these old needs. It appears that Linda has attempted to develop mirroring and twinship relationships with her female neighbor and with the two men with whom she tried to involve herself. However, the intensity of her needs and the urgency with which she attempted to have them responded to have been simply too intense in these relationships. In a self-psychological treatment, the job of the therapist would be to allow these needs to emerge in the therapeutic relationship and then to help Linda recognize to what her needs related. In Linda's case, a successful treatment outcome should allow her to develop a realistic appreciation of who she is, what she has missed out on, and what she has achieved. Probably the single most important change for Linda would be the development of her ability to appreciate herself and her accomplishments and to be able to accept this kind of recognition from others. With many patients, this is a slow process because of their hardened self-deprecation that is resistant to accepting the recognition offered by others. Linda probably falls into this category. The goal would be for the treatment process to allow Linda to develop a more realistic and resilient sense of self-respect and the ability to manage the ups and downs of her self-esteem.

A crucial aspect of psychoanalytic treatment is the development of insight. This includes the ability to recognize and understand what one is feeling and the ability to understand why one is feeling that way, and the ability to understand the feelings of others. Both aspects of insight seem to be noticeably lacking in Linda. An important mechanism of change and an important mechanism for maintaining that change would be the development of a spontaneous and effective insight. I would hope that Linda could develop a useful and effective insight into both herself and others.

REFERENCES

American Psychiatric Association. (2000). *Diagnostic and statistical manual of mental disorders* (4th ed., text revision). Washington, DC: Author.

Kohut, H. (1971). *The analysis of the self.* New York: International Universities Press.

Kohut, H. (1977). *The restoration of the self.* New York: International Universities Press.

Kohut, H. (1984). In A. Goldberg (Ed.), *How does analysis cure?* Chicago: The University of Chicago Press.

Mahler, M., Pine, F., & Bergman, A. (1975). *The psychological birth of the human infant.* New York: Basic Books.

Siegel, A. (1996). *Heinz Kohut and the psychology of the self.* London: Routledge.

Silverstein, M. (1999). *Self psychology and diagnostic assessment.* Mahwah, NJ: Lawrence Erlbaum.

4

Dialectical Behavior Therapy

Andrea Bloomgarden

OVERVIEW OF DIALECTICAL BEHAVIOR THERAPY

Dialectical behavior therapy (DBT), as developed by Marsha Linehan, is a relatively new treatment approach for borderline personality disorder (BPD) that draws heavily on cognitive-behavioral concepts and techniques but has a unique twist: the addition of ideas and practices common to Zen Buddhist monks. Linehan was interested in parasuicidal behavior (i.e., self-harming behaviors that are not meant to be lethal) and ultimately found herself working with the BPD population. She originally tried to understand why people self-harm and what she could do to help them. In the meantime, as part of her personal development, she began study with a Zen master and immersed herself in meditative practice and Eastern philosophy. With her desire to help people with parasuicidal behaviors, her knowledge of Zen Buddhism, and her cognitive behavioral therapy training, Linehan synergistically united these ideas and wrote *Cognitive-Behavioral Treatment of Borderline Personality Disorder* (1993). In this book she delineated a new treatment approach she calls dialectical behavior therapy.

The concept of dialectics has a long history in philosophy, where many have used it in other contexts (e.g., Marx & Engels, 1970, in their socioeconomic theory, Kuhn, 1970, in his theory of scientific change). Linehan (1993) briefly discusses the history of dialectics in her book (pp. 20–21). In the context of her theory, it can be summarized by "embracing of opposites." Applying dialectical thinking to the delivery of treatment is the art of DBT. Successfully doing it helps a person with BPD embrace opposite concepts, feelings, actions, and ideas.

Clients with BPD typically cannot do this at first because all-or-nothing thinking is a common information processing style. Usually people with BPD cannot conceive of being angry and loving toward the same person in the same moment. Similarly, they cannot imagine accepting themselves exactly as they are and viewing their "dysfunctional" behaviors as actually containing a bit of wisdom and functionality. When a person with BPD can truly embrace opposite concepts, ideas, and feelings in the same moment, a synthesis has occurred, and in this synthesis is the basis of healing from the disorder.

For example, a person's seemingly destructive behaviors may make sense in context. Embracing of opposites applies here because seemingly self-destructive behaviors are viewed as actually self-preserving from a DBT standpoint. If one were to truly understand the self-harming behavior in the full context of a person's life, there is good sense in the behavior, even in the current moment. This goes beyond a behavioral conceptualization that would propose that the behavior was reinforced in the past but is no longer useful. The dialectical view is that the behavior made sense in the context, and still makes sense right now. Thus, fully accepting a behavior as if it will never change, even knowing that one wants to change it, is one example of embracing opposites. Validating the current wisdom of the behavior in the moment rather than treating it as pathological is a crucial part of the DBT technique.

When a person engages a in what may normally be considered in other treatment approaches a "dysfunctional" behavior, from a dialectical standpoint there is "function within dysfunction; within distortion there is accuracy; in destruction one can find construction" (Linehan, 1993, p. 32). Rather than conceptualizing BPD as a disorder that causes many dysfunctional behaviors with underlying causes that need to be ferreted out and cured, a dialectical view presumes that individuals are "capable of wisdom with respect to their own life, although that capability is not always obvious or even accessible" (Linehan, 1993, p. 33). The goal of this treatment is to help the person find that wisdom, find the functionality that is presumed to be extant even if not apparent.

From a dialectical perspective, reality is constantly in flux, constantly changing, and so the therapist who embraces DBT works to help clients find functionality, find the inherent wisdom in their actions, accept themselves completely, and also try to make their lives better. This too is an example of embracing of opposites. One can recognize the need to stay the same, to accept oneself exactly as is, and also the need to change. They are opposites, but they exist simultaneously from a dialectical standpoint.

Delivering treatment in a dialectical way is crucial to the revolutionary new approach, so it is important to understand how it gets expressed in treatment. When Linehan was first developing her ideas, she had graduate students observe her sessions while she treated parasuicidal clients with cognitive behavioral therapy. She asked the students to identify helpful techniques as she tried to deliver treatment in a way that was most effective. She found herself experimenting with nontraditional procedures. For example, while normally using a warm, nurturant style of interaction with her clients, she often interjected with blunt, irreverent statements meant to throw them off balance in some way. Sometimes she unexpectedly used humor or played devil's advocate to exaggerate a point. This is a process she now calls dialectical because in her treatment style Linehan alternated among opposite ways of being with her client. As she introspected about what she was doing and why, she came up with an image of herself on a see-saw, sitting on one end with her client on the other end. Her interventions were in response to the client's position on the see-saw: She tried to say or do something in an opposite way that created balance, making the see-saw more level. In so doing, she hoped to help the client find a synthesis between opposing ideas, thus helping the client grow to a higher level of understanding.

When postulating the cause of BPD development, Linehan presumes a "biosocial" perspective on personality. This means that a combination of a biological predisposition and social/environmental factors, as well as their ongoing interaction over time, shapes personality expression. In particular, when an individual with a biological tendency to be emotionally vulnerable grows up in a certain kind of dysfunctional environment, which Linehan calls the "invalidating" environment, the result is likely to be the development of BPD. This is because the combination of these two factors leads to a dysfunction in the emotion regulation system, making the person less able to modulate affect, which is the fundamental problem that ultimately creates the characteristics commonly associated with BPD.

Being emotionally vulnerable, according to Linehan, means that the person is physiologically "wired" to be highly sensitive to emotional stimuli and capable of feeling and experiencing these stimuli with great emotional intensity. A situation to which an average person would have a slight emotional reaction would cause an emotionally vulnerable person to have a very strong reaction. The emotionally vulnerable person will also take longer to return to the original emotional baseline after the experience is over. Although the exact brain mechanisms that would cause emotional vulnerability are not known, some research suggests a low threshold for activation of activity in the limbic area, which is the brain area associated with emotion regulation, in individuals with BPD (Cowdry & Gardner, 1985; Cowdry & Gardner, 1988; Gardner & Cowdry, 1986; O'Leary, Brouwers, & Gardner, 1991). The net result is that such individuals need more help learning to soothe themselves and manage their emotions appropriately. When their family environment fails to give them that education, or even gives the opposite message and training, the individuals will develop the symptoms commonly associated with BPD.

In the case example, Linda's family dynamics fit the definition of an invalidating environment quite well. Linda's parents treated her in ways that were very hurtful to her, and it is presumed that she was also emotionally vulnerable. If she responded openly that she was hurt, as would be natural for such a child, she probably would have received a punitive response from her parents. This taught her that her feelings were wrong, that they must be suppressed, and that they were not to be trusted. Moreover, she might also have learned that perhaps she was to blame for feeling the "wrong thing." These are all hallmark effects of a sensitive person experiencing invalidation. For example, Linda's mother expected her underwear to be perfectly folded. What person (let alone a child) can always fold her underwear perfectly? When her mother inspected the drawer and found the one pair not folded "correctly," the mother dumped the whole drawer and made Linda redo all of it. What would have happened if Linda had cried and expressed her hurt instead of complying with her mother's demands? Her mother probably would not have said in a gentle tone, "I'm sorry Linda. I realize I'm expecting too much from a little girl," and then hugged her. Had her mother recognized Linda's legitimate emotional reaction of hurt and possibly shame, she would have been giving her daughter what Linehan calls a validating response. Giving Linda validation would have helped her return to emotional baseline more quickly and helped her to feel less intensely distressed. She would have ultimately learned how to give that positive experience of validation to herself, had she received it. However, Linda got the opposite. Her mother would probably have escalated in anger and been even more hurtful or maybe even violent in some way. Perhaps her mother would have dumped the whole dresser and made Linda redo everything or punished her for being defiant.

If a child's feelings are constantly invalidated by being shown that what she feels is wrong, stupid, or deserves punishment, she will learn to inhibit and even invalidate those feelings herself, eventually. She will also fail to learn how to regulate her emotion appropriately and will learn to suppress feelings and alternately explode. Moreover, the child will come to believe that her parents' perspective was valid and she was just a bad kid who wasn't good enough, thus damaging her self-esteem.

The case study contained other examples of how Linda's hurt feelings and upset were ignored or invalidated. Her father taught her that her needs were secondary to a man's in a relationship. She had "better learn how to accept sex with her husband," and not be a "frigid bitch" like her mother. Being told that her feelings and needs should be subjugated to someone else's meant that her feelings were not important or real. Linda's father was also extremely unkind when she was (essentially) sexually assaulted on a date and came home with a ripped blouse, only to have her father say, "I told you so." This invalidation and lack of compassion for her experience damaged Linda's self-esteem and failed to teach her any positive emotion-regulation skills. It also failed to teach her to feel compassion for herself or for others.

Another consequence of an invalidating environment is that Linda did not learn to grieve. Grieving is a natural process of allowing oneself to emotionally experience a loss, receive appropriate support, and eventually be able to accept a particular loss as a natural part of life. When successful grieving has occurred, the person can feel sad about something but accept it as something that happened in the past and can then feel reduced intensity of pain about it over time. If a person has appropriate support, loss and rejection can be tolerated. The individual who knows how to ask for support can also learn how to self-soothe. From a DBT perspective, Linda could not grieve any of her painful experiences in her family environment without receiving an invalidating or uncompassionate response from her parents, so Linda learned to ignore her feelings rather than soothe herself. Her affect management strategy thus became to ignore and deny feelings rather than to become aware of them, notice them, utilize appropriate soothing, and continue with normal functioning. Instead, Linda learned to prevent herself from experiencing loss as much as possible. Ignoring the feelings may have left her with a storehouse of unexpressed hurt, which she now expresses through anger. She is left with a tendency to be uncompassionate toward others and, because of her poor affect regulation, expresses anger in inappropriate ways. Linda also now avoids being in intimate relationships because of the intolerable feelings that come with being rejected. With no skills developed to manage rejection or loss, she has extreme reactions to it, for example, overdosing on pills after a failed romance. She has come to prefer anonymous relationships with men to prevent herself from feeling attachment, thereby preventing herself from experiencing unmanageable levels of loss.

The DBT treatment model is a very nonshaming, nonblaming approach. It begins by helping the client understand why she has the symptom pattern that she does, and also proposes ways that she will ultimately be able to change that. It is a cognitive behavioral approach with Buddhist philosophy woven into it. This approach employs a combination of change strategies that are standard in many cognitive behavioral therapy programs, but includes "acceptance" strategies that are equally important but not present in many other cognitive behavioral approaches. The acceptance strategies are the crucial ingredient that helps both the client and the therapist remain hopeful, when both might be frustrated or likely to give up hope if they believed the client would never get better.

ESSENTIAL CLINICAL SKILLS

One of the most important clinical skills necessary to deliver this treatment is that therapists must be willing to view Linda as a person who is trying her best, using the most adaptive skills that she was able to learn, and not perceive her as a mean, manipulative, or overly angry person. Even if the therapist at times gets annoyed or frustrated with Linda, the therapist's responsibility is to maintain a belief in the possibility for Linda to improve, and to remember that Linda is not a fundamentally bad person or trying to manipulate the therapist, even if the end result is that the therapist feels manipulated. The therapist must remain aware of the difference between Linda's ultimate effect on people and Linda's intentions, and must continue to respectfully view Linda as a person who is lacking skills, rather than a person who intentionally hurts or manipulates others. Thus, from a stance of compassion and respect for the wisdom in each of Linda's symptoms and seemingly maladaptive behaviors, the therapist must remain grounded in the ability to "radically accept" (as Linehan calls it) Linda at all times. At the same time, in a benevolent way, the therapist must urge and encourage Linda to work to make her life better. Linehan uses the analogy of a burn victim to describe the emotional sensitivity that individuals with BPD experience. Burn victims' surface skin is so sensitive that the slightest touch can be excruciating. The therapist can use the analogy to remember that when Linda acts angrily and impulsively, in truth she is reacting with extreme sensitivity, as a burn victim might respond to the lightest touch. Her seemingly over-reactive behaviors make sense in the context of the pain she feels. Linda may have been trying to avoid feeling hurt or rejection or may have been overwhelmed by unmanageable affect, and so she did the best she could to handle the situation. However, the therapist also needs to help her find more effective ways of managing these feelings. Linda needs help with her ability to regulate emotions and express affect appropriately because avoiding hurt or lashing out at others only further isolates and alienates her, which sustains her current symptom picture.

Therapists who use a DBT approach must be willing to get team support through a DBT consultation team. The team members support each other in their work because it is very taxing to maintain the aforementioned attitude at all times. Fellow team members validate and normalize each other's emotional reactions, remind each other when they have "anti-DBT" conceptualizations, and help each other get the support they need to get back on track for the betterment of both therapist and client. When therapists become judgmental, annoyed, and frustrated, they cannot be effective with the client. Therapists must be willing to accept their own fallibility, be humble enough to openly admit their lack of knowledge about how to proceed at times, and be willing to seek consultation from colleagues. Sometimes therapists get angry or feel inadequate when clients don't get better under their care. From a DBT standpoint, it is natural that a therapist working with Linda might feel such things at times and would need validation and support. Thus, the consultation group helps the therapist in a way that is similar to how the therapist's treatment helps the client. When the group validates the therapist's feelings, provides support, and offers practical suggestions, the therapist feels taken care of too. This ultimately helps Linda progress and helps the therapist remain hopeful for Linda even during times when things don't seem to be going well in Linda's treatment process.

The therapist must also be able to remain flexible. At times, the client may break a contract or act in some way that makes the therapist want to be rigid. The therapist must instead find the best balance between "unwavering centeredness" and "compassionate flexibility." For example, there will be times when Linda will ask to bend the rules, and the therapist needs to be willing to change and update rules that no longer make sense, but must also help Linda stay on track and must remain centered with the goals of Linda's therapy in mind.

The therapist must learn to artfully apply dialectical thinking. It may seem like a contradiction to say that the therapist accepts Linda fully and also encourages her to change, but this is an example of the embracing of opposites. Linehan purports that individuals grow to a higher level when they can synthesize opposite concepts and allow seemingly disparate ideas or feelings to coexist. For example, instead of feeling either attachment or abandonment, a person can feel attached and abandoned at the same time. If the therapist can think of Linda as perfect exactly as she is today (even if she just attempted suicide yesterday) and also remain committed to helping Linda change, then the therapist is skillfully using the dialectical concept. The art of this therapy is to be able to truly feel and convey full acceptance to Linda with all of her behaviors. Feeling accepted is an important part of Linda's healing process and provides the validation that she so badly needs and never got. In the same session, though, the therapist could help Linda remember her desire to change and urge her to use a skill she learned so that next time she can try not to engage in that symptom again. This is an example of using the dialectical concept—to validate, accept, and embrace the moment, but push for change too. From a DBT perspective, patients are doing the best they can, *and* they need to do better.

THERAPEUTIC GOALS

From a DBT perspective, there is a hierarchy of treatment targets for all clients. When doing outpatient therapy, the first stage is the pretreatment stage. The goals of that stage are to orient the client—Linda—to this type of therapy and to help her make a commitment to it. During that time, Linda would be educated about the biosocial theory that explains her symptoms, the course of treatment would be outlined, and she would learn about the therapist's interpersonal style. Linda would be allowed to ask any questions she wanted to help her be fully informed about the philosophy of the treatment and what the experience will be like. The best way to accomplish her goals would be to join a DBT skills training group where she would learn the skills she is missing to meet her goals. During her individual therapy, she would get help practicing and integrating these concepts. The group is more like a course than a group process experience, with notebooks, homework, attendance expectations, and practice in the skills she will be acquiring. Having the skills training occur separately from the individual therapy is ideal because it allows her a time and place to learn the skills, and then a place to integrate them into her life, with the therapist's assistance. An outline of therapeutic boundaries, such as appropriate use of telephone consultation, would be discussed. Gathering her clinical history would also happen at this stage. During this stage, Linda would make a decision to commit to therapy or not.

After the commitment is made, DBT provides a standard hierarchy of treatment targets about which Linda would have already been informed. Suicidal behaviors (including parasuicidal) are targeted first. According to the given history, this was not a reported symptom other than the one overdose. Treatment can only proceed to other issues if these most dangerous behaviors can be managed successfully. If these symptoms arise during the course of treatment, they always rise to the top of the hierarchy and are retargeted until there is evidence of the client successfully managing them.

The next set of targets are therapy-interfering behaviors. These are behaviors that prevent the therapy from working, such as missing sessions, feeling angry at the therapist but saying nothing, not doing homework, and so on. Linda may not have come to therapy with much motivation, given that she came in at her lawyer's urging, so a lack of interest in therapy or lack of commitment to herself to improve her life would be targeted here.

The next set of targets are quality-of-life–interfering behaviors. These are behaviors that ultimately decrease the quality of her life by getting her into trouble, creating crises, and making her life more difficult than it needs to be. Linda and the therapist would discuss this pattern and identify such behaviors. Examples from the case study include having sex with men she doesn't know, getting herself into legal trouble by purposefully hitting another car, and lashing out at coworkers. These targets are collaboratively defined as Linda begins to think about which behaviors she engages in that decrease the quality of her life.

After identifying these targets, learning of behavioral skills would be the next phase of treatment. Given that Linda would be in a skills group, she would be learning the skills simultaneously in group and practicing their application in her life, with the therapist's support. The skills are categorized into five main categories: core mindfulness, interpersonal effectiveness, emotion regulation, distress tolerance, and self-management. All of the modules will teach Linda the life skills she needs to reduce her loneliness, build healthy relationships, and manage her emotional life more effectively. Even during the stage of working on quality-of-life targets, the skills Linda is learning would help her address those targets more successfully.

Since Linda would be learning skills in group concurrently, individual therapy the therapist would work to integrate her learning of skills from the group into real situations in her life. The first goal for Linda would be for her to learn better interpersonal skills. She recognizes that her life is empty and that she lacks any close relationships at this time. She attributes that to reasons other than her own behaviors, at this time, because if she thought it were her own fault, she would probably be so emotionally crushed that she would become very depressed and suicidal. The therapist's role is to help her look at her life in a nonjudgmental way and have compassion for herself. She did not learn how to build mutually supportive, loving relationships because she did not learn that from her primary relationships with her family. But it is not too late to learn now. These are skills that she simply missed because of the way her family environment was for her. With a nonjudgmental attitude toward herself, Linda would probably be able to look more honestly at herself and recognize some of her behaviors that alienate people. The interpersonal skills module of the DBT skills training will be especially helpful to her because it teaches skills involved in building and maintaining mutually beneficial, respectful, and satisfying relationships. Skills training will certainly be a challenge, but she will need to do it to be able to change her relationships with her sister, neighbors, and potential relationship partners, and she will need to change to stop feeling "my life is empty." In fact, that belief is not a negative distortion at this point. In fact, her life is empty of close relationships. It is a given that this would be a collaboratively defined goal. If Linda did not agree that this was important, the therapist and Linda would explore to find what was most important to her to work on first. It would be my guess that building close relationships would be an important treatment goal.

A second important goal would be improved distress tolerance and emotion regulation, and the two modules by these names would help her. She employs shopping, bingeing, impulsive sex, and angry lashing out as coping mechanisms when she feels very distressed. All of these are destructive for her in some way, and so it would be important to identify and practice healthy ways to manage her distress. She would learn many techniques and practice them in the DBT group and in real-life situations. She would also learn "mindfulness" exercises in the mindfulness skills section, which would help her accept the moment and be able to tolerate painful experiences without having to act impulsively. She would need to learn these skills to counter the way she has learned to soothe herself when she feels emotionally wounded. She would learn these skills in group but would be asked to practice them in her life when situations warranting their use presented themselves. The individual therapy would be the place to work on that integration process, and an arrangement for telephone consultation with the therapist for practice during the week might also be part of the treatment plan.

ASSESSMENT

I would use the Dissociative Experiences Scale [DES; Bernstein & Putnam (1988)] to test Linda's level of dissociation because of her reported experiences of not remembering various activities. If she were highly dissociative, this would be important to know because perhaps mindfulness meditation could lead to further dissociating. She would need to learn grounding techniques, the ability to bring herself back from a dissociative experience, and would learn more about the circumstances under which she dissociates if these behaviors were present. If she scored above 25 on the DES, I would proceed with further assessment of dissociation using further scales or clinical interview. Given her loss of time, finding herself smoking when she does not smoke, and not remembering conversations, she could have a diagnosis of Dissociative Disorder Not Otherwise Specified or Dissociative Identity Disorder, so I would assess her carefully to determine a proper diagnosis. If either of these were present, they could lead to therapy-interfering behaviors (e.g., not remembering appointments) or quality-of-life–interfering behaviors, and assessment and management of these problems would be included in her treatment plan.

I would also assess for paranoid, narcissistic, or antisocial features in her personality disorder because of her severe lack of ability in relationships, lack of empathy for others, and lack of remorse. I would use clinical interviewing to assess the presence of any behaviors that might fit with those diagnoses by gathering more thorough information about her relationships with people throughout her life, her ability to empathize with others, her desire to be in relationships, and the like.

If there were qualities consistent with any of these diagnoses, further determinations would need to be made about Linda's treatment plan. There might be some changes in emphasis on which skills need more attention first, or different expectations of how Linda might behave in group that would be important to consider.

I would also gather more information about her impulsive behaviors. There was mention of shopping and binge-eating in the case study, so I would explore that further through interview and perhaps a checklist that might help her recognize her own degree of usage of these symptoms. It would be important to know how much she relies on these symptoms and in what situations she tends to use them. A functional analysis and behavioral chain analysis of these symptoms would be helpful. The therapist would help Linda to carefully analyze various episodes of these activities, learning about the antecedents and reinforcing consequences in the moment, and in her life context. After such analysis, the following questions could be answered: What function do these behaviors serve? What are the positive and negative consequences of engaging in them? What is the net effect of keeping them in Linda's behavioral repertoire? If they happen more than occasionally and have negative consequences for her, reduced reliance on them would be worked into the treatment plan. Dealing with addictions is part of the quality-of-life–interfering behaviors in the target hierarchy, so attention would be given to them and a plan for managing them would be developed. It is likely that she has addictive tendencies because she clearly lacks affect management skills and addictive behaviors are classic ways to soothe, distract, or otherwise avoid painful affect.

CONCEPTUALIZATION OF PATIENT

Linda is probably very lonely and sad, and also confused about why her relationships haven't worked out very well. She might think that the world offered her a raw deal and that, by chance, there is no one good around her. She doesn't realize how her lack of interpersonal skill contributes to, and emotion dysregulation leads to, her relationship problems. She probably feels deeply rejected on a regular basis and, in turn, believes that others are wrong, stupid, unkind, manipulative, or inadequate in some way. This is the best explanation she can come up with since she cannot yet look at her own contribution to why people treat her as they do. The case is riddled with this kind of external attribution. A few examples are that she believes the elderly people in the accident are manipulating for money, the school administration is "loading me with garbage" when asking her to have her letters to parents preapproved before being sent, her sister is distant because of her baby, and she can't understand why her neighbors dislike her. She probably has some form of a "poor me" or "why me" interpretation of failed relationships because she only sees others' parts and doesn't see what she does that contributes to it.

As a result, she probably often feels unhappy and in emotional pain. She may experience these feelings more as anger, based on the description of her behaviors, but underneath the anger would be sadness, loneliness, and feelings of rejection if she could be more emotionally honest with herself. Anger is a stronger, less vulnerable feeling and would have been more adaptive in her invalidating environment. She uses impulsive behaviors, for the most part to soothe and distract herself (e.g., shopping, bingeing, sex). She probably has no idea why she tends to overdo it when it comes to these behaviors and perhaps has a superficial understanding, such as "I just love to shop." After she engages in these behaviors, she may feel better in the moment but may feel shame, regret, and even upset when she must deal with the consequences. The trouble she gets into because of these behaviors becomes a quality-of-life issue.

She has come to believe that something is wrong with her, that she is fundamentally bad or defective in some way. Because she was often given messages of invalidation when growing up, she probably came to believe that something was wrong with her, rather than seeing how her parents' expectations and treatment of her gave her that message. She may also, or alternatively, be angry at the world for being unfair to her. Rather than feeling hurt, she may feel that the world is full of "jerks" who just don't understand or can't do anything right.

POTENTIAL DIFFICULTIES

There might be problems in the early stages of treatment because Linda did not come to treatment out of her own desire to make her life better. She could have problems at the precommitment stage and may not have much desire to engage in therapy at all. She might feel that she doesn't want to "waste time on this bullshit" because she is suspicious of others' motives and has difficulty trusting others. In therapy, she would have a nurturant therapist who accepts her behaviors and a group therapist (and members) trying to help her learn better ways of responding, and this might feel so foreign to her that it could be terrifying. Her thoughts might include "Why would these people care about me? This can't be real. They are trying to trick me into caring, and then they will abandon me." She might become so afraid of rejection and abandonment (which she often experienced in seemingly nurturant, loving, or caring relationships) that she might be drawn to sabotage it first by not showing up or by acting mean in hopes that others will let her go. If she started the therapy insufficiently motivated because her lawyer made her get an evaluation, even if she initially agreed to treatment, ambivalence may come through. Perhaps what she was being taught by the therapists would feel so overwhelming at first that she might want to quit therapy and just go back to her usual way of doing things.

She would probably be ambivalent about leaving, though, because the knowledge she would be getting about the causes of her suffering and the new skills provided would probably be very relevant and she would likely realize that. She might waver in her commitment to therapy, and the therapist would have to retarget therapy-interfering behaviors at various times. The therapist would have to remain very clear-thinking and understand the dialectical dilemmas: the desire to change and the desire to stay the same, the desire to face her fears and the desire to run from her fears. If the therapist gently points out these dilemmas and teaches her about the embracing of opposites, it might help her understand why she finds herself trying, in one way or another, to leave therapy when at other times she wants to stay and get better.

Linehan offers a number of techniques (Linehan, 1993) that could be used if Linda had problems with the commitment stage. For example, the therapist could go over the pros and cons of making a commitment to change, emphasizing her freedom to choose to continue with her life the way she currently lives it with full awareness of the likely consequences of that choice. Once Linda had made a commitment to therapy, the reasons for the commitment could be reviewed and the commitment renegotiated if there were appropriate changes that could make it more possible for Linda to commit, as long as they do not conflict with DBT principles or the therapist's limits. The therapist would need to be aware of shaping contingencies and review what might be most effective for reinforcing commitment and needs to generate hope by "cheerleading" Linda, with the goal of helping her reinstate her commitment.

The foot-in-the-door technique (offering little steps that she can commit to without emphasizing the difficulty) could be used to help Linda make a commitment to taking steps forward that she perceives as manageable for her. Even if Linda had agreed to commit at some point, it's not uncommon for ambivalence to come back at another point in therapy as fears of change or difficulty with the therapy process arise. There is a lower dropout rate for BPD clients in this type of therapy compared with the rate in other treatment approaches (Linehan, 1993), presumably because of the emphasis on helping clients remain committed to the therapy.

PROGNOSIS

If there were antisocial, narcissistic, or paranoid features to Linda's personality, any of these would worsen her prognosis for success. Based on the case history, it sounds as if something beyond borderline characteristics are there, and this means that she may have less potential to become fully functional interpersonally, or that the time it would take to accomplish this would be much longer than estimated.

If she did not have these additional features, and she were sufficiently motivated by her own readiness to change (not just coerced into a psychiatric evaluation by her lawyer), then she could probably demonstrate improvement in three to six months. She might also feel better right away, beginning with the orientation to the DBT biosocial theory, because she will learn that she is not fundamentally bad but that a "poor fit" between her environment and her biology caused her problems. She might be heartened to know about the positive outcome research for these symptoms and feel more hopeful rather quickly. If she were to learn and practice some distress tolerance skills, mindfulness, and emotion regulation skills, and also work on her interpersonal skills, she could begin to notice some changes in herself that would positively reinforce her efforts to change further. Once she learns the skills and applies them in her life, the long-term prognosis is good for her because she will have the skills she needs to make her life worth living. However, it is not clear from the presentation that she is sufficiently motivated, and in that case, no treatment will really be helpful until she feels that her own dissatisfaction with her life is strong enough to warrant the effort to change.

Assuming, however, that she really was motivated and that she did not have other personality disorder features, it would probably take a few years to be fully functional. I would expect that, even then, she might use some of her old symptoms at times. For example, she might resort to bingeing and shopping when feeling lonely or sad. Sometimes these symptoms can be hard to stop completely since societal messages frequently reinforce them. She might also be limited in her social functioning and may still have fears of allowing herself to be close, especially with men, and she would have to struggle to apply her skills in these relationships. If she could improve even one relationship (e.g., with her sister), she could begin to have a model for how relationships work, be able to receive feedback, and learn to recognize her effect on people.

TIMELINE

The skills training group goes through all four modules and would probably take about one year of treatment, during which Linda would go to group once a week and individual therapy once a week as well. The original outcome research reported in Linehan's book was based on one year of treatment in that manner. Once she completed the group, Linda and the therapist would assess what her therapy needs were. How well had she understood and integrated the information into her everyday life? Did she still need a lot of practice? What is still not working for her in her life? Most likely, even if she learned the skills, she still would need help applying them in context. So, a new therapy contract could be negotiated given her stated treatment needs if she wanted to continue. She could feasibly continue until she fully reached all of the goals she wanted to meet for herself. Thus, the length of treatment would ultimately depend on her desire to continue to change or her satisfaction with her current status.

SPECIFIC TECHNIQUES

I like to use humor with clients like Linda. She may have difficulty feeling any lightness or happiness, or even seeing the humor in anything. Whenever there was an opportunity to be lighthearted, I would try to incorporate that because she may not have had that experience with anyone. If she could learn to accept her limitations and laugh at herself in a compassionate way, she might be able to decrease her shaming, blaming, fault-finding way of conceptualizing things. This would be part of my "irreverent" way with her, which is a DBT concept that allows the therapist to use his or her own personality intuitively in ways to help the client see a point. Sometimes an exaggerated devil's advocate approach can be funny. For example, if she shared in therapy that she got so angry that she wanted to just go to the principal's office and curse him out or some such extreme behavior, rather than try to help her think of alternatives, I might say, "OK, let's imagine how that would go." I might egg her on and encourage her to embellish the event as she pictures it, and she might laugh when she realizes how absurd it might be if she actually did that. In my experience, clients like Linda have found that funny because they expected me to soberly encourage the "right," responsible behavior and are surprised when I tell them to go ahead and imagine it, and tell me how that would work. They raise their eyebrows in surprise and laugh as I soberly tell them to go ahead and enjoy that thought. In this way, I would be playing the devil's advocate because I would paradoxically encourage her to think of making the less functional choice, allowing her to fully play it out in her mind. However, as we exaggerated the scenario, she would see how, ultimately, that would not bring her what she wants, which is probably to be understood, respected, or heard by others. Perhaps she would laugh at the ridiculousness of taking such an action and feel lightened by the freedom to express it verbally without judgment from me, unlike what she would have expected from a therapist. I would only do that, however, if I felt sure that she understood it to be an exaggeration, had good reality testing, and recognized that I was not encouraging a harmful action. As long as I had assessed these abilities correctly, she would probably come to realize that she didn't want to make that choice. Similarly, if she had antisocial features and would derive sadistic pleasure from such a fantasy, I would certainly not use that technique. I would try to use my own strength, my ability to see humor in difficult situations and teach her that by modeling, if possible.

I would also use appropriate degrees of self-disclosure, if relevant, to go along with the irreverent stance. She might expect that no one else suffers the way she does, or that people like her will never succeed. It might help her if I occasionally acknowledged a perceived failing of my own and described how I handled it to help her see such experiences as part of the human condition, not a flaw of hers. I have found that clients like Linda have been surprised when I acknowledged that I, too, have gotten angry in my life and have not always handled it well, that

I have struggled in some way that was similar to what they experience. With her parents expecting her to be a super-responsible, perfect oldest child, she did not experience a nurturant, supportive, and validating relationship, and through self-revelation, I would be doing some repair work. Through my irreverent stance, I would hope to teach her that suffering is universal and that everyone has "dysfunctional" behaviors at times, which would give her hope and help her see herself as less different from others, instead of as a failed person who can't do anything right. Other techniques from DBT are to help her "make lemonade out of lemons" or help her see the kernel of truth in all behaviors so that she does not need to be so angry at herself or others.

I could imagine that if I tried that too much, or at the wrong time, that I could anger her or make her feel invalidated if I were joking when she was in a very serious mood about something. But if that happened, I would be prepared to respond flexibly to her need to be understood and would apologize for my lack of attunement at that moment. That, too, could be a healing experience, since her parents probably did not apologize for their invalidating behaviors.

I might also work on affect tolerance skills, using guided imageries to work on containing negative affect and building resources and qualities needed to manage affect. This is covered in DBT skills training to some extent, but I would draw from additional protocols from other related approaches (e.g., resource development or affect tolerance building) to supplement and see if she reports that it helps. If it did, we would continue it.

SPECIAL CAUTIONS

Linda would likely have feelings, problems, and issues in the therapeutic relationship with me, but in the DBT perspective, such problems are not called transference or countertransference but are categorized as therapy-interfering behaviors, which are the second most important set of targets after self-harm. If she ever had feelings toward me of any kind, she would know that she was allowed to talk about them and figure out a way to work through them with my help. Having feelings about the therapist is not therapy-interfering. In fact, such feelings are expected and can be very helpful. But having feelings, not talking about them, and instead having them come out in actions (e.g., missing sessions, being angry with me and not saying but showing it), is a therapy-interfering behavior. If that happened, I would point it out and we would talk about it.

The quality of the therapeutic relationship is of utmost importance and, at times, can be the only motivator for the client to fight to stay alive. If at any time either Linda or I had anything other than generally positive feelings toward each other and confidence in our ability to work together, we would need to talk about it. Her feelings and attributions about me would not be pathologized or dismissed as "transference." They might be about me as a real person or they might incorporate dynamics from previous relationships. If the feelings were getting in the way, the focus would be on how to resolve them between us. She would know from her orientation to raise such issues and that we would work together for her to feel more comfortable about them.

She might feel a strong attachment toward me and perhaps fear abandonment because it is uncomfortable to her to feel so attached. I might feel overly needed, exhausted, or perhaps worried about her at times. Having feelings in the context of this important relationship is normal, and I would let her know that it would be fine to feel whatever she did toward me and could talk about any of it with me. She would have been oriented about that early in the therapy, during the pretreatment phase when we discuss what therapy will be like, so the normalization of this aspect of therapy begins then. She would also have been informed of the limits of our relationship, specifically that we could never be friends, just therapist and client. If she were to question that or if there were times when it became a painful reality and a source of loss I would validate her loss feelings and help her deal with the grief rather than change the nature of our relationship. This is a painful reality, so I could use that as an opportunity to help her with healthy grieving about it. My own reactions to her as a person would get attention during my DBT consultation group. In the group, I would work to remain balanced so I could stay compassionate and grounded in my DBT conceptualizations and remain therapeutic for her should anything push me off balance.

She may have self-harm urges or even other-harm urges (especially if there is an antisocial component), and we would work closely to resolve such issues as a top priority whenever they came up. She would know that I expected her to tell me about such things from the beginning of therapy, during the pretreatment phase, and we would have a clear plan about how such issues were going to be handled. If safety could not be ensured in an outpatient setting, she would be referred to a hospital for a higher level of care if necessary.

AREAS TO AVOID

There is nothing I would choose to avoid. I don't agree with that idea, philosophically. I believe that patients have the right to talk about and work on any issue with me, and if there are areas of work that are beyond my expertise, I refer them to someone else, as needed. It is not for me to decide what not to work on, and if I discouraged Linda's interest in or attention to some aspect of her symptomatology, I think that would send a message that she was not fully accepted. I would consider that a therapy-interfering behavior on my part. Both therapist and client can produce therapy-interfering behaviors, and that would be one of them. If I felt that I didn't want to deal with some aspect of her treatment, I would need to examine that with my consultation group and figure out what caused me to feel that way. Depending on what the reasons were, I would decide what to do about it, but I would not continue to avoid the issue.

I would help Linda prioritize different symptoms so that she didn't try to do everything at once, or more than she could handle. But we would discuss it and organize the treatment so that if there were a problem, we could decide how it fit into the treatment depending on how severe and urgent the problem was.

MEDICATION

Medication might be helpful for Linda's depressed or anxious feelings, and I would support her going for a psychiatric evaluation. However, there are no medications for BPD per se, and I would help her understand which symptoms can be targeted by medication and which cannot. However, any medication that helped would be welcome, and I would encourage her to consider it.

PATIENT STRENGTHS

Linda's nurturance and cultivating of her bonsai plants would be something I would explore with her. What got her interested in this? Why does she do it? Is it hard work? How does she feel when doing it? This may be a way that she expresses a nurturant, caring, even loving part of herself, safely, with plants who don't talk back, mistreat her, or abandon her. If, in fact, this hobby represents that (and not some other thing like a competition to be better than others, etc.), I would try to help Linda build on the feeling she has for her plants and to broaden it to other creatures. Does she like pets? Where else can she allow herself to feel love and care gently for someone? I would want to work with that potential strength.

Linda demonstrates competence in her ability to teach fourth grade in a racially mixed environment as long as she has structure. Although she has not done well in the unstructured interpersonal realm, it sounds as if she can teach the children effectively. I would explore how she felt about that part of her life. Does she enjoy it? Does she feel successful at it? Can she derive good feelings from that aspect of her functioning? Does she enjoy the multicultural aspect of it? If so, that could be a source of self-esteem, if she can focus on awareness of that ability. If not, then we would look into why she stays in this job if she is not happy there. This is a quality-of-life issue.

She also completed a graduate degree while working and worked through college. She must be intelligent to have succeeded with little extra time to study. It is also a strength that she was so motivated to put herself through school that way. I would explore whether Linda feels proud of that. I would explore with Linda how it felt to be that motivated and see if she could feel that motivated about changing other aspects of her life and to conceive of her current personal growth as a graduate school for her life.

If Linda were to stay in therapy, I would reinforce her ability and willingness to look at painful aspects of herself. If she could do that, that is a great strength. I would help her to appreciate that about herself and see that not all people have the courage and commitment to try to change themselves.

LIMIT SETTING

Part of DBT is a "telephone consultation" agreement. The idea is that the individual therapist can be very helpful by coaching the client in the moment of a problem by reminding the client about possible skills to use to cope with the present stressor. Although that is the ideal telephone consultation arrangement, I prefer to plan for telephone consultation rather than just have clients randomly call me. The therapist needs to observe natural limits rather than set limits. My own natural limits are that since I am very busy, I do not like to get frequent random phone calls to which I am expected to respond right away. I cannot meet that expectation. The difference between a natural limit and setting a limit is that a natural limit is just a fact about the world. Philosophically, Linda would not be wrong nor wanting too much if she wished she could call me anytime and have me call her back. That would just be an expression of her wish or desire, which is not considered wrong or pathologized in any way. However, I cannot meet her needs all of the time, and so my inability to call back as Linda might like would be a natural limit. Instead, if Linda suspected that she would need a phone check–in, we would look at our books and schedule it at a given time that would be likely to be helpful. During a 15–30 minute check–in, I would help her apply a skill in a given situation. If she wanted to just "ventilate," I would ask her what skill she needed to use, try to help her get back on track, and "cheerlead" her into helping herself in that moment. I charge for that time and would tell her that. At one point, I did not charge for telephone time, but I found that if I had too many check–ins I would feel resentful, tired, or worn out. Sometimes three or four clients in a given week needed check–ins, and I used to accommodate calls for free. I don't pretend that planning the consultation or charging for it is the best for the patient, or for "setting a limit," but it is a natural limit of mine. I am a busy person who is very attentive and caring toward my clients, and I need to take care of myself. Thus, I prefer to schedule and have telephone time paid for. However, I think it may help keep the conceptual boundaries clearer to plan and charge, to help the client remember the context of the relationship. It could also be helpful for Linda to learn to delay gratification and work on something herself until she can get the additional reinforcement from her therapist. I think there are pros and cons to both ways of handling telephone consultation.

Another important boundary issue that could be relevant with Linda is verbal abuse. Since she tends to express her feelings angrily and without compassion for others' feelings, she might be verbally abusive to me. Although I might accept some lack of skill on her part, I would not allow myself to be verbally abused and would let her know that the first time it happened. Verbal abuse is covered in my informed consent process at the beginning of therapy, and I discuss it in the pretreatment phase. I consider it a therapy-interfering behavior, and we would work on it from that perspective. On a few occasions, I have had clients who were verbally abusive who thought they were entitled to treat me that way because they paid me. Now I include this briefly in my informed consent form, and then if the issue ever comes up, I reference it. It is a natural limit for me as well, but it would also be helpful for Linda to know that people (even therapists) have feelings and that even talking meanly to others will have a negative effect on her relationships with people.

SIGNIFICANT OTHERS AND HOMEWORK

If at all possible, I would involve Linda's significant others. If any of her family would come (e.g., sister, parents), I would encourage it. I would not necessarily plan for regular family therapy, given her stage of life and their current relationship. If anyone were willing to get involved in her treatment to some degree, though, it would most likely be helpful. It would help me to observe Linda's relationship dynamics and interpersonal behaviors in context. I could also help determine if any of the relationships had potential for improvement if she worked on changing her behaviors toward these individuals. It would also provide an opportunity for Linda to practice better interpersonal skills with me present so that I could help her see how she gets off track, or positively reinforce and encourage (i.e., "cheerlead") when she is on track. If we tried it and together determined that it was not helpful, we would discontinue it.

Regarding homework, she would have weekly homework from her group from the DBT workbook. However, I usually come up with homework in addition in a collaborative manner. I would ask if she wanted more homework or just ask her to share the homework she already had from the group. Since the group is focused on homework and feedback about the homework, I would not want to duplicate their work but would simply be interested in her experience, her attempts to apply new skills, and her stuck areas where she needed help from me. I would go over her Diary Card with her, which is a homework assigned by her group that clients use daily to check off whenever they have a symptom and/or use a new skill they learned. Doing so would reinforce the group work, help me find out about her symptom level, and let her know that I care and am paying attention to her growth and development.

TERMINATION ISSUES

Termination would happen when Linda felt ready to leave, unless she left early because she didn't really feel ready to make a commitment to therapy. When she felt satisfied with her life and wasn't in need of changing anything else, we would have to deal with her feelings of loss in leaving the relationship. Linda would probably feel a great deal of sadness and wonder if she could do it on her own. We might plan a slow tapering schedule, first every other week, then once a month for a while to help her adjust to the change. We would talk about all that she had accomplished, and I would help Linda to feel proud of how much she changed her life if she didn't feel that already. Loss issues might still be triggered, and it might feel hard to imagine not seeing me anymore. We would talk about what that was like for her and how she might cope with that. She would take her time and taper until she felt ready to really be on her own.

With regard to relapse prevention, Linda would need to know what her early warning symptoms would be, and we would define them together. For example, she might start to feel more depressed or find herself bingeing. She would need to pay attention to all issues in her life if symptoms were starting. If Linda were ready to leave, she would likely have some quality relationships in her life, so she would have people she could talk with to help her figure out what is going on for her. She would need to use those relationships before seeking therapy again. She might be able to get back on track if she is talking about what is going on and using the skills she learned.

MECHANISMS OF CHANGE

At the end of therapy, Linda would know about her temperament, be more able to take care of herself, and be aware that she is a very sensitive person in the world. Rather than feel bad about that, angry or otherwise emotionally overwhelmed, she would now know how to ride the tide of a feeling and would have many skills to cope with that uncomfortable experience. She would also now be supporting herself through her feelings and helping herself manage, rather than being her own worst enemy by not making good decisions, acting impulsively, or otherwise being destructive to herself.

She would also know about how her "invalidating" family environment left her with many skill deficits. This would help her to not feel like a horrible person who is often rejected. It would help her nonjudgmentally accept what happened to her. She does not need to blame her parents because their upbringing was based on the same principles. They too were doing the best they could, and they too had skill deficits, which they passed on to her. Their way of parenting was not a good fit for her. Rather than focusing on blaming anyone (herself or her parents), she would understand that sensitive children feel very hurt by such environments, and they fail to learn needed skills. She can learn these skills now, and it is never too late to learn.

If she could accept this premise, she could have an open mind to learning whatever she needs to that will help meet her goals. If she would like better relationships, then there are a lot of interpersonal skills in the DBT group and manual for her to learn. If she really learned to apply them, her relationships with people will have improved.

Secondly, if she could learn to tolerate painful moments and grieve appropriately, she would no longer need to act in self-destructive and impulsive ways. These are skills, and she could learn them by practicing the mindfulness exercises and learning about healthy grieving. During the course of her treatment, she would learn to have compassion for herself and the pain she endured as a child. Compassion would first come from her therapist, but then she would be able to give that compassion to herself. This could be a challenge if she had developed antisocial or paranoid traits because then issues of trust and lack of compassion are more deeply entrenched and she may have to really struggle to change this about herself. She would have to really want to change and recognize the value of doing so. That would be up to her. The DBT approach offers skills, but clients must decide to make the commitment to try to accept themselves and at the same time make the effort to change. The therapist can offer hope, "cheerlead," and help clients make a commitment, but ultimately clients must choose. Linda has a choice about what she wants to do with her life, and if her present way of being is unsatisfying enough to her, perhaps she will really work on herself.

REFERENCES

Carlson, E. B. & Putnam, F. (1988). Bethesda, MD: National Institute of Mental Health.

Cowdry, D., & Gardner, R. (1985). Self-destructing behavior. *Psychiatric Clinics of North America, 8*(2), 389–403.

Cowdry, D., & Gardner, R. (1988). Pharmaco-therapy of borderline personality disorder: Alprazolam, carbamazepine, trifluoperazine, and tranylcypromine. *American Archives of Psychiatry, 54*(2), 111–119.

Gardner, D., & Cowdry, R. (1986). Positive effects of carbamazepine on behavioral dyscontrol in borderline personality disorder. *American Journal of Psychiatry, 143*(4), 519–522.

Kuhn, T. S. (1970). *The structure of scientific revolutions.* Chicago: The University of Chicago Press.

Linehan, M. (1993). *Skills training manual for cognitive-behavioral treatment of borderline personality disorder.* New York: Guilford Press.

Marx, K., & Engels, F. (1970). *The Communist Manifesto.* Selected works (Vol. 3). New York: International Universities Press.

O'Leary, K., Brouwers, P., & Gardner, D. (1991). Neuropsychological testing of patients with borderline personality disorder. *American Journal of Psychiatry, 148*(1), 106–111.

5

Cognitive Behavioral Therapy

Gina M. Fusco and Jack Apsche

OVERVIEW OF COGNITIVE BEHAVIORAL TREATMENT

Cognitive behavioral therapy (CBT) is extensively used as a short-term psychotherapeutic treatment modality for a wide range of mental disorders. Although treatment may require more intensive intervention than with Axis I disorders, CBT has in the past several years become an increasingly effective intervention in the treatment of borderline personality disorder (BPD) (McGinn & Sanderson, 2001). Some writers have also suggested that CBT may have some distinctive advantages over other therapeutic approaches (A. Beck, Freeman, & Associates, 1990; A. Beck, Freeman, Davis, & Associates, 2003; Freeman, Pretzer, Fleming, & Simon, 1990). Recent studies have demonstrated that CBT in combination with formal problem-solving skills training (PSST) reduces self-injurious behaviors (Raj, Kumaraiah, & Bhide, 2001). Most therapists, however, agree that BPD can be one of the most challenging, complex (Layden, Newman, Freeman, & Morse, 1993) and "vexing" disorders to treat (Trull, Stepp, & Durett, 2003).

Specific cognitive approaches to the treatment of borderline personality disorder include A. Beck, Freeman, Davis et al., 2003; Perris, 1994; Linehan, 1987; Turner, 1989, 1992; and Millon, 1987. A. Beck et al. proposed a cognitive behavioral treatment strategy aimed at decreasing and improving impulse control and dichotomous thinking, increasing control over emotions, addressing assumptions, and strengthening the identity of the patient.

Ironically, although several studies have been published about treating individuals with BPD, little empirical research examining the effectiveness of cognitive therapies in the treatment of BPD exists (Trull, Stepp, & Durrett, 2003). Koerner and Linehan (2000) suggest that specific cognitive behavioral treatment based on Linehan's dialectical behavior therapy model demonstrated a lower dropout rate, fewer inpatient psychiatric days, lower self-reported anger, and significantly less self-injurious behaviors than the rate for those who had received "treatment as usual." Anecdotally, Freeman, Pretzer, Fleming, & Simon (1990) state, "when properly applied, Cognitive Therapy can be effective with Borderline Personality Disorder" (p. 181).

The major thrust of CBT is toward the understanding and identification of patient's behavioral patterns and the precipitating and accompanying cognitive processes. Cognitive processes include current and automatic thoughts, self-statements, perceptions, appraisals, attributions, memories, goals, assumptions, standards, and beliefs. Simply, cognitions influence behavior, emotions, and physiological states without a linear connection that thoughts equal feelings (Freeman, 1992).

CBT is a relatively structured approach to treatment and is based on the collaboration between the patient and the therapist. It is an active, directive, time-limited approach that focuses on the present (A. Beck, Rush, Shaw, & Emery, 1979). Distressing emotional states and/or dysfunctional behaviors are conceptualized as the result of the interpretation by the individual and how the individual makes assumptions (McGinn & Sanderson, 2001). DeRubeis and Beck (1988) write that in order to understand emotional disturbance, the cognitive aspect of the upsetting situation must be the focus of change. Therefore, cognitive behavioral approaches examine how stimulus is perceived, interpreted, categorized, and responded to. These responses tend to be patterned responses reacting to learned beliefs, assumptions, expectations, and held beliefs. The overarching goal of CBT, therefore, is to change or alter those beliefs that have led to distress or dysfunction.

MAJOR TENETS OF COGNITIVE BEHAVIORAL THERAPY

A core tenet of CBT is that one's basic assumptions play a central role in influencing perception and interpretation of events and in shaping both behavior and emotional responses (A. Beck, Freeman, et al., 1990; Beck, 1976, 1987). These basic assumptions or rules that govern individual thought and behavior develop over years and are called schema. Schema guide every aspect of the individual's life. They provide meaning and structure to a world that is bombarding our senses with information, and they are created through years of development. They provide the blueprint or the template for beliefs through which receptive information is processed and filtered. This method of organization is in accord with an already existing system complete with rules and meanings. From these basic beliefs, automatic thoughts are generated. Automatic thoughts are the immediate conscious stream of thoughts that are generated from schema. Automatic thoughts can be rational though still dysfunctional, biased, or distorted. CBT therefore aims to help patients change these dysfunctional thoughts and, by testing and challenging these thoughts, alter the underlying schema (McGinn & Sanderson, 2001).

Frequently Encountered Schema in the BPD Patient

Generally, patients with BPD typically maintain numerous schema that may be in opposition to each other or incongruent. Layden, Newman, Freeman, & Morse (1993) agree with Young's (1990) description of characteristic maladaptive schema for the BPD patient, stating that the most frequently encountered BPD schema are dependence, lack of individuation, emotional deprivation, abandonment, mistrust, unlovability, and incompetence. These schemas are typically compelling and pervasive and may have caused significant disruption and dysfunction for the patient. From these dysfunctional schema, cognitive distortions such as dichotomous (black and white) thinking and catastrophizing are common cognitive processes (e.g., automatic thoughts) present with the BPD patient (A. Beck, Freeman, Davis, et al., 2003).

Accessing and Identifying Schema

Intrinsic to treatment success is the edification of the concept and impact of schema that govern behavior, thoughts, and feelings. A. Beck and Weishaar (1986) write that cognitive psychotherapy is "a collaborative process of empirical investigation, reality testing, and problem solving between the therapist and patient" (p. 43). Additionally, the therapist and patient identify those problems or dysfunctional areas that occur in problem situations that are generated from these schema.

Several useful aids for identifying schema such as the Cognitive Conceptualization Diagram (J. Beck, 1995) and the Incident Chart (Fusco &

Freeman, 2003) can help organize how schema impact the patient's functioning in a patterned and predictable way. Automatic thoughts are also identified through direct therapeutic intervention. The therapist can teach the patient to ask, "What was just going through my mind?" (J. Beck, 1995, p. 10) or to record thoughts on the daily record of dysfunctional thoughts (A. Beck, Rush, Shaw, & Emory, 1979) or on the more recent dysfunctional thought record (J. Beck, 1995). Once problem areas are identified, the patient and therapist determine whether to target the associated schema, whether change can occur, and which level of change is necessary.

Techniques

Strategies are aimed at reducing the symptoms directly, learning new skills, and improving ability to cope with problematic situations that can lead to emotional dysregulation (McGinn & Sanderson, 2001). Methods may include cognitive and behavioral techniques or a combination, such as relaxation, assertiveness training, and cost-benefit analysis. Collaboration, a fundamental principle in CBT, umbrellas the treatment paradigm and can be especially powerful in creating and maintaining therapeutic rapport and the associated treatment gains that such rapport generates.

CLINICAL ATTRIBUTES

The clinical skills and attributes key to successful treatment with a patient with BPD include skills that foster collaboration, rapport, and consistency. J. Beck (1995) writes that many of the attributes essential for the cognitive behavioral therapist are consistent with Rogerian theory and include genuineness, empathy, and remaining nonjudgmental. In addition, the ability to create trust and rapport with the patient is essential. Rapport building begins with the first contact with the patient and continues throughout the entire therapeutic process. Empathic statements, active listening, and correct summaries and reflection encourage rapport and help build therapeutic alliance (J. Beck, 1995).

Based on an accurate case conceptualization, therapists are able to understand past behavior, explain current behavior, and anticipate future behavior (Freeman, 1992). Therapists must be adaptive, flexible, and creative when applying treatment interventions to meet the specific needs of the patient (American Psychiatric Association [APA], 2001). Therefore, in-depth knowledge of specific cognitive and behavioral interventions that will guide patients through self-discovery are necessary to help lead the patient to change (Weishaar, 1993).

Bandura (1969) maintains that learning can also occur through the observation or imitation of others' behavior. Therapists therefore become a significant role model because patients often emulate patterns of values, beliefs, and behaviors of the therapist. Cognitive behavioral therapists have the opportunity to demonstrate healthy boundaries, structure, and an inquisitive nature. They can also demonstrate patience, tolerance, consistency, and the ability to withstand ambiguity and ambivalence, key problems for the patient with BPD.

Inherent in treatment with BPD is the patient's difficulty in engaging in the therapeutic process because establishing trust and intimacy are significant obstacles (Freeman, Pretzer, Fleming, & Simon, 1990; Koenigsberg, 1995; Mays, 1985). The patient with BPD may manifest these difficulties within the therapeutic relationship with themes of abandonment, entitlement, idealization and devaluation of the therapist, and anger management problems. It is therefore essential that the therapist maintain an objective stance, maintain focus, and be able to withstand emotional and reactive expressions (Freeman, et al., 1990). By maintaining a supportive yet firm stance, the therapist creates the necessary holding environment as espoused by Winnicott (1965). It is also imperative that the therapist not personalize these intense and highly charged interactions, but rather apply these behaviors to the ongoing case conceptualization. Applying information from these exchanges to the case conceptualization represents an ability not only to remain married to the original case conceptualization but to be flexible enough to alter or adjust the conceptualization to assimilate new data. The therapist needs to communicate clearly, assertively, and truthfully to the patient in order to reduce misunderstandings. Additionally, the therapist has the unique opportunity to follow through or remain consistent with the patient, which, anecdotally, appears to be sorely lacking in the life of the patient with BPD. This contributes to the building of trust, with the goal of generating a safe environment that promotes attempts to try new behaviors, challenge distortions, and ultimately produce change.

THERAPEUTIC GOALS

An overarching goal necessary for any potential treatment for Linda is to develop rapport and a collaborative relationship. Without the development of such a relationship, treatment is doomed to failure. Linda has a long history of mistrusting others. She jumped to the conclusion that her husband was unfaithful when in reality he was late, and she maintained a firm belief that neighbors "dislike me." It will be important for the therapist to challenge these strongly held schema by remaining consistent, empathic, and engaged in the therapeutic relationship.

The initial goal for Linda is the elimination of suicidal and parasuicidal behaviors. This goal would remain throughout treatment. In the past, Linda has demonstrated that when schema relating to abandonment are activated, she lacks adaptive coping skills to manage the emotional overload. For example, when she refused sexual intimacy with her boyfriend, his remarks about other women caused her to beg, "Please don't leave me," and subsequently to threaten to kill herself. Treatment related to this goal may include learning adaptive coping skills rather than self-injury. Linda's coping skills need to include learning how to self-monitor for catastrophized thoughts related to abandonment or for dichotomous thinking that may include thoughts such as "the only way to prevent him from leaving is to threaten to kill myself." Once these thoughts are identified, Linda may learn to access supports (call her therapist, talk to a supportive friend, go to the emergency room), try relaxation techniques, challenge catastrophized thinking (e.g., "I'm all alone"), or turn her emotions down (Fusco & Freeman, 2003).

Another goal for Linda would be to help her to specifically identify her tendency to engage in dichotomous thinking. This polarized thinking has triggered Linda to react in dramatic, impulsive, and risky ways.

Additional goals for Linda include reducing her propensity to be impulsive. She has engaged in promiscuous sexual interactions with strangers, sporadic spending, and binge eating, and she has reacted with rage and been vengeful toward others. By understanding and becoming aware of the patterned chain of events that leads her to be impulsive, she can then create the opportunity to change or alter the pattern. The chain of events includes identifying and intervening with the following: what triggers lead her to be impulsive (e.g., feelings of rejection, abandonment); the evaluation and challenge of distortions related to triggers; learning stopping techniques; contemplating consequences; and, finally, learning to choose better adaptive responses (A. Beck, Freeman, et al., 1990). Learning to be particularly aware of times when she is vulnerable to triggers can also help her prepare to effectively cope.

Self-monitoring will benefit Linda throughout treatment. Linda's treatment plan should include self-monitoring for worsening Axis I symptoms such as anxiety and depression. Relaxation techniques can assist with reducing arousal associated with anxiety. As Linda has few intimate attachments, she often experiences feelings of isolation and abandonment. These feelings trigger painful experiences of emptiness (e.g., "my life is empty"), which have led to impulsive and dangerous behaviors. For example, rather than searching for the excitement or "rush" of meeting strangers in bars, she may learn how to cope with emptiness in healthy ways. She may try to validate herself (e.g., concretely identifying those things that affirm her identity) by thinking about her positive role as a teacher. These self-affirming thoughts contradict distortions that she is empty and without direction or purpose.

Linda's schema related to abandonment and mistrust may be the most difficult to modify. It is suggested that each goal be subjected to collaborative scrutiny, in that realistic goals, realistic levels of change, and a realistic end product will more likely create a beneficial therapeutic outcome.

ASSESSMENT

Structuring treatment for Linda can be a difficult process. This, in part, is due to the comorbid presentation of Axis I pathology, which can often mask or cloud more long-standing problems. Linda has symptoms of anxiety and depression that may not be the product of the affective instability that is associated with BPD. Assessment should include examining clusters of traits that are particularly specific to BPD. Fusco and Freeman (2003) suggest these traits include a crisis-prone style, heightened sensitivity, catastrophic thinking, and dichotomous thinking. As with any comprehensive assessment, Linda's assessment should also include reviewing her medical history, developmental and historical background, psychosocial history, level of functioning, and mental status. By completing a comprehensive assessment, the therapist can formulate better and more viable treatment strategies that address Linda's specific treatment needs. Overall, the assessment process needs to be comprehensive and flexible and should always include assessment for high-risk behaviors.

Poor coping and problem solving, combined with a borderline personality style, intense affective states, heightened sensitivity, and erratic behaviors, tend to enlarge simple stressors into more formidable crises. Therefore, Linda's inability to manage or cope and her tendency to wrestle with crisis on a daily basis affect her overall functioning (Freeman & Fusco, 2000). This is particularly important to assess because Linda's history includes high-risk behaviors and suicide attempts.

Assessment within the CBT framework includes assessing for the patient's schema that are relevant to the BPD diagnosis and to the prior and present dysfunction that the patient is experiencing. Freeman (1992) suggests that assessment of schema also should include integrating into treatment where these schema fall within the activity-inactivity spectrum. Layden, Newman, Freeman, & Morse (1993) state that schema assessment include viewing how the schema affect the presenting problems, the types of crises that emerge during treatment, and a review of the most negative experiences in the past that impact the present. Freeman (1992) suggests the use of the critical incident technique, which prompts the patient to identify a stressful situation in detail, thus eliciting the accompanying automatic thoughts and related schema. Comprehensive assessment provides a greater understanding and awareness for the patient about how he or she responds to activated crisis-mode schema. This awareness provides a greater opportunity to tackle entrenched patterns that may have caused distress or dysfunction.

CONCEPTUALIZATION OF PATIENT

Linda's past and present behaviors, affective components, and cognitions are consistent with patients diagnosed with BPD. Personalitywise, Linda exhibits a pervasive pattern of instability with interpersonal relationships, identity problems, affective instability, and impulsivity, which are identified as key elements of BPD (APA, 2000). Linda demonstrates problems with interpersonal relationships in all areas of her life, including familial, intimate, social, and occupational spheres. Throughout her life, she has struggled to be stable within a changing environment, never quite forming or maintaining a consistent sense of self. Key to Linda's diagnosis are her demonstrated problems with affective changes, reactivity, and impulsivity. The compounding nature of these traits has caused Linda many problems. For example, when the driver in front of her refused to allow her passage around his slower-moving vehicle, the combination of her intense anger and impulsive style resulted in her deleterious actions. This enraged state caused her to "lightly bump" his car to "give him the message." Linda has also had frequent verbal and physical outbursts, had numerous episodes of indiscriminate unprotected sexual encounters, and, when stressed, has impulsively threatened suicide.

In addition to meeting the *Diagnostic and Statistical Manual of Mental Disorders* (fourth edition, text revision) (APA, 2000) criterion for BPD, Linda exhibits clear heuristic markers that identify a personality disorder (Layden, et al., 1993). These markers include an ego-syntonic style, an unawareness of the impact of behaviors on others, difficulty establishing therapeutic rapport, an all-or-nothing thinking style, difficulty moderating affect, and what appears to be a low motivation for change. Linda's exhibition of these traits confirms a personality disorder diagnosis. As part of the cluster B spectrum (APA, 2000), Linda also exhibits traits consistent with narcissistic, antisocial, and histrionic personalities. For example, Linda's narcissism is demonstrated in her complete lack of compassion and empathy and her grandiosity and entitlement toward the elderly couple involved in the car accident.

Her relationship schema include themes of abandonment, problems with dependency, and a vacillation of how the other is viewed. For example, in response to her tendency to devalue and alternately idealize her ex-husband, she experienced a stormy, conflicted marriage. Her behaviors in response to these activated beliefs caused her to act and react without a consideration of potential consequences. She alternates expressing her aggression to others and to herself, including harmful acts toward others (destroying property, fighting, arguing) and toward herself (suicidal threats, gestures, and attempts). Linda's treatment for this behavioral dysregulation may involve learning to stop (deep-breathing exercises), finding the continuum of grays between the "all bad" or "all good," and choosing more adaptive responses.

Linda exhibits an unstable affective state, a trait consistent with BPD patients. Her moods vacillate and are intense and often piqued by innocuous or, at best, minimal stressors (e.g., car driving slowly in front of her). She also reports Axis I symptoms of depression and anxiety. She reports this anxiety as jumpiness and agitation and recognizes that she is easily angered. Most patients with BPD are highly sensitive, and this sensitivity of the Axis II BPD personality often causes and exacerbates Axis I symptoms. Mood changes have caused Linda to behave in often irrational and, at times, dangerous ways. Treatment may include learning to self-monitor for mood changes and the related thoughts that appear to trigger those changes.

Layden, et al. (1993) write that common distortions for the BPD patient include dichotomous thinking, catastrophic thinking, labeling, jumping to conclusions, overgeneralizing, mind-reading, fortune-telling, and emotional reasoning. Particularly evident in Linda's case is a theme of dichotomous thinking, especially in the realm of interpersonal relationships. She also catastrophizes and jumps to conclusions in response to internal and external stimuli that cause her difficulty. Treatment will involve challenging these distortions, weighing the evidence to determine how realistic they are, and forming new interpretations and assumptions. Overall, Linda's case conceptualization includes a pattern of heightened reactivity, a crisis-prone style, and the cognitive, behavioral, and affective components consistent with the BPD diagnosis.

POTENTIAL PITFALLS

The major pitfall in Linda's treatment would be the potential for the simultaneous activation of conflicting schemas. Conflicting schemas create a major therapeutic impediment. Ambivalence generated from schema conflict creates difficulty in developing and maintaining a collaborative relationship. For example, Linda may both idealize and devalue the relationship with her therapist. As a result of these schema, conflicts, emotional instability or dysregulation may occur. A. Beck, Freeman, et al. (1990) suggest that dichotomous thinking is particularly problematic because it contributes to the patient's unrealistic evaluation of situations and interpersonal relations. The patient experiences cognitive distortions that evaluate life in terms of mutually exclusive experiences (black and white; good or bad) rather than experiences falling on a continuum. This thinking creates a cascade of events that includes confusion, a diffusion of thought that ultimately leads to powerful emotional reactions. Linda may become intensely attached to her therapist, but if she perceives any rejection or criticism, she may at the same time experience intense rage directed at the therapist. The slightest of norm- or limit-setting might be interpreted as an attempt to control or devalue and be subject to an extreme and angry reaction. This can create a no-win or difficult situation for the therapist. If not managed effectively, the devaluation of the therapist may become so compelling that Linda may prematurely terminate treatment.

The potential success of CBT with Linda relates to the therapist's ability to develop and maintain this collaborative relationship. The therapist needs to continually enlist Linda into a commitment to treatment and the treatment plan. Part of this commitment is an agreement not to engage in suicidal or self-injurious behaviors. Without such an agreement, therapy most likely will reflect and mirror the chaos prevalent throughout the patient's life.

Another difficulty when treating Linda is her demonstrated inability to manage crises. It is important for the therapist to be clear about how emergencies will be managed, in particular, how after-hours emergencies will be handled. Early in treatment with a patient with BPD, the therapist often is subjected to "tests" by the patient to determine how the therapist manages the crisis. It is important for the therapist to be available to work effectively during these early phases. To prevent negative countertransference and as a means to remain grounded, the therapist may need to seek additional supervision, peer support, or consultation. Following through and consistency are vital. For example, if the therapist makes an agreement with the patient that the patient will not engage in self-injurious behaviors and the patient does self-injure, the therapist needs to act upon prior agreements in the event these behaviors occur. An example would be to follow through with hospitalizing the patient after the patient self-injures. The therapist must be clear about these boundaries and not vacillate or waver in response to requests for new contracts.

Linda's history provides evidence that cognitive distortions will most likely precipitate anger, rage, impulsivity, and emotional deregulation. These distortions create feelings of emptiness and pain, which may be acted out within the therapy. To avoid misunderstandings, it is imperative that the therapist be explicit and direct in outlining the agenda for the session, explaining the logic for particular treatment interventions, and eliciting feedback. For example, when the therapist attempts to gain compliance with homework, Linda could possibly misinterpret or distort the rationale for the homework ("Why am I being punished?," or "My therapist doesn't think I get it"). The selection of specific agreed-upon assignments that are directly related to the session is suggested to avoid such a problem. As Linda has difficulty with her moods, she can easily appreciate the rationale of completing a mood log. She may also be receptive to completing a dysfunctional thought record (DTR), which would record the specific automatic thoughts that precipitate such mood changes.

PROGNOSIS

The level of coping and adaptation Linda will reach depends on the ability of the therapist to develop a collaborative relationship. Linda will express distrust, undoubtedly as a "test" for the therapist, either wittingly or unwittingly (Pretzer, 1990). She may push limits to test her therapist's resolve and to try to prove she won't be abandoned. As the therapist remains consistent and supportive while challenging Linda's catastrophized interpretations of the relationship (e.g., "If my therapist can't see me now, she'll never see me!"), Linda will learn that she is able to cope when immediate needs cannot be met. She will also gain an understanding that limits do not necessarily translate to abandonment.

It is key that Linda understand the relation between her emotional dysregulation and her dichotomous thinking. By understanding that her perception of the world is directly related to how she reacts to the world, Linda can choose to challenge or alter her thinking patterns. The direct byproduct of challenging these held patterns is a change in her behaviors. For example, she may learn to appreciate that every situation is not black and white but consists of many shades of gray. By self-monitoring, she could begin to understand how thinking in absolutes has fueled her rage toward others. Linda may learn more about herself by completing homework related to self-monitoring and, more specifically, the DTR (J. Beck, 1995).

Linda may also identify that her dichotomous thinking is related to her expectations of others. When Linda's expectations are not met, she tends to immediately devalue others to an extreme level. For example, when some of her students did not perform well on assignments, Linda's expectations of the children's parents were unrealistic and extreme. This led to the devaluation of the parents and, in all-or-nothing style, precipitated an angry and vengeful letter. Helping Linda incorporate the grays of the situation (e.g., parents may not spend many hours doing homework with the child but provide a loving and safe home) will contradict these extreme views and thus prevent irrational interactions and reactions. As a means of helping Linda identify the grays, Beck, Freeman, et al. (1990) suggest operationalizing the polarities (black versus white) and categorizing what (e.g., people or situations) is included within these polarities. Definitively categorizing opposite extremes allows the therapist and patient to examine the category's validity and to challenge these beliefs by exploring the more realistic continuum that exists between them. This methodology could help Linda move from just identifying dichotomous thinking to active schema modification.

At the close of therapy, with the ability to self-monitor for dichotomous thinking, suicidal and parasuicidal thinking, and mood changes,

Linda is likely to have improved function. As she learns to monitor her thinking and feelings, she will gain the opportunity to have a more balanced and functional lifestyle. This will help improve her functioning within interpersonal relationships and her occupation, as well as her overall interpretation of the world. As she continues to examine her held beliefs and assimilate contradictory evidence, she will become better equipped to manage crises. She may learn alternative means of coping and how to access her strengths and resources.

TIMELINE

Generally, patients who enter outpatient psychotherapy require 1.5 to 6.5 months of weekly outpatient sessions. Personality disorder diagnoses warrant additional sessions (J. Beck, 1995). The CBT timeline for treatment of a patient with BPD is longer than the normal average of 6 months for other psychological disorders. Based on the goals of treatment and the volatility that Linda has exhibited, Linda would most likely benefit from psychotherapy for a year, at minimum. In support of this time frame for the specific treatment of BPD, the APA states, "substantial improvement may not occur until after approximately 1 year of psychotherapeutic intervention has been provided" (2001, p. 4).

Appointments may need to be scheduled for additional times during the week and to accommodate crisis situations. Linda may require additional sessions to support her through particularly high-risk times (e.g., new relationship) or when she is experiencing intense anxiety due to challenging strongly held beliefs. The length of the sessions should be 50–60 minutes. Freeman, Pretzer, Fleming, & Simon (1990) note that if therapists do not take into account the very features that cause dysfunction for the BPD patient (interpersonal difficulties), effective treatment may be compromised. In other words, it is important to explore not only Linda's assumptions about the length of therapy but also the therapist's.

Discussing the treatment parameters provides an opportunity to demonstrate cognitive behavioral theory. The therapist can elicit Linda's automatic thoughts when the therapist proposes the limits and structure of therapy. For example, Linda may experience dichotomous thoughts such as "My therapist should always be there for me; otherwise she doesn't care." The therapist can use this opportunity in many ways. The therapist might ask Linda to describe the emotions associated with these thoughts, demonstrating the connection between thoughts and feelings.

The therapist might also demonstrate that the therapeutic relationship is not based on extreme polarities but exists along a continuum.

The therapist may also need to commit time to generating referrals to additional and adjunctive therapies that may benefit Linda. For example, Linda may benefit from a self-help group that addresses binge eating, or the therapist may need to consult with a psychiatrist or primary care physician to ensure consistent and comprehensive treatment is provided. The APA (2001) states that of the studies that demonstrate effective treatment for BPD, all modalities include three components: weekly sessions with an individual therapist, weekly group sessions, and meeting for consultation or supervision for the treating therapist. The therapist may also need to anticipate, particularly in Linda's case, time required for court appearances or providing her employer with mandated updates.

SPECIAL TECHNIQUES

Standard cognitive therapy techniques include, but are not limited to, anxiety reduction techniques, problem-solving skills, activity scheduling, graded task assignments, cognitive restructuring, self-monitoring, communication and listening skills, rational responding skills, decatastrophizing, and challenging dichotomous thinking. Techniques can be utilized as homework or within the session. Techniques such as imagery, impulse control, assertiveness training, and rehearsal include more behavioral components but can also access the cognitive (Layden, Newman, Freeman, & Morse, 1993). However, CBT utilizes many techniques that focus on cognitions, behaviors, and physiological and emotional aspects of the patient. CBT allows for the individual needs of the patient because techniques are adapted to the functioning level of the patient. In addition, patients may benefit from variations of a known technique. Dattilio and Freeman (1992) and Freeman, Pretzer, Fleming, & Simon (1990) provide an extensive list and explanation of specific techniques that can be utilized in cognitive therapy.

As a means to foster the therapeutic alliance, A. Beck, Freeman, et al. (1990) suggest that the therapist implicitly acknowledge and accept the patient's difficulty in trusting. It is hoped that distrust will diminish over time through consistency, congruency, and empathy from the therapist. Therefore, the initial potentially beneficial strategy to implement with Linda would be to create a technique that includes building trust. For example, a scale of 1 to 10 to measure trust at the beginning and end of every session could gauge Linda's trust of her therapist. This could easily be included as part of the transition from agenda-setting and during feedback at the end of each session. The key to successful utilization of this technique is to define operationally what the varying levels are within this scale. As a means of applying the scale to the therapeutic relationship, the therapist might ask Linda to compare the therapist's ranking on the trust scale with that of someone in her life who ranks higher. The therapist can then learn the specifics of how Linda interprets trust, and how trust is earned. Trust can also be demonstrated by providing coverage for those times that the therapist may not be available. This includes making specific arrangements to manage crisis and emergency calls.

Cognitively, several techniques can be utilized. The key to successful utilization of these techniques is the use of guided discovery and Socratic questioning to derive information and to not trigger intense emotional responses before the patient is prepared. This strategy involves using simple, focused questions to move the patient toward a desired goal (either insight into a behavior's antecedents or recognition of a particular behavior). The Socratic dialogue makes the session easier for the patient but requires the therapist to carefully frame questions and responses.

An important consideration for any technique would be to address and identify the patient's dichotomous thinking through a review of automatic thoughts. Automatic thoughts could be accessed by asking Linda to keep a DTR (J. Beck, 1995). This technique requires that the patient not only understand the rationale of the assignment but agree to complete the record. Linda has shown that she is organized and diligent with work, and she may approach the assignment in the same assertive way. By reviewing Linda's DTRs, the therapist may quickly identify themes of dichotomous thinking. Developing continuums or gradations on a continuum in the form of a disputation is useful for both homework and real-time therapy exercises.

A careful review of a completed DTR may reveal beliefs that are inherently flawed and will therefore be rejected. These beliefs can be tested within the therapy session. For example, if Linda's therapist can honestly accept Linda for who she is and communicate this effectively through empathy and concern, Linda could be provided with an invaluable experience of acceptance and validation. It would be useful to compare this acceptance to the rejection that Linda has experienced in the past, such as the rejection from her parents. If possible, it would be helpful for Linda to review her thinking and emotions involved in both experiences. Often, patients have clear situations of dichotomous thinking and emotional extremes surrounding the situations of their rejection. If trust and a collaborative relationship have been established, these extremes are useful to plot on a continuum of dichotomous thoughts and associated feelings. Plotting a continuum also provides a concrete means of viewing how such cognitive distortions can generate intense emotional states.

SPECIAL CAUTIONS

Ongoing assessment for potential acts of self-harm, suicidality, and aggression toward others should occur throughout treatment. Linda has also demonstrated dissociative symptoms where potential harm could occur (she did not remember going out to buy cigarettes).

As a crisis-prone individual, Linda appears to be highly reactive to stressful situations. She becomes easily agitated and is not able to apply healthy coping strategies (e.g., "I get overwhelmed by a lot of the things that I do."). For example, when a married colleague wanted to end the affair he was having with Linda, feelings of intense rage, despair, and abandonment drove her to threaten to tell everyone at school and his wife about the affair. Linda did not consider the ramifications of how the married colleague, his wife, or their employer might react to this information. Later, the man's wife actually threatened to kill Linda if she contacted her husband again. Linda's automatic thoughts may have been dichotomous, with themes of vengeance, such as "If he won't be with me, I'll ruin him!"

It is therefore imperative that the therapist continually assess for any indicators of potential self-injury or suicidal ideation. It is vital that the therapist understand the patient's motivation for any self-injurious or suicidal thoughts. Assessment must also include whether Linda can manage her safety without external intervention such as hospitalization (APA, 2001). An agreement from Linda to report any thoughts of self-injury or hopelessness must be part of the treatment plan. In addition, Linda and her therapist should create a predetermined safety plan (e.g., calling the therapist, contacting a safe person, going to the emergency room) to activate in the event she experiences self-injurious thoughts.

Self-monitoring allows Linda to make a choice about how she will react. She may examine her physiological indicators of stress (e.g., arousal symptoms such as rapid breathing, tense muscles); her affective indicators (e.g., feelings of rage or despair); her behavioral indicators (e.g., calling repeatedly, walking, pacing); and her cognitive indicators (e.g., cognitive distortions such as dichotomous thinking and cata-strophic thinking). For example, Linda reports that she was stressed because she was running late the morning she hit the elderly couple. If she was skilled in self-monitoring, she may have noticed that she was experiencing a racing heart, feeling rageful, driving aggressively, and having thoughts such as "They're purposely driving slowly to prevent me from getting where I need to go." (personalization). Testing these automatic thoughts for validity can allow Linda to identify themes repre-senting underlying schema related to rejection and invalidation. Her interpretation that she is not important to the other driver may have led her to the drastic conclusion, "I'm not important, so no one loves me." This thought created a cascade of intense emotions. Had she recognized that her crisis-prone style often produces negative conse-quences, she may have been able to apply some basic techniques to slow down the process. For example, she could have taken some deep breaths to reduce arousal and taken a moment to "turn down" her rageful feelings, choose an action other than driving aggressively (such as pulling over), and finally challenge the cognitive distortion of person-alization with competing thoughts such as "it's more likely that, as an elderly couple, they're comfortable driving slower." Once Linda identifies distortions, attempts to modify related schema can occur.

Many of Linda's resistances in therapy would most likely be a product of dormant schema becoming activated within the therapeutic relation-ship. These may include issues relating to trust, abandonment, and vacillating feelings toward the therapist and the therapy itself. There may be a fear of change that contributes to noncompliance, which can sometimes lead to early termination (Pretzer, 1990). Linda may have dichotomous thinking toward the therapist. For example, if the therapist is on vacation, Linda may interpret this as "She's never there for me," alternating with beliefs such as "She is always there for me and would do anything for me." These powerful beliefs are likely to become acti-vated when Linda is stressed or during a challenging time in therapy. Key to navigating these stressful situations with the patient is for the therapist to remain focused, retain appropriate boundaries and struc-ture, and utilize the forming case conceptualization. The therapist can then be prepared to predict how the patient may or may not be able to manage a situation and can also proactively prepare the patient with anxiety-reduction techniques and self-monitoring skills.

Often, powerful countertransference occurs when treating a patient with BPD. As the cognitive patterns of a patient with BPD exhibit intense beliefs such as dichotomous thinking, fears of abandonment, feelings of unlovability and betrayal, and a general mistrust of the world, the therapist is often the recipient of these intense emotional transference reactions. Layden, Newman, Freeman, & Morse (1993) suggest that to encourage therapeutic empathy, therapists should continually remind themselves of the "emotional baggage" (p. 117) that the patient is trying to live with and manage. In addition, the therapist may also be the object of projected feelings or rage, mistrust, and abandonment that at times can subjectively be felt as manipulative. The therapist needs to remain ever-vigilant not to internalize these manipulations. Newman (1990) writes that therapists who may feel victimized or manipulated are more vulnerable to thoughts toward the patient that are contraindicative and counterproductive. Layden, et al. (1993) suggest that these types of manipulations are not to be avoided or dismissed, but rather taken seriously. Pretzer (1990) writes that the therapist must remain genuine, honest, and empathic to the unpleasant emotional experiences of the BPD. In this way, the collaborative working relationship is maintained and continued treatment gains can occur.

AREAS TO AVOID

Obvious immediate issues include the establishment of rapport and agreed-upon parameters and limits of therapy. The focus of Linda's therapy is largely related to identifying, managing, and coping more effectively with intense affective changes. Therefore, the primary treatment focus would be for Linda to examine her patterns of relating to herself and the outside world. Until she is able to clearly identify and self-monitor effectively, family interactions and issues may not be the immediate or even short-term focus of treatment. As there appear to be "hot" cognitions (J. Beck, 1995) related to these interactions, it would seem to be contraindicated to address these interactions early in the treatment. These issues could be addressed later (if they become more relevant).

Although her emotional traumas (e.g., her parent's blaming her for being victimized sexually) may be related to current schema, these past events may not be impacting her daily functioning. The underlying schema that are a result of these experiences may in fact be the culprit in creating ineffective coping strategies. However, the APA (2001) warns that too much attention on past trauma instead of current functioning can actually derail therapy. Therefore, particularly emotionally laden experiences with her family should be initially avoided unless they are relevant to her daily functioning.

Other areas that may be avoided are issues related to Linda's choice about whether to have a family. Linda laments on several occasions the difficulty she experiences with children and the subsequent tension with her sister who is currently pregnant: "My sister has no interest in me because of her having a baby." Because Linda is experiencing many identity issues, it may not be therapeutically beneficial to discuss her ambivalence or feelings about becoming a parent. Although her indiscriminate sexual encounters would be a primary issue because they create dangerous situations, they may be better addressed as impulsive behaviors she may wish to change. Evaluating and weighing whether she wants to be a parent may be better approached when a more clear and established sense of self is present.

An expectation that was evident within Linda's family was demands for perfection. It may not be beneficial to address these parental rules initially because they may fuel Linda's feelings of threatened rejection and abandonment. The therapist might validate and recognize Linda's need to get things "just right" rather than categorizing the perfectionistic tendency as an issue in treatment. This prevents Linda from experiencing the painful, shameful emotional experiences that were a result of not meeting parental and familial expectations. It provides emotional validation.

Generally, areas to avoid would be emotionally laden familial experiences that trigger powerful, compelling schema typical of the borderline diagnosis.

MEDICATIONS

Cognitive behavioral treatment does not preclude use of medications within psychotherapy. Pharmacotherapy is often utilized as an adjunctive form of treatment with the aim of ameliorating key symptoms of BPD, including affective instability, impulsivity, transient psychotic symptoms, and self-injurious behaviors. Pharmacotherapy generally is used to manage state symptoms and trait components that cause chronic vulnerabilities such as impulsive temperament (APA, 2001).

Medication may be required to manage Linda's prominent symptoms of anxiety and depression. She would benefit from a psychiatric evaluation to determine whether medication is warranted. Linda experiences intense rage reactions, impulsivity, and mood lability, dimensions on both Axes that may be receptive to medication.

As with any implement of a treatment intervention, suggesting the initiation of medication may produce adverse or negative assumptions by Linda. It is important for the therapist to elicit Linda's automatic thoughts related to taking medications and to work with Linda to determine their validity. Linda may have thoughts such as, "If I need medication, I must have failed," or "My therapist thinks I'm crazy." Many patients hold the view that medication is for "lunatics" or "mental patients" and are fearful of the associated stigma. Linda may also have unrealistic assumptions about negative side effects or may hope for a "miracle cure." Because some medications are more toxic than others, patient compliance with treatment amounts and filling prescriptions, potential for substance abuse and self-harm must always be assessed. If the patient is prescribed medication, it is imperative that continued medication management occurs throughout treatment. Patients' beliefs that they are incapable of managing without the support of their medication should be challenged. The APA (2001) advises that there are three dimensions evident in the BPD presentation that can be addressed with medication: affective instability, impulsiveness, and perceptual problems.

Medication can be utilized as a powerful support to the treatment of BPD. However, it requires a complete, thorough evaluation by trained medical personnel who integrate the psychological background, history, and vulnerabilities of the patient with BPD. Linda may benefit from medication because she presents both Axis I and Axis II symptoms. (For a fuller description, see APA, 2001.)

PATIENT STRENGTHS

Linda has many strengths that can be accessed in therapy. First, despite numerous challenges in her interpersonal life, she has maintained steady employment. Although she has experienced some difficulty in her work situation, she is aware of the specific requirements of her job and is able to function within those parameters accordingly. Additionally, she has maintained a residence, also suggesting a level of awareness of fulfilling the basic requirements of living as an independent adult.

Second, Linda has responded well to interventions or direction from an authority figure. For example, when advised she was required to complete a psychological evaluation for court, she complied. She has attended the necessary counseling sessions suggested by her employer as a result of the letters she sent to parents. In addition, she has followed her employer's directives to not send any additional letters to parents. Her ability to respond to authority and directives implies that within therapy, she may be responsive to limit-setting, adhering to emergency procedures, and imposed structure.

Third, Linda demonstrates insight into some of the basic issues with which she is struggling. She easily identifies that she has experienced depression and anxiety and at times feels overwhelmed and agitated. She states that she is easily angered and is "jumpy" and says "Little things just bug me and I react." Also, she is able to identify areas consistent with the BPD diagnosis. For example, she recognizes she has difficulty with her identity and experiences emptiness and what appears to be transient suspiciousness. She states, "My life is empty," "There's nothing in my life," and "My neighbors dislike me."

Because Linda exhibits some insight into areas relevant for both the present Axis I and Axis II symptoms (depression, anxiety, and BPD traits), her propensity for further understanding and awareness is evident. She more than likely can learn to identify automatic thoughts, related schema, and their subsequent cognitive, affective, and behavioral counterparts. This insightfulness allows for easier access to the underlying core schema that generate and produce these symptoms. The insight that Linda demonstrates can also be utilized as a gateway to further insight into deeper and more complex schema, which can then be subjected to collaborative empiricism in order to determine their validity.

LIMIT-SETTING

Because difficulty with interpersonal relationships presents considerable problems for the patient with BPD, boundary issues and limit-setting become major components of psychotherapy. Driven by activated schema that may include themes of abandonment, rejection, and vacillation, patients often respond to these beliefs by violating and testing limits and boundaries with the therapist. These violations can cause much distress for therapists because they may impact their daily schedule or even their personal life with late-night calls, intrusive interruptions, or unreasonable requests for additional time. In its extreme form, limit testing can include threats of suicide or self-harm or threats against another person. It is vital that the therapist retain appropriate boundaries. Higher levels of care may need to be pursued, and the therapist must remain vigilant that the therapeutic relationship is strictly professional.

Linda has demonstrated poor boundaries within her interpersonal life, including with her family, romantic interests, and friends and within her occupation. Linda clearly has poor boundaries with romantic partners, as exemplified in her intense, reactive, and impulsive sexual interactions with strangers she meets in bars. Her choice of partners also represents poor boundaries because she chooses men who are otherwise committed or unavailable. Within the social sphere, her attempts to create an intense connection with a neighbor failed. Within her job, Linda demonstrates poor boundaries by writing derogatory letters to parents that go beyond her role as an educator. Understanding key schema relating to these boundary violations are intrinsic to successful negotiation of more appropriate boundaries. For example, within the romantic sphere, her automatic thoughts are flagrant with dichotomous thinking, which may include "This man is paying attention to me, so I can be intimate with him," which is generated by core schema that may state, "I am basically unlovable" or "I can't be alone." Automatic thoughts generated by these core schema, combined with an impulsive style, create examples of poor boundaries and ultimately represent an ongoing threat of danger.

Linehan (1987) suggests that clear and concrete limits be disseminated to the patient at the beginning of therapy and be part of a contractual arrangement. This may include, but is not limited to, scheduling issues, availability of the therapist, emergency procedures, aggression, verbal abuse, personal questions and/or physical contact with the therapist, and termination. Limits can be delineated in a supportive, nonthreatening manner and can be framed as a means of creating mutual respect between two adults (Layden, Newman, Freeman, & Morse, 1993).

During times of distress, patients can be reminded and supported to respect these contractual agreements and learn to work within these boundaries. Similarly, by maintaining this agreement, patients can begin to generalize their experience to other relationships. This directly contradicts dichotomous beliefs that may state that limits are equated with rejection, abandonment, or devaluation.

Limit-setting becomes extremely important when suicidal behavior or threats or undiminished ideation require the treatment plan be changed. Because most patients with BPD tend to vacillate in their actual intent to die, clear and understandable limits such as the patient agreeing to the treatment recommendations set by the therapist are necessary to retain patient safety, determine ethical decisions, and recognize when assistance and/or supervision for the therapist may be required. Part of setting limits includes advising the patient that ambiguous or vague responses to questions about suicidal thoughts will not be tolerated and may require that additional steps to endure patient safety may need to occur (Fusco & Freeman, 2003).

SIGNIFICANT OTHERS/HOMEWORK

At this time, Linda does not have a significant other. She has been in several transient, even indiscriminate, interactions with men, but overall she has been unable to maintain any long-term romantic relationship in her life. Regarding her family, Linda's parents have relocated to Florida and would not be available to participate in therapy. In addition, her siblings do not appear to be a major part of her life and would probably not be a part of the treatment. Perhaps at a later date, if Linda expresses an interest, meeting with her parents (perhaps by phone) could occur. However, a determination needs to be made whether this type of meeting would be appropriate, beneficial, and not contraindicated.

The therapist needs to remain flexible in the event that Linda may begin a romantic relationship in the future. Because Linda's predominant issues relate to interpersonal difficulties that include themes of abandonment, rejection, and impulsivity, the introduction of a significant other into her life will dictate whether the treatment plan needs to be altered.

Homework assignments are a key element of CBT. Homework should be designed to support the work that is completed within the session to outside of the session (Freeman, 1992). As the patient learns new exercises and means of challenging dysfunctional thoughts and behaviors, homework allows the opportunity for practicing these in daily life. Initially, homework should be designed as a means of gathering additional information via self-monitoring. For example, Linda may have captured the automatic thought that stated, "These parents do nothing for their children," prior to engaging in negative type behaviors (writing derogatory letters). As the therapy progresses, Linda can practice interventions and techniques that she has learned to manage these powerful thoughts, especially when specific distressful situations occur (Fusco & Freeman, 2003). The assignments should be individually tailored to match Linda's skills. Linda should easily tackle the DTR because she has been a very successful student and is able to understand abstract concepts.

Linda's out-of-session homework would most likely include techniques and activities designed to help her identify and modify dichotomous thinking. Using the DTR would help Linda learn how to self-monitor and would provide concrete descriptions of dichotomous thinking. The homework can be utilized as an aid to demonstrate the potential continuum of thinking that lies between her two extremes. Linda would also benefit from homework assignments that address her mood changes and lability. Assignments could include recording her moods on a mood log, along with the specific events or thoughts that tend to precipitate a mood change.

For example, Linda may have interpreted her neighbors' actions of not curbing their dogs as a threat. She responded by literally stalking her neighbors without actually processing what the realistic harm would be. The therapist would encourage Linda to examine the situation and whether it presented a true threat. Overall, homework is an invaluable tool in CBT, and Linda would benefit from its results.

TERMINATION

Termination can be very difficult for the patient with BPD. Themes of abandonment, dependency, trust, and unlovability may become activated and compelling when the patient faces termination. Linda has demonstrated that these are powerfully held and active schema. When significant relationships have come to an end in Linda's life, she has regressed to self-injurious, threatening, and decompensated behaviors. The therapist will need to consider this dynamic when creating Linda's treatment plan.

If patients have been able to engage in a collaborative, supportive relationship with the therapist, a new and formidable task of separating from the therapist can escalate into a crisis situation. As a result, patients may relapse to their held patterns of reactions, including acting out as a means to keep the therapist involved, creating new issues, requesting additional sessions, or exhibiting extreme anger as a reaction to feelings of rejection and abandonment. In Linda's case, she has demonstrated physical aggression, self-injury, and vengeful acts and has destroyed property.

Collaboration between Linda and her therapist will help establish an agreed-upon termination date. This date can be subject to change if discussed in a collaborative, supportive manner. Automatic thoughts about the projected or pending termination should be elicited by the therapist so that distortions can be disputed or tested for their validity. Automatic thoughts may represent strongly held schema, such as "I need my therapist to get through this," or "I'll never be able to do this on my own." The therapist can help Linda to challenge these distortions so that she can utilize the cognitive techniques she has learned in order to dispel, dispute, or contradict dysfunctional thinking.

Relapse prevention should include a means of self-monitoring and identifying when Linda is beginning to experience an exacerbation of symptoms. These symptoms have in the past led to dysfunctional thinking and high-risk behaviors. As part of a comprehensive case conceptualization, relapse prevention planning should be predictive in nature. The plan should anticipate what may cause distress or decompensation for the patient. Interventions to prevent relapse may include carrying prior homework assignments, bibliotherapy, examples of healthy coping in high-stress situations, names and phone numbers of supportive individuals, reminders of the chain of events that lead to impulsive behaviors, and—most importantly—a safety plan for patients who have a history of high-risk behaviors. Linda would benefit from all of these. In addition, relapse prevention should include a component that concentrates on Linda's intense affective states, which have caused many problems in the past. These interventions can be written on a small notepad to allow for easy access in the event of a stressful situation that may challenge her ability to cope. It would be more effective to taper off the therapy contacts rather than simply ending. The rate of tapering should be a collaborative decision between the patient and the therapist. As patients are tapered off therapy, they may begin to experience greater confidence to manage stressful situations without their therapist (Layden, Newman, Freeman, & Morse, 1993). Pretzer (1990) suggests that therapy should be tapered off gradually from weekly to biweekly to monthly sessions and, if necessary, to biannual sessions. Pretzer also suggests at least 3 months are needed to prepare the patient for termination. Achievement in managing stressors between sessions provides evidence that the patient is able to maintain therapeutic gains independently. This contradicts dependency and incompetency schema. When therapists encourage self-support and accessing alternative supports, patients may not necessarily experience painful abandonment and rejection issues through termination. Instead, they experience increased self-efficacy and self-esteem.

MECHANISM OF CHANGE

Automatic thoughts are the pathway and inroad to underlying schema. Linda's thinking is laden with dichotomous thoughts and beliefs, suggesting that she has many early maladaptive schemas consistent with BPD diagnosis (Young, 1990). These schema include dependence, lack of individualization, emotional deprivation, abandonment, mistrust, unlovability, and incompetence. Prevalent throughout Linda's life are expressions of these related schema that, when activated, compel and powerfully drive her behavior. At times, these beliefs have caused Linda very negative consequences, which have led to legal, social, and interpersonal problems.

Addressing Linda's dichotomous thinking should reduce the frequency and intensity of the emotional deregulation associated with schematic activation. Linda's affective instability is directly related to the distortions created by the all-or-nothing thinking. Episodes of emotional and affective instability are functionally related to her anger and rage reactions. If others are not completely in alignment with her beliefs, she clearly thinks, "If they're not with me, they're against me!" This dichotomous thinking is central to her indemnity problems and her constant feelings of devaluation and invalidation.

A second major mechanism of change for Linda is addressing and modifying her impulsive style. Linda's impulsive style has created much distress in her life, such as legal charges, mandated therapy, indiscriminant sexual encounters, and poor coping skills. By learning to self-monitor, Linda can subsequently make choices based on an awareness of how to react rather than a conditioned response set.

A final major mechanism of change for Linda is a successful and collaborative therapeutic relationship. Interpersonal difficulties are a major component of the constellation of characteristic patterns for those with BPD, which inherently creates therapeutic treatment obstacles. In addition, her therapist will be continually seeking her participation and feedback to ensure that Linda receives what the therapist has determined to be the major goals and issues to be addressed in treatment. Because contradictory schema are evident within the BPD presentation, the therapist's ability to maintain consistent and predictable boundaries can dispute the patient's contradictory beliefs, which alternate between idealization and devaluation of self, therapist, and the relationship. Because therapy represents a microcosm of the patient's life, positive interactions with the therapist can subsequently be generalized to outside relationships.

These powerful mechanisms of change allow patients to make informed, aware, and cognitively processed responses and reactions to stressful events. The experience of incurring self-knowledge would provide Linda valuable information to use in situations that have in the past caused difficulty. With continued collaboration and therapeutic alliance, challenging of distorted thoughts, and realistic goal-setting, Linda will be able to empower herself to experience a more fulfilling, balanced, adaptive, and healthy life.

REFERENCES

American Psychiatric Association. (2000). *Diagnostic and statistical manual of mental disorders* (4th ed., text revision). Washington, DC: Author.

American Psychiatric Association. (2001). Practice guidelines for the treatment of patients with borderline personality disorder. *American Journal of Psychiatry, 158*(10), 2–52.

Bandura, A. (1969). *Principles of behavior modification.* New York: Holt, Rinehart & Winston.

Beck, A. (1976). *Cognitive therapy and the emotional disorders.* New York: International Universities Press.

Beck, A. (1987). Cognitive therapy. In J. K. Zeig (Ed.), *The evolution of psychotherapy* (pp. 149–178). New York: Brunner/Mazel.

Beck, A., Freeman, A., & Associates. (1990). *Cognitive therapy of personality disorders.* New York: Guilford Press.

Beck, A., Freeman, A., Davis, D., & Associates (2003). *Cognitive therapy of personality disorders* (2nd ed.). New York: Guilford Press.

Beck, A., Rush, A., Shaw, B., & Emery, G. (1979). *Cognitive therapy of personality disorders.* New York: Guilford Press.

Beck, A., & Weishaar, M. (1986). *Cognitive therapy.* Philadelphia: Center for Cognitive Therapy.

Beck, J. (1995). *Cognitive therapy basics and beyond.* New York: Guilford Press.

Dattilio, F., & Freeman, A. (1992). Introduction to cognitive therapy. In A. Freeman & F. Dattilio (Eds.), *Comprehensive casebook of cognitive therapy* (pp. 3–12). New York: Plenum Press.

DeRubeis, R., & Beck, A. (1988). Cognitive therapy. In K. S. Dobson (Ed.), *Handbook of cognitive-behavioral therapies* (pp. 273–306). New York: Guilford Press.

Freeman, A. (1992). The development of treatment conceptualizations in cognitive therapy. In A. Freeman & F. Dattilio (Eds.), *Comprehensive casebook of cognitive therapy* (pp. 13–26). New York: Plenum Press.

Freeman, A., & Fusco, G. (2000). Treating high-arousal patients: Differentiating between patients in crisis and crisis-prone patients. In F. Dattilio & A. Freeman (Eds.), *Cognitive-behavioral strategies in crisis intervention* (2nd ed., pp. 27–58). New York: Guilford Press.

Freeman, A., Pretzer, J., Fleming, B., & Simon, K. (1990). *Clinical applications of cognitive therapy.* New York: Plenum Press.

Fusco, G., & Freeman, A. (2003). *Borderline personality disorder: A therapist's manual to taking control.* New York: Norton.

Koenigsberg, H. (1995). Psychotherapy of patients with borderline personality disorder. *Current Opinion in Psychiatry, 8*(3), 157–160.

Koerner, K., & Linehan, M. (2000). Research on dialectical behavior therapy for patients with borderline personality disorder. *Psychiatric Clinics of North America, 23,* 151–167.

Layden, M., Newman, C., Freeman, A., & Morse, S. (1993). *Cognitive therapy of borderline personality disorder.* Boston: Allyn & Bacon.

Linehan, M. (1987). Dialectical behavior therapy: A cognitive behavioral approach to para-suicide. *Journal of Personality Disorders, 1,* 328–333.

Mays, D. (1985). Behavior therapy with borderline personality disorder: One clinician's perspective. In D. Mays & C. Franks (Eds.), *Negative outcome in psychopathology and what to do about it.* New York: Springer.

McGinn, L., & Sanderson, W. (2001). What allows cognitive behavioral therapy to be brief: Overview, efficacy, and crucial factors facilitating brief treatment. *Clinical Psychology: Science & Practice, 8*(1), 23–37.

Millon, T. (1987). On the genesis and prevalence of the borderline personality disorder: A social learning thesis. *Journal of Personality Disorders, 1,* 354–372.

Newman, C. (1990). Therapy-threatening behaviors on the part of the cognitive-behavior therapist in the treatment of the borderline patient. *Behavior Therapist, 13*(9), 215–216.

Perris, C. (1994). Cognitive therapy in the treatment of patients with borderline personality disorder. *Acta Psychiatric Scandanavia, 89* (suppl 379), 69–72.

Pretzer, J. (1990). Borderline personality disorder. In A. Beck, A. Freeman & Associates (Eds.), *Cognitive therapy of personality disorders* (pp. 176–207). New York: Guilford Press.

Raj, A., Kumaraiah, V., & Bhide, A. (2001). Cognitive-behavioural intervention in deliberate self-harm. *Acta Psychiatrica Scandinavica, 104*(5), 340–345.

Trull, T., Stepp, S., & Durrett, C. (2003). Research on borderline personality disorder: An update. *Current Opinion in Psychiatry, 16*(1), 77–82.

Turner, R. (1989). Case study evaluation of a bio-cognitive-behavioral approach for the treatment of borderline personality disorder. *Behavior Therapy, 20,* 477–498.

Turner, R. (1992). Borderline personality disorder. In A. Freeman & F. Dattilio (Eds.), *Comprehensive casebook of cognitive therapy* (pp. 215–222). New York: Plenum Press.

Weishaar, M. (1993). *Aaron T. Beck.* London: Sage.

Winnicott, D. (1965). *The maturational process and the facilitating environment.* New York: International Universities Press.

Young, J. (1990). *Schema-focused cognitive therapy for personality disorders: A schema-focused approach.* Sarasota, FL: Professional Resource Exchange.

6

Rational Emotive Behavior Therapy

Windy Dryden

WORDS OF CAUTION

Before addressing the task at hand (how to approach the treatment of Linda P.), I would like to offer some words of caution. First, it is difficult to write about a case when perhaps the most important information is missing, that is, patient response to the therapeutic approach and the therapist. It may be that after I described rational emotive behavioral therapy (REBT) to Linda, she would consider it to be an inappropriate treatment approach for her, in which case, I would refer her to an experienced clinician representing another approach. The approach to Linda's treatment described below is based on the assumption that she has given her informed consent to work with me in REBT treatment.

Second, not all REBT therapists practice the same way. There is much diversity in independent variables, as I discovered when I asked several leading REBT therapists to outline their idiosyncratic practice of REBT (Dryden, 2004). Thus, the therapy description in this chapter reflects my own idiosyncratic practice of REBT therapy.

Third, rather than writing from an ideal perspective—how I might approach Linda's therapy if ideal conditions were in place—I chose to use a realistic perspective—how I would approach Linda's therapy given the actual conditions of my practice. With the exception of a few facilities dedicated to the treatment of patients with severe personality disorders, patients with borderline personality disorder (BPD) are treated under conditions where the ideal is compromised by realistic constraints. These constraints include my particular practice as an REBT therapist.

My major work is as an academic and psychotherapy trainer, and I also coordinate a hospital-based, group-oriented REBT/cognitive behavior therapy program. Further, I have a small private practice where I see individuals and couples, but—largely for practical and logistical reasons—I do not run groups in my private practice, although conjoint individual and group therapy for patients with BPD can often be useful. Also, there is no private, ongoing REBT group for patients with BPD to which I could refer Linda.

RATIONAL EMOTIVE BEHAVIOR THERAPY: A BRIEF DESCRIPTION

Rational emotive behavior therapy (REBT) was founded in 1955 by Albert Ellis. As such, it is the longest established of the cognitive behavioral therapies (Dryden & Ellis, 2001). While it shares a number of theoretical and practical elements with other cognitive behavior therapies, it also has its unique features, some of which are particularly relevant in working with patients with BPD.

Basic Theoretical Tenets

Some of REBT's general theoretical tenets are particularly relevant to BPD:

- Rigid and extreme beliefs are at the core of much psychological disturbance, and flexible and nonextreme beliefs are at the core of psychological health.
- Psychological disturbance is either ego in nature (that which relates to the person's estimation of herself) or non-ego in nature (that which does not relate to the person's estimation of herself).
- Psychological solutions to ego disturbance involve the patient making flexible preferences about the self and holding an attitude of unconditional self-acceptance.
- Psychological solutions to non-ego disturbance involve the person making flexible preferences about internal discomfort and external frustration and holding "non-awfulising" beliefs (e.g., "this frustration is bad, but not awful"), high frustration tolerance beliefs (e.g., "it's a struggle to tolerate this frustration, but I can tolerate

it and it's worth it for me to do so"), and accepting beliefs ("it's bad that you are frustrating me, but you are not a bad person for doing so") about such uncomfortable and frustrating conditions.

- Irrational (i.e., rigid and extreme) beliefs about internal or external adversities tend to lead to unhealthy negative emotions, dysfunctional behaviors, and distorted cognitions, while rational (i.e., flexible and nonextreme) beliefs about the same adversities tend to lead to healthy negative emotions, functional behaviors, and realistic cognitions.

- Beliefs, emotions, behaviors, and nonbelief inferential cognitions are interdependent psychological processes and influence one another in often complex ways. Thus, if you believe that significant others must approve of you and you are less worthy if you are not approved of (belief), then you may feel anxious about the prospect of being disapproved of by someone significant to you and depressed if you think you have been disapproved of by that person (emotion); may avoid this person or act in ways that are designed to appease her (behavior); and may think that if this person disapproves of you, then others are bound to, as well (nonbelief inferential cognition). And if you think that a number of significant people will disapprove of you (nonbelief inferential cognition), then you may avoid or appease them (behavior), feel anxious when you see them (emotion), and believe that you are less worthy if they disapprove of you (belief).

- As in cognitive therapy, REBT theory distinguishes between core irrational beliefs and specific irrational beliefs. A core irrational belief is a general belief held by the person about a central realm of her personal domain (Beck, 1976), across relevant situations, and which accounts for psychological disturbance in these situations. A specific irrational belief can either be a specific example of a core irrational belief or a specific belief in a particular situation that is not representative of a core irrational belief.

- People have metapsychological problems (i.e., psychological problems about psychological problems), and the existence of these metapsychological problems can impede people's progress toward overcoming their original psychological problems.

- Humans are biopsychosocial organisms and can be influenced for better or worse by their biological heritage and by the environments (past and present) that they inhabit. Ellis's (1994a) view is that in psychological disturbance people are more influenced by biological factors than by environmental factors, and this is particularly so for patients with BPD (Ellis, 1994b).

- Potentially, humans can learn many skills to help themselves become and stay psychologically healthy (Ellis, 2001). However, they may not do so for a number of reasons: (a) They do not know what these skills are and need to be taught them. (b) They know what these skills are but stop themselves from acquiring them because of the irrational beliefs that they hold in relevant areas. In this case, they need to be helped to identify, challenge, and change these irrational beliefs. (c) They may know what these skills are but have one or more deficits that prevent them from acquiring them. In this case, they may need remedial help and/or appropriate medication to address these deficits before they can be expected to acquire these skills.

Views of BPD

REBT holds that patients with BPD have a number of cognitive, behavioral, and interpersonal deficits and distortions to which they are biologically predisposed and which are exacerbated by their early and later environment (Ellis, 1994b). They are frequently reared abusively by their parents, one or both of whom may have distinct psychological problems of their own. These patients therefore have a double handicap: They are biologically predisposed to severe disturbance, and they are exposed to a noxious interpersonal environment. As if this were not enough, patients with BPD are further handicapped. Having easily disturbed themselves about life's frustrations (of which more later), they disturb themselves about their disturbances; thus, they may make themselves anxious about their anxiety and self-hatingly depressed about their depression, to name but two metapsychological problems. They tend to have great difficulty moderating their disturbed feelings long enough to deal with them productively. Also, because they often act in grossly dysfunctional ways toward themselves and others, they are exposed to greater frustrations than are patients who are less disturbed. Thus, when they harm themselves, they physically handicap themselves either temporarily or permanently and are thus less able to perform tasks that they could perform if they had not harmed themselves, thus creating more frustration for themselves. When they treat others badly, these others respond by moving against them or by moving away from them (Homey, 1950), with the result that they are exposed to increased interpersonal frustration and discomfort. Because patients with BPD do not in general deal well with frustration and discomfort, they are likely to disturb themselves about these frustrations and discomforts that they have done much to bring about.

Given these multilayered problems, patients with BPD need to accept themselves with their problems and work hard consistently on these problems if they are to be significantly helped by REBT or any psychological therapy. However, a further handicap is that they find it difficult to accept themselves and find it inordinately difficult to commit themselves to the often uncomfortable process of psychotherapeutic change due to their low frustration tolerance, which drives them to seek short-term solutions that are self- and relationship-defeating in the long term.

Thus, REBT therapists who take on patients with BPD need to have realistic goals and need to work on themselves using REBT if they are to be a reliable and therapeutic long-term resource with these patients.

Basic Practice

Contrary to what is often thought, REBT therapists are very mindful of developing good therapeutic alliances with their patients, and this is particularly important in working with patients with BPD. Dryden (1987) was the first to show how the practice of REBT could be informed by Bordin's (1979) working alliance theory, and DiGiuseppe (1995) developed this in his work with patients with anger problems. This work is particularly relevant to therapy with patients with BPD, who often describe feeling unhealthily angry and often express this anger in dysfunctional ways.

REBT can be seen as psychoeducational in nature in that its practitioners are explicit about the assumptions that they make about how people disturb themselves and what they can do to un-disturb themselves. In doing so, effective REBT therapists are prepared to make compromises with respect to these assumptions and work with what patients are prepared to accept rather than attempting to ram classical REBT down their patients' throats (Dryden, 1987). If we bring the alliance principle to the principle of psychoeducation, we get the principle of "informed allies" which I consider to be the gold standard of the working relationship between therapist and patient to which REBT therapists should aspire (Dryden, 1999b). When this is achieved, therapist and patient are working together, both informed about what each has to do to help the patient achieve his or her goals. Developing an informed alliance is particularly problematic with patients with BPD. Does this mean that REBT therapists should avoid trying to develop such relationships with these patients? Far from it! REBT therapists need to model attitudes of high frustration tolerance, persistence, and acceptance if they are to be in any way successful in working productively with patients with BPD.

REBT is perhaps best known for its emphasis on disputing patients' irrational beliefs. DiGiuseppe's (1991) comprehensive analysis of the disputing process showed that REBT therapists have at their disposal a variety of disputing styles (Socratic, didactic, metaphorical, and humorous), four major disputing targets (demanding beliefs, awfulising beliefs, low frustration tolerance (LFT) beliefs, and depreciation beliefs), three major types of disputing questions (empirical, logical, and pragmatic), and varying levels of specificity (very specific to very abstract). Disputing irrational beliefs is an art that takes dedicated practice and imagination. It also requires a quick brain because patients are likely to come up with a variety of doubts, reservations, and objections to surrendering their irrational beliefs and acquiring alternative rational beliefs and therapists need to respond quickly, tactfully, and persuasively to clients' queries.

REBT is a multimodal approach to therapy in that its practitioners use a variety of cognitive, imaginal, behavioral, emotive, and interpersonal techniques to help clients to weaken their conviction in their irrational beliefs and strengthen their conviction in their rational beliefs (Ellis & MacLaren, 1998)

REBT is a form of theoretically consistent eclecticism in that its practitioners are prepared to borrow techniques from other therapeutic approaches, but use these techniques in a manner consistent with REBT clinical theory (Dryden, 1987).

REBT therapists recognize that there are different types of psychotherapeutic change (Dryden & Neenan, 2004). They prefer to help clients work toward belief change, but when this is not possible for whatever reason, they are prepared to help their clients achieve other types of psychotherapeutic change such as inferential change, behavioral change, or environmental change (Dryden & Neenan, 2004). The ability to compromise is particularly important in working with patients with BPD.

DESIRABLE CLINICAL SKILLS AND ATTRIBUTES

Therapeutic work with patients with BPD is challenging. The first challenge concerns the therapist's skill. The psychopathology of patients with BPD, including interpersonal oversensitivity and low frustration tolerance, often calls for a very skillful response on the part of the therapist, particularly in developing and maintaining an effective therapeutic alliance and in delivering RFBT concepts and techniques. For example, in developing a therapeutic alliance, the task-oriented, active-directive style traditionally associated with REBT can alienate some patients with BPD and needs to be modified with an increased emphasis on communicating accurate empathy and on encouraging the patient to see that there is hope for a better life. The latter needs to be based on a realistic and agreed-upon appraisal of the patient's strengths, since patients with BPD generally have poor tolerance for vacuous, Pollyanna-ish statements of hope.

With respect to the delivery of REBT concepts and techniques, some patients with BPD can react adversely if the therapist phrases an REBT concept in a way that is unacceptable to the client or if the therapist explains a concept in an authoritative manner. It is the latter that is the turn-off for such patients. I clarify to patients that I want to use language that is acceptable to them and want to avoid unacceptable language. I ask them to educate me when I get things wrong from their perspective, and then they can tell me honestly and without rancor that my use of language needs improvement. Consequently, I usually portray therapy as a mutual educational experience to patients with BPD. I let them know that I have some concepts and techniques that patients have generally found helpful that I will share with them if they are interested. I stress that they may find some of these techniques helpful and others unhelpful. From their side, I stress that patients with BPD need to teach me how to make these concepts and techniques most useful for them and to teach me which *they* find helpful and which unhelpful. On this latter point, I help patients to see that the best way to judge the usefulness of concepts and techniques is to give them a proper trial. This can help to raise their philosophy of low frustration tolerance about some aspects of the therapy.

Working with patients with BPD is not only professionally challenging but often personally challenging. These personal challenges occur in three major areas. First, it is important for REBT therapists to manage their own feelings effectively, particularly their feelings of unhealthy anger. Therapist unhealthy anger stems partly from the accurate inference that patients with BPD can act aggressively towards the therapist, but largely from the irrational belief that the patients must not do so. In order to change these feelings of unhealthy anger, therapists need to challenge and change this belief to a rational belief that acknowledges that it would be desirable if these patients were cooperative and noninsulting, but sadly they don't have to be this way. Instead, given the nature of these patients, it is important to remember that they should empirically act at times in ways that are personally challenging to their therapists. Reviewing this rational belief in this way will lead therapists to feel healthy anger, and this realistic and contained feeling will help them to respond constructively to the patient.

Second, it is important that REBT therapists maintain a self-accepting philosophy in their work with patients with BPD because these patients often threaten the self-esteem of their therapists in a number of ways. For example, it is well recognized that patients with BPD swing from deifying to devilifying significant others. Maintaining a self-accepting attitude in the face of patient criticism and scorn is crucial if therapists are to maintain an effective therapeutic equilibrium.

Finally, it is very important that REBT therapists be persistent in working with patients with BPD. The progress that such patients make is variable, and they often slip back after making strides forward. An attitude of persistence is important in a number of ways. First, persisting with patients with BPD clearly keeps therapists in the therapeutic setting. Second, therapist persistence serves as a good model for patients with BPD in that it shows them that they can persist at helping themselves. Third, therapist persistence helps to calm the abandonment fears of patients with BPD. In order to be persistent, REBT therapists need to maintain a philosophy of high frustration tolerance.

It is clear, then, that in order to practice REBT effectively with patients with BPD, REBT therapists need to practice REBT effectively with themselves.

TREATMENT GOALS

REBT theory argues that there are two forms of psychological disturbance: ego disturbance and non-ego disturbance. In regard to ego disturbance, an important goal would be encouraging Linda to accept herself unconditionally for her problems so that she can address those problems effectively. If necessary, I would help her to see that unconditional self-acceptance does not promote resignation or complacency as some patients mistakenly think. Some patients are quite happy to acknowledge that they have BPD, while others resist this diagnosis. My hunch is that Linda would resist this label, so I would encourage her to accept herself for her problems, however she sees them. I would also explore other areas where Linda is likely to depreciate herself either explicitly or implicitly and encourage her to accept herself instead. These areas are likely to be interpersonally focused.

However, most of the work that I envision myself doing with Linda would be in the domain of non-ego disturbance. The goal would be to help her accept others as fallible human beings who sometimes make egregious errors and to tolerate better the frustration of having her wishes thwarted by others. In particular, I would want to help her act less impulsively when others break her rules. I would further encourage her to see that when she is less impulsive, she gets less frustration in her life, while if she acts impulsively on her angry feelings, she will get more frustration in her life. Another goal would be to help her manage her disturbed feelings better and develop a range of self-protective behaviors when she feels disturbed.

There are areas where the therapeutic goals would impinge on both ego and non-ego disturbance. Thus, there is much evidence that Linda is demanding of others with whom she is involved and fears abandonment when others withdraw from her in response to her interpersonally aversive behaviors. Thus, an important goal would be to help her relate better with others so she is more interpersonally rewarding. In particular, I would want to help her go more slowly in the developing stage of relationships, since there is evidence that she is impatient for certain relationships to proceed quickly. Second, I would want to help her to appreciate aloneness and to see that she can still be with herself when others are away from her or leave her. Also, I would want to help her to accept herself when she is left by others.

There is evidence that therapists have more ambitious goals for their patients than their patients have for themselves (Maluccio, 1979), so this may be the case for Linda P. On the positive side, however, the complaints that she is bringing to therapy (beyond the immediate legal situation) are significant and encourage me in the hope that I would be able to engage her in a meaningful discussion of at least some of my major goals for her long-term well-being. However, therapy would begin with her goals rather than mine.

FURTHER INFORMATION NEEDED

While REBT therapists do not carry out a formal case formulation with all their patients (as do cognitive therapists), it is my practice as an REBT therapist to complete such a formulation with patients with complex and difficult problems such as patients with a personality disorder. I refer to this activity as formulating a UPCP (understanding the person in the context of his or her problems [Dryden, 1998]). The following are the therapist's tasks in conducting a UPCP-based assessment and includes the information I am likely to seek from Linda:

- Obtaining basic information and utilizing initial impressions
- Developing a problem list
- Identifying goals for therapy
- Developing a list of problem emotions "Cs"
- Developing a list of problem critical "As"
- Identifying core irrational beliefs
- Identifying dysfunctional behavioral "Cs"
- Identifying the purposive nature of dysfunctional behavior
- Identifying ways in which the patient prevents or cuts short the experience of problems
- Identifying ways in which the patient compensates for problems
- Identifying metapsychological problems
- Identifying the cognitive consequences of core irrational beliefs
- Identifying the manner of problem expression and the interpersonal response to these expressions
- Identifying health and medication status
- Developing an understanding of relevant predisposing factors
- Predicting likely responses to therapy
- Negotiating a narrative account with the patient

CONCEPTUALIZATION OF LINDA IN THE CONTEXT OF HER PROBLEMS

While a full conceptualization of Linda's problems depends on a full UPCP-based assessment, from the information provided, the following should be regarded as hypotheses about Linda's functioning.

Personality

In Beck's view, patients' personalities can be usefully understood in terms of how the patients deal with autonomy and sociotropic issues

(A. Beck, Epstein, & Harrison, 1983). Regarding autonomy, Linda can function well at work within a structure, but not when given independence. When given autonomy, her rigid demands about how others must behave come to the fore and she acts on these rigid beliefs. Rather than compromise and alter the tone of her notes to parents, she chooses not to write them at all. This is typical of the black and white split in the personality of many patients with BPD.

From a sociotropic perspective, Linda is able to function well when she is on her own, but when she is in relationships, her difficulties come to the fore. When relating to significant others, she over-attaches and responds poorly (e.g., crying and begging) when she perceives others may be losing interest in her. She is insecure in close relationships and shows this in the form of jealousy, rage, and anxious, clinging behavior, which understandably leads others to withdraw from her physically or psychologically. This withdrawal activates a disturbed reaction to being "abandoned." This reaction is characterized by Linda disrespecting the boundaries of others, a pattern of behavior that has predictably poor results interpersonally. There is little sense from the case study that Linda can clearly see her role in the demise of her relationships, and an important therapeutic task would be to encourage her to see this role and to take responsibility for it without self-blame.

Behavior

There is evidence that Linda's behavior is dominated in problem areas by impulsiveness. Indeed, the episode that led to her referral was an example of an angry, impulsive action (bumping the car). Her impulsiveness is also shown by her overspending and by bingeing on food and sex. On the other hand, she has made only one suicide attempt. This suggests that she either does not have frequent suicidal impulses or that she is able to resist them. I would need to discover which.

Affective States

Linda reports depression, anxiety (for which she is particularly seeking help), anger and impatience, jealousy, and insecurity. She also reports feelings of emptiness (common in patients with BPD) and spacing out (a dissociative response which she uses to deal with anger-related hurt).

Cognitions

Assessing cognitions really needs to be done in the context of the therapist-patient dialogue. In the absence of this dialogue, the following points are made tentatively. There is some evidence that Linda holds the following general irrational beliefs.

- "People must do the right thing" (particularly with respect to her parents and her neighbors).
- "I must be in control" (she is overwhelmed by work when she is not in control).
- "I must be perfect and be in control of myself."
- "When I am with a man, I must have contact with him when I want to, and I can't stand it when I don't get what I want."
- "I can't bear to be left" (when she is, she considers that she has been abandoned).
- "I must get rid of my emotional pain quickly" (leading to impulsive action).

In addition, she seems to think that interpersonal relationships are inherently conflictual and that men can't be trusted and are only after sex (but idealized her husband before marriage). These two cognitions are best seen in REBT theory as general distorted inferences.

POTENTIAL PITFALLS AND DIFFICULTIES

Psychotherapy with patients with BPD can be fraught with pitfalls and difficulties, and I would be concerned if I did not experience any with Linda because this would indicate to me that I had not engaged her at an emotionally meaningful level.

The therapist must determine whether Linda is seeking therapy for help with her legal case alone. My own practice in such cases, and this has little to do with REBT as a therapeutic approach, is to separate therapy from legal report writing. I usually make it quite clear at the outset of such cases that if I am to take the person on for therapy, I will not write a report that can be used by that person in court. If the person and/or the lawyer wants such a report, I recommend that it needs to prepared by someone not concerned with the patient's treatment. I would explain this to Linda at the very outset before I agreed to be her therapist. Then, if she chooses to seek therapy with me, it would be because of what she could gain from it therapeutically and not what she could gain from it legally.

Another possible pitfall may be Linda's response to an active-directive therapeutic approach. Some patients with BPD do not respond very well to a driving form of active-directive REBT, and I would watch Linda's response to my active-directive interventions. In doing so, I would be influenced by my cognitive therapy colleagues and seek feedback from Linda about this aspect of therapy (as well as other aspects).

The success of any therapeutic approach with Linda would depend on the extent to which she can be encouraged to stand back and reflect on her experience in a meaningful way. I would need to guide her so that she avoids crashing on the rocks of Scylla (acting mindlessly on her impulses) and Charybdis (spacing out). If I considered that I could not do this or if Linda thought that a different type of therapy or therapist would help her to do this, I would refer her. Patients with BPD often have a problem with unhealthy anger and often express their angry feelings to their therapist when they consider that he or she has done something wrong or let them down in some way. If Linda expresses her feelings of unhealthy anger toward me, this could be an obstacle in therapy in two main ways. First, it may prove an obstacle if I respond counter-therapeutically. This would be the case if I held an irrational belief about her anger (e.g., "I have tried to help her; therefore she must be appreciative and not rant at me"). Second, it may prove to be an obstacle if I am not able to help her to stand back and reflect on her experience. I will probably fail in this attempt if I do not offer Linda a genuine empathic response to her anger.

Another potential pitfall to therapy would be a failure to carry out agreed-upon homework assignments. Burns and Auerbach (1992) showed that completion of homework assignments predicts a good response to cognitive behavior therapy. Linda may not complete self-help assignments for various reasons, one of which would be my failure to negotiate such assignments with her properly. I may fail to spend enough time negotiating such assignments with Linda, fail to ensure that they she clearly sees that carrying them out will help her to achieve her therapeutic goals, or fail to help her identify and troubleshoot obstacles to homework completion. Another reason why Linda may not complete assignments would be because she holds one or more low frustration tolerance (LFT) irrational beliefs (e.g., "I shouldn't have to do these assignments," or "Carrying out homework assignments is too difficult for me."). Unless I help Linda to raise her frustration tolerance for self-help, she will achieve only limited gains from REBT.

A final pitfall in REBT with Linda is patient burnout with REBT concepts. With frequent use of REBT concepts, they eventually will lose their impact with her and may even become meaningless to her. She may become annoyed at their very mention. To prevent this from happening, I would encourage Linda to come up with her own terms for REBT concepts and use those instead.

Immediate and Long-Term Functioning

Predicting the outcome of a therapy before it has commenced is difficult because the best way to know how a patient will respond to REBT is empirically: to begin REBT and observe the patient's response. Obviously this will not do here, but there is some evidence in the case study that Linda thrives in a structured environment, and she therefore may do well with a structured therapeutic approach such as REBT.

If therapy was successful, Linda would be able to tolerate her disturbed negative feelings and deal with them productively rather than act impulsively; she would be able to think rationally and act appropriately when others act badly toward her; and she would be able to respect the boundaries of others. Further, she would be able to develop and maintain respectful relationships with people and deal with interpersonal rejection with self-acceptance. Whether she was able to maintain and even capitalize on these gains would depend on the extent to which she practiced her REBT self-help skills.

TIMELINE

My experience in working with patients with BPD is that those who acknowledge the full extent of their difficulties and are motivated to address them do well in long-term REBT of about 2 to 3 years. Those who don't fully acknowledge their problems and think that they are less disturbed than they are will only commit themselves to short-term treatment, but will return to therapy when they think they need further help. Obviously, one can do more with the former than the latter. Assuming that I can encourage Linda to acknowledge the full extent of her problems and assuming that her wish for treatment is not based only on a desire to be helped with her legal case, then treatment might last for about 2 years, with once-a-week sessions lasting the standard 50 minutes. This assessment is based on the understanding that she has a haven to turn to as an alternative to self-harm and impulsive action since I do not operate a practice where I can respond quickly to emergency situations nor do I permit patients to telephone me out of hours.

SPECIFIC TECHNIQUES EMPLOYED

As an REBT therapist, I would, of course, use a range of cognitive, emotive, behavioral, and imaginal techniques associated with the practice of REBT (Ellis & MacLaren, 1998). These are largely geared to encouraging patients to change their irrational beliefs to rational beliefs (belief change), but others are employed to further inferential change, behavioral change, and environmental change if belief change in general or on specific issues is either resisted by the patient or for other reason not possible.

I would make it clear to Linda that our joint task is to determine which techniques she finds helpful and which not helpful. To counter her impulsiveness, I would encourage her to give each technique a fair test before making a decision on its potential usefulness. Although REBT has a number of standard techniques, my own practice is to find idiosyncratic ways of using them with my patients. Since REBT is a persuasive therapy, I would determine how Linda has been productively influenced in the past and draw upon this knowledge in planning and executing my interventions. In a similar vein, I would determine which influence attempts Linda has found aversive in the past and would seek to eliminate these from my practice. I should add, however, that such clinical thinking is informed by my professional ethical code and my assessment of the long-term impact of my persuasive interventions. Also, as noted above, I have been much influenced by the work of my cognitive therapy colleagues in asking for feedback on the interventions that I use so that I can practice a personalistic approach to REBT with Linda (A. Beck, Rush, Shaw, & Emory, 1979). However, because there is some evidence that Linda responds well to structure, I may encourage her to read through my REBT patient workbook (Dryden, 2001) to determine whether she might find it a useful resource. This workbook presents some of the most commonly used REBT techniques in an accessible way so that patients can learn to use these methods themselves. Each

...nique is fully described and exemplified, full instructions are given for its use, common difficulties in using the technique are outlined and discussed, and advice concerning how to avoid these problems is provided.

As Ellis and MacLaren (1998) clearly documented, many REBT techniques are used to encourage patients to change their irrational beliefs to rational beliefs, and standard REBT techniques focus on disputing irrational beliefs and encouraging clients to act and think in ways that are consistent with their developing rational beliefs and inconsistent with their irrational beliefs. If I considered that Linda was reactant to direct disputing methods, I would encourage her to see irrational beliefs and rational beliefs as a set of choices, each with short- and long-term consequences for her and the people in her life. I would work carefully with Linda to identify those consequences and help her to choose whether she wanted to commit herself to thinking rationally or irrationally on the basis of this cost-benefit analysis. Assuming that she wanted to think rationally, I would then work with her to identify the techniques that could best help her do that.

On the basis of my experience of using REBT with patients with BPD, I would predict that the process of therapy with Linda would not go smoothly. I would help her to realize this and not disturb herself about it. In particular, it is likely that she would have a series of doubts, reservations, and objections about a range of rational concepts and about the process of therapy based on a variety of misconceptions and on other irrational beliefs (Dryden, 1995; 2001). I would patiently work with Linda to identify and examine her doubts and reservations and help her to correct these. While it is difficult to predict what Linda's reservations might be, an example might be "if I accept that others are not bad people for doing bad things (the REBT principle of other-acceptance), then I am condoning what they do."

In addition to these regular REBT techniques, I would probably try to help Linda in some or all of the following ways:

- I would suggest methods to encourage Linda to engage with her "observing ego" without spacing out. The choice of such methods would be made according to Linda's experience of being able to stand back and reflect on her experience. The purpose of these methods is to encourage her to use cognitive behavioral techniques instead of self-defeating impulsive action.
- I would teach Linda various mindfulness techniques to help her to accept and stay with her thoughts, images, and feelings rather

than desperately trying to get rid of them (Segal, Williams, & Teasdale, 2002). However, I would use these techniques after I had taught her the REBT principle of acceptance, which advocates acknowledgement that a psychological experience has happened, that it is unpleasant, and that the best way to deal with it is to allow it to be until it disappears.

- I would help Linda to identify and role-play difficult interpersonal scenarios. Before the role-play, I would help her devise constructive ways of thinking and behaving in these situations that may not be in her repertoire. Then I would have her role-play with me. This would be best done in a group setting because other group members could have valuable input into the process.
- I would encourage Linda to imagine being on the receiving end of her own interpersonal behavior and ask her how she would like to be treated in these situations. I would then discuss the concept of relationship rules and have her formulate rules that might elicit more favorable interpersonal responses from people. I would then encourage her to experiment acting in ways that are consistent with these rules and to dispute any irrational beliefs that interfere with her doing so. Because of the delicate nature of this work, it would probably take place late in therapy.
- It is clear that Linda does not have a sense of healthy boundaries with respect to self and others. Perhaps as part of the work on the development of relationship rules, I would introduce this concept. Then, I would encourage Linda to identify how she would like others to respect her boundaries, help her develop healthy ways of thinking and acting when others encroach on these boundaries, and help her see that others would probably appreciate her respecting their similar boundaries. This would then lead to a discussion of what would stop her from respecting others' boundaries and how she could surmount these obstacles. Again, due to the sensitive nature of this work, it would probably take place late in therapy once Linda and I had developed a solid therapeutic alliance and had successfully weathered a number of therapeutic storms.

SPECIAL CAUTIONS

Working with patients with BPD almost always involves special cautions and I would imagine that my work with Linda would be no exception.

It is difficult to predict with any certainty what these areas may be, but from the information provided, I would imagine that transferentially, Linda may try to sexualize our relationship. If so, I would show her that I accept her as a person, but I would bring the issue into focus and explore the reasons why she thinks she is doing this. From my perspective, I would see such behavior as being determined by one or more of a number of factors: a need for familiarity, an idea that this is the only way that she can get attention from a male, and/or the idea that she needs love and attention from a significant male and sex is the only way that she can get this. Once we have identified and focused on her "sexualizing" behavior, I would put forward the above as hypotheses for her consideration and would work with the issue that she resonated with, helping her to consider the advantages and disadvantages of the issue and to identify alternative, more constructive behavior. I would also help her formulate healthy alternatives to any irrational beliefs that we discovered as a part of our exploration and help her question both sets of beliefs using empirical, logical, and pragmatic arguments.

If she continued her sexualizing behavior toward me, I would immediately bring this to her attention, remind her of the work that we did on the issue, and encourage her to challenge and change her irrational beliefs there and then.

I would also predict that Linda would show in one or more ways her oversensitivity to rejection in our relationship. In such episodes I would first help her to describe my behavior that she took as rejection. I would empathize with her in that if that is what I did, I could understand her feelings. I would then ask her if she would like to deal with such situations more healthily. If so, I would help her to identify her feelings in these situations (often feelings of hurt), to tolerate these feelings long enough to identify the irrational beliefs that underpin them, to challenge and change these irrational beliefs, to construct alternative, healthier rational beliefs, and determine how she could act on these beliefs. If she was willing, I might suggest that we role-play such "rejection" scenarios.

I would then help Linda to understand that her core irrational beliefs about rejection lead her to infer rejection in ambiguous situations and that her alternative rational beliefs about rejection would lead her to be more accurate in her inferences about rejection. Only then would I encourage her to test her inferences about rejection from me and other significant people in her life. This strategy is based on the REBT view that inferences are best questioned after the person has had some measure of success in reevaluating his or her irrational beliefs. However, because REBT is a flexible therapy, I could envision situations in which I would help Linda to test her inferences before questioning her irrational beliefs.

With respect to counter-transference feelings, I would follow the usual stance that my feelings may be either a reliable guide to how others respond to Linda interpersonally or a sign that I am disturbing myself about Linda's behavior both inside and outside therapy. If the former is the case, I might begin by disclosing my reaction and asking Linda how she imagined others felt about similar behavior. If she could see the unconstructiveness of her behavior, we would then use REBT techniques to challenge irrational beliefs and devise more constructive ways of behaving. If not, I would leave the issue to another time.

If my feelings toward Linda were unhealthy, I would use REBT on myself to identify, challenge, and change my irrational beliefs about her behavior. I would also seek supervision on my work with her so that I could get an objective view on what was going on between us.

From the case study, I would judge that Linda posed a minimal risk to herself. Nonetheless, when we focused on issues concerning self-care, I would review possible threats to her well-being, both sexual and nonsexual, and intervene according to the REBT model by identifying and challenging irrational beliefs and then identifying and strengthening alternative rational beliefs by acting in ways that are consistent with them.

AREAS TO AVOID

There are no areas that I would avoid or would not address with Linda, but there may be areas that she may wish to avoid addressing. If this is the case, my response would be guided by two principles: the primacy of the therapeutic alliance and the importance of challenging, but not overwhelming.

As many commentators have observed (e.g., Bordin, 1979), the development and maintenance of an effective alliance is an important contributor to the outcome of psychotherapy, and this is true even for a technically oriented approach such as REBT. Thus, I would have the primacy of the therapeutic alliance in mind if I raised areas that Linda may not wish to address. In doing so, I would explain to Linda the principle of challenging, but not overwhelming. For therapy to be effective, patients have to deal with issues they find painful and would rather avoid, but these areas are only dealt with when patients consider them a challenge but not overwhelming. I would stress to Linda that while I may sometimes bring up areas that she would rather not face, she is in ultimate charge of what she chooses to work on and I will respect her decision, although I may challenge it from time to time. I would also stress that I will help her to raise her tolerance level for painful emotions before we deal with painful issues.

ROLE OF MEDICATION

The role of medication in the treatment of patients with BPD is to be decided by those trained to prescribe such medication, and in Britain this means psychiatrists. It is likely that in Britain Linda would have been referred to me by a psychiatrist, and in this case I would liaise with the referring psychiatrist over medication. As Linda's therapist, I would have two concerns with respect to her taking medication, which I would discuss with her psychiatrist. First, would she use her medication inappropriately to manage her feelings? If so, this would interfere with the work I would do with Linda on healthy affect regulation, and I would ideally want to help her raise her tolerance level for negative feelings before she takes medication, although this might not always be possible. Second, is there a risk that she might overdose on her medication? If there is, then medication might be withheld until this risk is minimal.

LINDA'S STRENGTHS

Linda has a number of strengths apparent in the case study:

- Linda did well at school and at college. This suggests that she is intelligent and that she can be persistent.
- Linda saw education as way out of her environment. This shows that she can think long term and put into effect a long-range plan.
- Linda functions well in her job when she has a well-defined structure in which to operate.
- Linda looks after her bonsai trees. This suggests that she is caring and can put her caring into practice in the long term.

- Linda has chosen to live away from children. In doing so, she shows that she knows what is in her healthy best interests and is able to act on this knowledge.

I would also interview Linda carefully concerning past successful attempts at coping with difficult situations and difficult feelings. If she considers that she has not had any success at coping, I would attempt to discover anything that she has done that has helped her to refrain from harming herself. I would then use this information to help her to see that she can help herself and that we can build on even small, temporary successes at self-help. In addition, I would seek out healthy features of her disturbed emotional and behavioral reactions. Thus, although she operates on a number of rigid demands, these demands are unhealthy transformations of flexible desires, and her stalking behavior of men shows persistence, albeit of an unhealthy kind.

I would draw upon these strengths singly and in combination in my discussions with Linda about the principle of transferable skills. This principle states that patients often have and use constructive skills in important areas of their lives but don't often realize that they can transfer such skills to other, more problematic areas of their lives. Thus, if we are focusing on an area in which her problem is lack of persistence, I would refer to an area where she has demonstrated persistence and discuss with Linda what it would take for her to transfer her ability to persist. This might lead to a discussion about the importance of goals and putting up with discomfort in order to achieve them. Thus, I would watch for ways to show Linda that she has strengths that she is not using in problem areas. This would lead to a discussion of the obstacles that prevent the transfer of skills, and perhaps allow Linda to overcome such obstacles.

BOUNDARIES, LIMITS, AND LIMIT-SETTING

Setting suitable boundaries and limits with patients is a central ingredient to most approaches to psychotherapy, and this is perhaps even more important with patients with BPD because they often have had their own boundaries encroached upon or breached by others or have breached the boundaries of others. Establishing clear boundaries and explaining the limits of therapists are helpful for a number of reasons. Boundaries help patients know what they can expect, and thus they don't have to engage in testing limits (often a test to see if the therapist is strong enough to cope with the patient). Explaining limits helps patients understand that the therapist is a person and not some impersonal object without feeling that the patient can treat badly and will absorb the treatment without effect. An understanding of these issues helps patients see that they can help the therapist (who is helping them) by keeping within the limits, and that breaking the limits compromises the therapist's ability to serve as therapist.

I do not claim to speak on behalf of REBT therapists and am discussing only my own set of limits. There is nothing in the REBT approach that pertains to this issue. My view is that if I am not able to work within a set of firm but fair boundaries, my therapeutic value for my patients is compromised and I cannot be fully helpful to them. If a patient with BPD telephones me at home in the middle of the night in crisis, my sleep is disturbed as is my wife's, thus affecting the quality of my personal and professional life. Psychotherapy as a profession is demanding enough at the best of times and is even more so for those of us who work with patients with severe disturbance. In addition, my private practice is but one part of my busy professional schedule, and patients need to respect my time so that I can perform all my professional duties. Some may argue that because of these conditions I should not work with patients with BPD, and I have some sympathy with this view. However, I have worked effectively with patients with BPD who have respected the following points, which I would spell out to Linda at the outset when discussing a treatment contract.

- *Fees.* I expect to be paid for every session at the end of the session. I will not renegotiate my fee once treatment has commenced. Fees will be paid unless 24 hours' notice is given.
- *Sessions.* Each session will last for 50 minutes, and the patient will leave promptly at the end of the session.
- *Extra-therapy contact.* I will not respond to any attempt to contact me between sessions other than to reschedule a session that the patient wishes to cancel. If Linda is in distress and considers that she is at risk, she should contact someone chosen jointly by Linda, her psychiatrist, and me.
- *Self-harming behavior.* If Linda is prepared to make a contract not to self-harm herself with me, I would ask her to make one, but only if she considers that doing so would be helpful and appropriate. Some patients with BPD find that the prospect of making

such a contract increases their sense of being unsafe, and if this is the case, I would not ask Linda to make one. However, I would want her to commit to work toward refraining from self-harm in the long term and would tell her that I would prioritize issues that render her more vulnerable to engaging in self-harming behavior.

If Linda does not agree with the above points, I would not take her on as a patient. Once she has agreed to these principles, I would regard instances of her counter-therapeutic behavior as threats to her recovery and attempts to render me therapeutically impotent and would deal with them as such with her. In particular, I would encourage her to reflect on what she was experiencing prior to her attempting to violate our agreed boundary. I would deal with this issue with empathy and show Linda that I accept her as a person but that I will not tolerate her behavior. From there, I would help her to identify, challenge, and change the irrational beliefs that underpin such behavior. Continued boundary violations would lead me to terminate the therapy relationship with Linda and refer her back to her psychiatrist.

INVOLVEMENT OF SIGNIFICANT OTHERS AND THE USE OF HOMEWORK

From the case study details about Linda, her life, and her family situation, involving her significant others in therapy does not seem feasible. She lives in Chicago and her parents live in Florida, and thus while there might have been some value in holding family sessions late in Linda's treatment (if both Linda and her parents agreed and if the therapeutic agenda was clear), it is not practicable. If Linda's sister lives near her, joint sessions with Linda and her sister may have some value, since Linda considers that she is being neglected by her sister. Again, this would happen late in Linda's treatment and only if both parties agree and the therapeutic agenda is clear.

I would definitely use homework assignments with Linda because they are an integral part of REBT. Maxie C. Maultsby, Jr. (personal communication), the noted rational psychiatrist, once said that effective therapy is, in essence, effective self-therapy because if patients do not use what they learn in therapy sessions, they will not benefit in any meaningful, lasting way outside therapy sessions. I would tailor the use of these self-help assignments with Linda and collaborate with her in their selection. I would draw on the entire range of homework assignments that REBT therapists traditionally use (Ellis & MacLaren, 1998), the content of which would depend on what Linda and I discussed in therapy sessions. Many of these homework assignments would likely be designed to encourage Linda to

- accept herself (Dryden, 1999a)
- overcome her feelings of unhealthy anger with respect to the behavior of others (Dryden, 1996)
- express healthy feelings of anger in an assertive and respectful manner
- contain her disturbed feelings long enough to deal with them in productive ways rather than impulsively striving to get rid of them quickly through self-harm

RELAPSE PREVENTION AND TERMINATION

I would certainly use relapse prevention methods with Linda. In particular, I would do the following:

- Help her to distinguish between a lapse (a slight and temporary return to a problem state) and a relapse (a complete and more enduring return to a problem state). I would further encourage her to see that lapses are inevitable in the change process and are valuable in that they are an opportunity for Linda to use her developing REBT self-help skills. During this process, I would encourage her to "de-awfulize" lapses and even to take the horror out of a relapse should she be very anxious about the prospect of relapsing.
- Encourage her to develop a list of vulnerability factors. Vulnerability factors are those to which she would likely respond with unhelpful, pretherapy behaviors, thoughts, and feelings. I would then help Linda prepare to face such vulnerability factors by coaching her on how she could use what she has learned from therapy in such situations. This preparation would include discussion, roleplay, imagery methods and practice of such responses until Linda considered herself ready to face the vulnerability factors in her own life environment. Throughout this process, I would encourage Linda to face situations that were challenging but not overwhelm-

ing for her to face, which would help her build up her emotional muscle (Blythe & Garcia, 1977).

- Help her to identify, challenge, and change core irrational beliefs; encourage her to develop alternative core rational beliefs; and encourage her to strengthen them by acting and thinking in ways that are consistent with these healthy beliefs and by refraining from acting in ways that are consistent with her core irrational beliefs.

As Linda improves, I would encourage her to take more responsibility for her self-change. One way that I would do this is to decrease the frequency of therapy sessions (after significant work on relapse prevention). Initially, we would meet every 10 days rather than weekly, then once every 3 weeks, then monthly, etc. At each point, the change would be a joint decision and I would monitor her responses to decreasing therapist contact. In fact, I would raise abandonment as an issue if she does not mention it herself. If she says that she does not feel abandoned, we would explore the thoughts that protect her from this experience and encourage her to use this experience as a template for her other relationships, especially with men.

Termination implies that therapist and patient will never see one another again, which is probably not realistic, particularly in work with patients with BPD. Although terminating with such patients does bring their issues with abandonment into sharp relief, it may also deter them from returning to therapy for additional help should they require it. In my experience, even BPD patients who do well in therapy will require additional therapeutic input from time to time. Terminating with such patients tends to discourage them from seeking help from the therapist.

Therefore, when the time was right, I would discuss with Linda how she wants to manage the self-help process in the long term and what role I might have in this process. She might choose to see me infrequently on a planned basis, or she may want to contact me when she has tried but failed to use her self-help skills effectively and needs a consultation to determine why her attempts to help herself have failed.

If therapy does not go well and Linda is one of those patients with BPD who just will not help herself, then I would accept this grim clinical reality and keep seeing her if it helps to prevent self-harm. In such a case, I would continue to try to encourage Linda to help herself and would increase the time between sessions to back up my encouragement with action. In this case, I may not formally terminate therapy with Linda. I would still raise the abandonment issue, and how she would deal with it, by discussing various scenarios with her, such as my retirement from clinical work or my moving away.

MECHANISMS OF CHANGE

Mechanisms of change are the means by which change is effected. If Linda does benefit from REBT, which change mechanisms may have helped to bring about this benefit? Since I have answered this question elsewhere in this chapter, I will summarize my response here. For therapy to be successful:

- Linda and I need to develop and maintain an effective therapeutic alliance.
- Linda needs to first understand the importance of ongoing self-help and then needs to implement this principle.
- Linda needs to assess and deal with her problems using the REBT model of change, which includes the following elements:

  —identifying and tolerating her unhealthy negative feelings (at "C") rather than acting impulsively to get rid of them
  —using her disturbed feelings to identify what she was most disturbed about in the specific situations (at "A")
  —identifying the irrational belief (at "B") that mediates between "A" and "C"
  —challenging and changing this irrational belief and formulating a rational alternative to it
  —acting in ways consistent with this rational belief
  —correcting any remaining cognitive distortions at "A"

- Linda needs to implement the above specific REBT-based change mechanisms in specific situations and to generalize this more widely in her life. Linda needs to identify, challenge, and change her core irrational beliefs. As previously noted, whether Linda would be able to do this would depend on the extent to which she took responsibility for her own long-term well-being and the extent to which she was able to overcome obstacles to self-care.

REBT theory views clinical phenomena as acting interdependently rather than independently. Nonspecific and specific change mechanisms have their power largely because of their interdependent influence. The specific mechanisms that will be most therapeutic for Linda can only be determined after the fact.

REFERENCES

Beck, A. T. (1976). *Cognitive therapy and the emotional disorders.* New York: International Universities Press.

Beck, A. T., Epstein, N., & Harrison, R. (1983). Cognitions, attitudes and personality dimensions in depression. *British Journal of Cognitive Psychotherapy, 1*(1), 1–16.

Beck, A. T., Rush, A. J., Shaw, B. F., & Emery, G. (1979). *Cognitive therapy of depression.* New York: Guilford Press.

Blythe, B. T., & Garcia, E. J. (1977). *Developing emotional muscle.* Athens, GA: University of Georgia.

Bordin, F. (1979). The generalizability of the psychoanalytic concept of the working alliance. *Psychotherapy: Theory, Research and Practice, 16,* 252–260.

Burns, D. D, & Auerbach, A. H. (1992). Does homework compliance enhance recovery from depression? *Psychiatric Annals, 22,* 464–469.

DiGiuseppe, R. (1991). Comprehensive cognitive disputing in RET. In M. E. Bernard (Ed.), *Using rational-emotive therapy effectively: A practitioner's guide* (pp. 173–195). New York: Plenum.

DiGiuseppe, R. (1995). Developing the therapeutic alliance with angry clients. In H. Kassinove (Ed.), *Anger disorders: Definition, diagnosis and treatment* (pp. 131–149). Washington, DC: Taylor & Francis.

Dryden, W. (1987). *Current issues in rational-emotive therapy.* Beckenham, Kent: CroomHelm.

Dryden, W. (1995). *Preparing for client change in rational emotive behaviour therapy.* London: Whurr.

Dryden, W. (1996). *Overcoming anger: When anger helps and when it hurts.* London: Sheldon.

Dryden, W. (1998). Understanding persons in the context of their problems: A rational emotive behaviour therapy perspective. In M. Bruch & F. W. Bond (Eds.), *Beyond diagnosis: Case formulation approaches in CBT* (pp. 43–64). Chichester: Wiley.

Dryden, W. (1999a). *How to accept yourself.* London: Sheldon.

Dryden, W. (1999b). *Rational emotive behaviour therapy: A personal approach.* Bicester: Oxon: Winslow.

Dryden, W. (2001). *Reason to change: A rational emotive behaviour therapy (REBT) workbook.* Hove: Brunner/Routledge.

Dryden, W. (Ed.). (2004). *Idiosyncratic REBT.* Ross-on-Wye: PCCS Books.

Dryden, W., & Ellis, A. (2001). Rational emotive behavior therapy. In K. S. Dobson (Ed.), *Handbook of cognitive-behavioral therapies* (pp. 295–348). New York: Guilford Press.

Dryden, W., & Neenan, M. (2004). *The rational emotive behaviour approach to therapeutic change.* London: Sage.

Ellis, A. (1994a). *Reason and emotion in psychotherapy* (Revised and expanded edition). New York: Birch Lane Press.

Ellis, A. (1994b). The treatment of borderline personalities with rational emotive behavior therapy. *Journal of Rational-Emotive and Cognitive-Behavior Therapy, 12*(2), 101–119.

Ellis, A. (2001). *Feeling better, getting better, staying better.* Atascadero, CA: Impact.

Ellis, A., & MacLaren, C. (1998). *Rational emotive behavior therapy: A therapist's guide.* San Luis Obispo, CA: Impact.

Homey, K. (1950). *Neurosis and human growth.* New York: Norton.

Maluccio, A. N. (1979). *Learning from clients: Interpersonal helping as viewed by clients and social workers.* New York: Free Press.

Segal, Z. V., Williams, J. M. G., & Teasdale, J. D. (2002). *Mindfulness-based cognitive therapy for depression: A new approach to preventing relapse.* New York: Guilford Press.

7

Borderline States and Individual Psychology

Mark H. Stone and Nicole M. Hoffman

Although borderline features were observed and discussed in psychoanalytic papers by Moore (1921), Reich (1925), Oberndorf (1930), Glover (1932), Kasanin (1933), Fine (1989), and others writing at this time, Stern (1938) is thought to be the first to use the term *borderline* explicitly. A more contemporary application of the term has often been attributed to Knight's classic paper (1953). This is ironic, inasmuch as Knight wrote, "I have no wish to defend the term 'borderline state' as a diagnosis" (p. 97). Knight went on to make succinct but insightful observations about the borderline state: "The patient is quite sick but not frankly psychotic" (p. 94) and added, "making the [diagnostic] decision is difficult." Further, in his opening paragraph, Knight stated that a borderline diagnosis "conveys more information about the uncertainty and indecision of the psychiatrist than it does about the condition of the patient" (p. 94).

Today, the condition is labeled as "Borderline Personality Disorder," a syndrome whose essential features are described as "a pervasive pattern of instability of interpersonal relationships, self-image, and affects, and marked impulsivity that begins by early adulthood and is present in a variety of contexts" (DSM-IV-TR, 2000, p. 706).

An excellent history and classic depiction of historical views of what is now designated as borderline personality disorder can be found in Chapter 1 of Stone's *The Borderline Syndromes* (1980). Stone describes a "diagnosis cube" whose three dimensions show how the borderline condition (1) occupies an intermediate location between the neurotic and psychotic states; (2) can be viewed from the schizophrenic, schizoaffective, and manic-depressive perspectives; and (3) presents with an additional variety of personality subtypes. A genetic predisposition may also contribute to this condition.

Alfred Adler, Freud, and their contemporaries had not yet treated the borderline condition as a separate entity, but they addressed the condition. Adler's theory and clinical work, known as individual psychology, speak directly to the diagnosis and treatment of this disorder.

TREATMENT MODEL

Genesis of the Condition

Inferiority complex is the most well-known concept from Adler's writings (Adler, 1983; Ansbacher & Ansbacher, 1956). It is fundamental to his theory of psychopathology, and Adler (1929) explains its development. A child begins life as probably the most dependent of the species. Years of maturing are required to reach productive independence. In the formative years of development, the small physical stature and developing maturity of the child can easily be overwhelmed by adults and by the demands of life. Gradually, a sense of accomplishment evolves as skills and competency emerge, especially when fostered by good parenting and supported by the assistance of helpful teachers and others. Meeting the challenges of life becomes possible. The problems of growing up are increasingly resolved. Meeting life's challenges moves from a possibility to a reality. This results in an adult who, in turn, can foster development in others.

What if a sense of inadequacy (physical and/or mental, real and/or imagined) pervades? What if, instead of receiving nurturing, a child suffers from continuing adversity with little or no help or guidance from parents or others? What if a child is excused from developing independence and responsibility? Then life's challenges may appear as seemingly insurmountable obstacles to avoid because no opportunity of success appears possible and because failure is anticipated. A sense of inferiority may result that dominates behavior and causes "distance"[1] to be placed between the challenges of life and the child. This results in self-defeating behavior and produces an ever-increasing fear of failure.

Whether the course of personal growth is enhancing or frustrating, a distinctive pattern of looking at life develops. It is a subjective perspective, a resulting leitmotiv producing a unique, apperceptive view of self, others, and the world. This unique perceptive is called "Life Style" in individual psychology. Adler frequently cited novelists and dramatists such as Dostoevsky and Ibsen as "psychologists" who insightfully portrayed and explored the Life Style of their characters (Stone, 2000).

Adler used a quote from Seneca to introduce his second book, *The Neurotic Constitution* (1983): "It is not what happens that afflicts the person, but it is the opinion about this thing which afflicts the person" (Hadas, 1961, p. 89). His point in using this quote was to show that it is our perception of events rather than the events themselves that deserves our attention. Life Style reveals such apperception.

Adler's contentions are substantiated today. Garber and Seligman (1980) summarized an extensive laboratory research program and concluded, among other things, that the less individuals feel in control, the more likely they are to develop cognitive and emotional deficits that undergird self-defeating behavior. Beck and colleagues (Beck, 1967; Beck, Rush, Shaw, & Liese, 1979) also identified idiosyncratic schema in the patients from his clinical studies. Schema ruled their behavior.

How persons cope with inferiority belies the central strategy guiding a person's behavior, i.e., Life Style. If a person with weak vision pursues a vocation requiring substantial visual acuity, that person risks something due to his or her condition. Nevertheless, one may choose and pursue a goal that challenges one's endowment. Difficulties with vision are subordinated to the pursuit of a challenging goal. Another person might choose never to try because to do so would appear to be courting failure. People are creative in the ways they address their goals.

Another way to cope with a sense of inadequacy is to create self-delusions by which to assuage inferiority feelings (Stone, 1997, 1999). People sometimes develop ingenious means to avoid feeling overwhelmed by fear about the problems of life. These fabrications, denoted as "fictions"[2] in individual psychology, can be modest or extensive. Fictions are part of the self-created "working orders" in an individual's Life Style. Adler wrote, "I readily follow the ingenious views of Vaihinger (1983) who maintains that historically ideas tend to grow from 'fictions' (unreal but practically useful constructs) to 'hypotheses' and later to 'dogmas' " (p. 169). Adler meant that normal persons can create and use fictions as useful expedients, but some persons reify fictions and use them dogmatically.

Fictions can guide a person's negative coping. Treated unfairly in a past singular incident, a person may choose to incorrectly generalize from this experience. The unfortunate incident is converted into a generalization. It becomes a distorted "motto" for guiding subsequent behavior. All bias develops in this manner. While past experience can be a useful guide to subsequent behavior, one can also fabricate personal distortions and draw inaccurate conclusions. Fictions can become powerfully embedded in the mind to direct attitudes and behavior. Kant (1964) wrote, "The only feature common to all mental disorder is the loss of 'sensus communis' (common, communal sense) and the compensatory development of a 'sensus privatus' (private sense) of reasoning" (p. 16).

Adler frequently commented upon the need for a person to adopt "common reasoning" as opposed to "private reasoning" in solving problems. This is not meant to oppose individuality and creativity, but to show that undue reliance upon private reasoning is egocentric and prone to isolate the person from effectively communicating with others (Ansbacher & Ansbacher, 1978).

Early recollections are an important part of Life Style assessment. The collection and interpretation of early recollections (ERs) can reveal the dominating mental images constructed about the self, others, and the world. One's Life Style is a construction. To recollect is to take stock of one's memory, which is itself a construction of self-selected information (distortions) chosen as significant to one's life. ERs are indicators of how we perceive life. Our earliest recollections constitute the working bank of information that guides our perceptions. Early memories have value to the person, whether or not they are true. When they are true and valid, the person gains insight into the larger sphere of human activity. When they are falsely constructed, they give a biased, egocentric viewpoint. Early recollections help build a Life Style and contribute to the working plans for living (Eckstein, Baruth, & Mahrer, 1982). They signify what has been selected to focus upon, to guide action and to direct behavior. Munroe (1955, p. 428) identified Adler's Life Style assessment using ERs as the first projective test.

The Fictive Goal

Life Style assessment seeks to determine the goal that guides behavior. This goal is usually hidden and not recognized by the individual. May (1970) wrote, "My concept of myth is very much what Adler had in mind by guiding fiction." It is a tenet of individual psychology that all behavior is goal directed. Adler said, "The goal of mental life becomes its governing principle, its causa finalis. Here we have the root of the unity of the personality, of the individuality of a person. It does not matter what its origins may have been. It is not their origin, but their end, their ultimate goal, that constitutes their individual character" (in Ansbacher & Ansbacher, 1956, p. 94).

We appear to know the ostensible goals in our lives, but our hidden goal may not be self-evident. It is usually hidden because to bring it to conscious recognition might be painful. Hidden goals stem from feelings of inferiority and remain hidden because they excuse action when we lack the courage to persist where failure might be possible. A hidden goal isolates these contingencies. The consequences of not facing them are, of course, just as bad. They keep one from experiencing more of life and enjoying the advantages accruing from more opportunities. Individual psychology addresses the hidden goal and related aspects in treatment: "We aim to remove such errors through conversation, explanations, words and thoughts, to change the person who has become asocial into a fellow man" (Adler, 1983, p. 11). Adler's approach to explicating errors resulting from a faulty Life Style is similar to the disputing of irrational beliefs as practiced in rational emotive behavior therapy (Ellis & Harper, 1975).

Adler's mention of changing a person from an asocial stance to a fellow-being is very important in individual psychology. A spirit of cooperation with others is the hallmark of mental health. It stands in contrast to its opposite condition, a retreat from this challenge. Involvement with fellow humans in productive activities defines a positive adaptation to life. Avoiding productive endeavors by withdrawal, whether modest or extreme, physical or mental, results from feelings of inferiority.

"Social interest" or "social feeling"[3] is the sine qua non of mental health, as defined in individual psychology. Social feeling means that the person has joined the human sphere and chooses to make a contribution to furthering the well-being of everybody. Personal involvement in the social milieu—family, community, nation, and beyond—is considered an indicator of "normality" in individual psychology.

Clinical Approach

Life Style assessment guides treatment in individual psychology, but Adler made the following suggestions in describing his clinical approach:

Three or four phases of psychotherapy have variously been identified and de-
scribed . . . though . . . not all the phases are always represented. As we see it, the phases
are: (1) establishing and maintaining a good relationship with the patient; (2) gathering
data from the patient to understand him, to have source material for interpretation,
for conceptualizing his life style; (3) interpreting the data: (4) provoking therapeutic
movement, change of behavior (in Ansbacher & Ansbacher, 1947).

Most of the difficulties encountered in life are problems of relating to others, and Adler wrote, "Psychotherapy is an exercise in cooperation and a test of cooperation. The first rule is to win the patient; the second is never to worry about your success" (in Ansbacher & Ansbacher, 1956, pp. 340–341). This approach shows how "social" psychology is an integral part of the theory and practice of individual psychology. Psychotherapy is a cooperative task.

Feelings of inferiority are compensated for by attempts to move to a position of superiority. Adler wrote, "We soon perceive a greater or lesser degree of the feeling of inferiority in everyone, together with compensatory striving towards a goal of superiority" (in Ansbacher & Ansbacher, 1956, p. 2).

Whatever the circumstance or situation, inferiority can be seen whenever a person strives to achieve a superior position. This does not mean that people should not work toward excellence; rather, it means they should not strive for a façade of dominance over others. The need to have something or be somebody, to be bigger, better, or faster, are obvious examples. Striving for this kind of superiority arises from feelings of inferiority. It is ultimately futile.

Instead, one needs courage to meet life's challenges and endeavor to persevere. Beethoven's Heiligenstadt Will is an outstanding example (Kalischer, 1926). His will is in the form of a letter to his brothers. Approaching mid-life, with his most productive years ahead of him, Beethoven found himself almost completely deaf. There is no worse fate for a musician. Deafness also left him bereft of friends. Yet he wrote that rather than end his life, he would make yet a greater, even more courageous effort to continue to compose, and, in the next 25 years, completely deaf, Beethoven produced his greatest works.

THERAPEUTIC GOALS

Linda has shown continuous movement in distancing herself from just about everyone. This may happen with her therapist unless the therapist prepares ahead for its possible occurrence. As Adler said, relationship is paramount. This will be a challenge to the therapist. As Linda might express it, if only she was aware of her condition, "Either I have something to do with this state of affairs, or it is necessary to assign responsibility to some external cause, to my environment and/or to other people." She is unlikely to initiate this matter for consideration in treatment. Her history reveals a wholesale disparagement of others. This is done in order to protect her self-esteem. Where feelings of inferiority are found, there will simultaneously exist the asserting of superiority as a compensatory mechanism. Her therapist may be next on her hit list unless attention is given to understanding this apperceptive device.The therapist will need to foresee this attack in order to prepare for its occurrence and not be caught off guard.

The therapist must provide a safe environment for Linda so that she will not misperceive herself as under attack whenever issues about her and her behavior are discussed. She will have the tendency to personalize any such comments as attacks on her. The therapist must not react when attacked by Linda but should always meet any such attacks by responding in a calm and friendly way. The therapist has a "re-parenting" role and needs to soothe and re-educate Linda on how to address her problems. This approach can help Linda get beyond her attacks and move to a more cooperative spirit. A firm but continually supportive approach is necessary.

Adler said that the therapist must "win over" the person. Linda may struggle and resist such efforts, but they remain essential goals for the therapist. The therapeutic encounter is a "social experiment" for the client. The therapist engages the client by a style that keeps prominent a sense of caring and support. Therapy is provided in a manner similar to parents in dealing with their children. There will be difficult times, yet through it all a parent always seeks to promote a sense of caring. If Linda can establish a working relationship in treatment, it can be carried over into other domains. This makes the relationship a primary goal of treatment for Linda (Rogers, 1957; Shulman, 1982).

FURTHER INFORMATION NEEDED

Life Style assessment will provide information to help the therapist conceptualize the case, and, in turn, later serve as useful information for Linda. Life Style assessment will include Linda's recalling of her environment, parents, siblings, and the family atmosphere. Ecological and constitutional factors will be examined. Developmental lines and cultural influences are explored. The elements of Life Style analysis are almost the same as the ones that Anna Freud (1965) included in *Normality and Psychopathology in Childhood*. Particularly important will be Linda's account of her childhood. Her unique interpretation of these matters will show the "spin" Linda puts on her past experiences.

The therapist will gather Linda's early recollections to further understand the unique perspective she gives to the life she experienced. Her case history provides what might be one example, the account of her mother inspecting the children's rooms and finding in Linda's room "a pair of panties 'incorrectly' folded." If this were a recollection, the therapist would inquire further about Linda's feelings regarding this incident and, even more important, speculate about whether she formed any compensatory behaviors as a result of this incident or from others she experienced.

The case study also reports that she "was expected to take care of her siblings." Perhaps some recollection about these matters will help the therapist see how Linda transformed these parental expectations of her when she was a child into a hidden goal for subsequent behavior. As Richard III (Shakespeare, *Richard III*, Act I, line 28) put it, "and therefore, since I cannot prove a lover, . . . I am determined to prove a villain," so might Linda have made declarations to herself about what would happen, based on how she perceived mother's treatment of her.

Understanding Linda's perceptions of her mother's demands might help the therapist understand Linda's subsequent ways of behaving. Did she see the demands as excessive and unfair, and did she feel put-upon? The truth behind the mother's actions won't be known, but the therapist can ask Linda how she interpreted them. They serve as experiences that can be revisited in treatment when Linda is ready to look at matters from more than one perspective.

CONCEPTUALIZATION OF PATIENT

The first use of Life Style assessment materials will be to assist the therapist to understand Linda's latent issues. Later, when Linda is deemed ready, this material can be interpreted to her in a manner that will give her better insight into herself. What the therapist uncovers are Linda's "private logic" and "fictional goal." These are what guide Linda's behavior. The therapist seeks to know them to understand Linda and then to help her examine these matters when the therapist guides her to try more useful strategies and helps her have more productive interactions with others. Timing is important, and the therapist must watch for opportunities to make inroads and avoid times when such activities would be counterproductive, especially in early sessions. The therapist also needs to serve as a personal "cheerleader" and encourage Linda's efforts to understand herself and her behavior so that she can engage in more useful social interaction.

The case study showed that Linda is intelligent. She has earned a teaching degree and a master's degree. She has a responsible teaching position. The therapist should try to mobilize these assets. Linda needs to hear that she has strengths.

A useful exercise in Life Style assessment is to hypothesize the fictive goal of the client. This helps the therapist conceptualize the case, but it should be conveyed to the client only when, and if, the client can gain useful recognition of its value. The following are some hypothesized paraphrases of Linda's private logic and fictive goal:

- You have to take charge to get what you want because, in this world, everybody is looking out for number one.
- If I don't take care of myself, nobody else will.
- There really are a lot of jerks in the world.
- Why do people make trouble for me? Don't they have anything better to do?
- I am going to do what I want and to hell with everybody else.

An important theme for Linda is "everybody else." She has no part in, let alone responsibility for, what has happened in her life. For her to accept such responsibility, Linda would probably feel required to accept every bit of it. She has an either/or mentality operating. Either it is all her fault, or none of it is. She may at times have wondered whether she does have some responsibility for what has occurred in her life, but she has compensated for such a nightmare by taking the completely opposite approach: none of it is her responsibility. Caught in her either/or thinking that the fault is all hers or all others', Linda chooses others. Deep down, Linda may wonder if it could be all her fault. This is what her mother conveyed in the bedroom scene, and it may be how Linda was made to feel early in life. Now, to keep this inadequacy from overwhelming her, she adopts the opposite, superior view, and acts like nothing is her responsibility. This is a posture that Linda won't reveal, except, perhaps, to someone she can trust. If the therapist can merit her trust, there is the possibility that Linda can recognize that she need not take all the blame or feel overwhelmingly inadequate and inferior. Instead, she can learn to make her own way, be responsible for only her own acts, and reestablish contact with others in a productive manner.

POTENTIAL PITFALLS

The first steps for Linda in making changes will probably occur in treatment sessions. How Linda responds to a friendly, supportive environment will be the first clue. She may see it for what it is, or she may remain suspicious and constantly test the therapist the way adolescents test their parents. The length of time Linda takes to develop initial security in treatment will be a clue about how long her treatment can be expected to last. If her style is deeply ingrained, it will be difficult for her to even begin to make steps to change.

Other situations may arise in which Linda could make changes. These will be the ones that appear less threatening to her, making it more possible for her to risk a new approach. The therapist should be watchful for what these might be in order to encourage Linda and should also be aware of the areas that are most threatening to Linda and least amenable for movement.

PROGNOSIS

Linda will challenge the therapist. This requires that the therapist be in charge of his or her Life Style. Supervision may be needed to clarify matters. Getting "stuck" in therapy is often a sign that the working relationship is foundering and in jeopardy. Not all of the blame rests on the client. Calling someone "borderline" often elicits agonizing sighs among fellow therapists. Labeling is not helpful in treatment. It frequently signifies a superior status on the part of the therapist. This is counterproductive to working with Linda and frustrates a true understanding of her condition.

Therapists can easily become frustrated and perplexed by people like Linda. Expressed or hidden, these feelings can emerge in various ways. Linda will be quick to spot them, and she may go a step further and make them up out of nothing. It is important to be aware of such possibilities so as not to be taken off guard. However, a calm manner and firm but fair limits will usually be tolerated by even the most upsetting of persons. The important matter is not to respond inappropriately. This may require not scheduling Linda's sessions at the end of a long day or at taxing times during the week. Adherence to a regular time is required.

Therapy with Linda might be rough going. She already has a way of coping, which serves to safeguard her self-esteem. Trying other approaches and working out other strategies may appear threatening to her. The first steps of change may be slow and laborious. It is important for the therapist to maintain a strong, positive affirmation of Linda's capability to succeed even when setbacks occur.

TIMELINE

As treatment progresses, the major goal would be to help Linda "to realize what she is doing and to transfer her egocentric interest to social life and useful activity" (Ansbacher & Ansbacher, 1956, p. 40). "Social life" here does not mean getting out more for a good time, but productively interacting with others in useful ways. For Linda, this means learning to develop better relationships with her students, their parents, colleagues, people in the condominium, and those driving on city streets. It might be best to begin with the area where Linda has the most competency and success. The work environment would perhaps be the best and safest area to begin making changes. Linda can rely on her teaching competencies and perhaps not be as threatened in this environment. Later she can move to other relationships. Intimacy will be the most difficult.

Linda could work toward establishing a better environment with her students, their parents, and her colleagues at work. The degree of success achieved at this stage will be a gauge by which to estimate the time required for more complex relationships.

SPECIFIC TECHNIQUES

The therapist must first provide much support and encouragement and work on having a good relationship with Linda. It is important to set reasonable boundaries and be quietly firm on important matters, but above all the therapist must work to build a good relationship with Linda. Rogers (1957) specified "unconditional positive regard" as one of the necessary and sufficient conditions for therapeutic change.

A second goal is to identify Linda's assets and capitalize on them. Begin with her strengths and try to promote a more and broader application of them. Find even minuscule examples of productive movement and use them to encourage Linda to continue in this manner. Any of Linda's modest attempts to change should be encouraged.

Individual psychology identifies three main tasks in life: building lasting friendships, addressing an occupation, and participating in a loving relationship. Friendships are lacking in Linda's life. She may require education on how to make and retain friendships. She also needs to know and appreciate that friendships require sustained effort. Extensions from what has been learned in treatment sessions may be employed to help Linda gain insight and appreciate the work involved. Linda has achieved an important career goal and is in a place to make a important impact in the lives of her students. She seems, however, to be her own worst enemy, and, consequently, she needs to examine why she is pursuing self-defeating behaviors that could cost her her job, or at least bring her grief at work. The goal is to help her learn to be more effective as a teacher. Linda seems to know what to do, but she turns it all against herself instead of turning things in her favor. It is probably not her teaching skills that are lacking but that she is misapplying them to her detriment. She needs help to see what she is doing. Her attempts to find love have resulted only in one-night stands. She needs to learn how to move more usefully into these relationships. In this area, too, Linda acts in an all-or-nothing mode. The therapist should recommend that she refrain from sexual encounters until she has moved through the successive stages of a loving relationship. Linda needs to be helped to postpone big decisions until she is at the proper stage.

Linda needs to be guided in how to make proper overtures to others. Her efforts seem to vacillate between overreacting in the extreme and withdrawing completely. She needs to learn, and practice, a repertoire of skills to help her communicate with people. She also needs to learn how to express her ideas and feelings to others without becoming fearful of what they think. Linda overreacts as compensation for not knowing how to communicate honest differences.

SPECIAL CAUTIONS

The therapist needs to be especially conscious of his or her impact on Linda. She may resist or engage in any number of activities to deprecate the therapist and depreciate treatment. Linda may have a love-hate relationship with her therapist. Her ultimate weapon will be to leave treatment. Therapists can lament the way patients with borderline personality disorder act; such lamentations are counterproductive. Therapists need to be aware of transference/countertransference issues, but individual psychology doesn't use these terms. According to Adler (1927), "what the Freudians call transference (so far as we can discuss it apart from sexual implications) is social feeling. The patient's social feeling, which is always present in some degree, finds its best possible expression in the relation with the psychologist" (p. 247). The therapist must establish a bond with the patient to facilitate movement. Progress in therapy is best achieved in a spirit of cooperation and facilitation among the participants. The issues of relationship between client and therapist must be addressed whether or not we use the words *transference* and *countertransference*. The therapist must be prepared to face Linda's confrontations all through treatment. Lapses back to past behavior do not mean Linda failed. They indicate that she is in a working mode, and the therapist must support her efforts and help her pick herself up when she slips. Expect relapses. They are part of the change process.

AREAS TO AVOID

The three life tasks are work, friendships, and intimacy, and Linda's treatment should follow this order. The work environment is likely the easiest place for Linda to begin to change. She has the most preparation to be successful in this domain. Consequently, the therapist should postpone moving too quickly with Linda into issues with friends and not encourage pursuit of intimacy at this point. Therapy should help Linda move gradually to achieve a new viewpoint by achieving successful interaction with others in modest stages. The therapist should not provide personal information, and the authors do not recommend self-disclosure except of a general type, such as, "Yes, Linda, people can feel sad when something awful happens."

MEDICATION

We do not see evidence of an immediate need to medicate on the basis of the case history. Linda, however, may also complain of difficulty sleeping, problems with digestion, etc., which upon further assessment may suggest medication, as appropriate. Treatment along the lines of individual psychology does not preclude any other medical treatment. Adler's approach was biologically based and followed what today would be known as a biopsychosocial approach.

PATIENT STRENGTHS

Linda is intelligent and educated. She can respond to reason and follow a line of discussion. In a supportive environment, Linda may even come to solicit more information. But whenever she feels challenged, it will not be surprising to see her revert to old behaviors. A cognitive, rational approach can be followed in treatment. She can be expected to evaluate the goals of therapy, to prioritize topics to work on in treatment, and to offer reasonable feedback.

She holds a responsible job and renders an important service in educating children. These are vital for our society, and Linda can be supported and encouraged in having chosen such a profession.

LIMIT-SETTING

Linda needs to keep regular appointments and be helped to see that order and reason are the best tools for her. Treatment goals should be worked out cooperatively. Linda needs to be helped without the therapist "solving" her problems for her.

As treatment progresses, additional goals can be developed to further encompass the major issues in her life. But the therapist must also prepare for resistance throughout treatment. Adler wrote, "I expect from the patient again and again the same attitude which he has shown in accordance with his life-plan toward the persons of his former environment, and still earlier toward his family. At the moment of the introduction to the physician and often even earlier, the patient has the same feelings toward him as toward important persons in general" (Ansbacher & Ansbacher, 1956, p. 336).

INVOLVEMENT OF SIGNIFICANT OTHERS

Linda's history does not indicate that family is available or that she has close friends or a significant relationship with anyone. We think it best to give Linda "center stage" and provide her maximum attention. One way to involve others eventually is to have Linda make new overtures to old colleagues, students, and parents. She can then bring her reports of these interactions back to her sessions and report on how they went and how they could be improved.

TERMINATION

Linda shows a long history of self-defeating behavior. The prognosis is for a long, slow course of treatment. She may regularly fall back into her old ways of behaving and make it appear, to herself and to her therapist, that all her work has been in vain. Change needs to be measured in small steps so that expectations do not get ahead of action for client and therapist. Change is probably more frightening than difficult. Bugental and Bugental (1984) described fear of changing as "a fate worse than death." A relatively long treatment will likely be required for Linda, and she may interpret termination as abandonment.

MECHANISMS OF CHANGE

Adler (1970) once added a fourth task to the three life tasks already mentioned—creative endeavor (schopfeische Gertaltung). Linda's creative energy can be mobilized productively for her benefit. She used it in the past to create self-delusions and misperceptions that brought her to this place in her life. Now her constructive energy needs to be mobilized to bring her to a better accommodation with herself and others.

NOTES

1. Distance. *Distance* connotes some purposeful "separation" inserted between the self and an anticipated act or decision. The intensity of this separation can range from modest discomfort to immobilization.
2. Fictions. Adler derived foundation and support for this concept from the German philosopher Hans Vaihinger and his work, *The Philosophy of "As-If,"* subtitled, *The Theoretical, Practical and Religious*

Fictions of Mankind. The book documented ingenious mental constructions. Adler appropriated the fiction to describe self-delusions constructed to excuse behavior.

3. Social Interest or Social Feeling and translations of Gemeinschaftsgefuhl, the criterion of mental health in individual psychology. The idea is as old as man and expressed in many forms. Stone (1997) has reviewed and discussed some of them.

4. Life Style. Life Style assessment strategies are further explained in Eckstein et al., 1975; Morris, 1978; Mozak & Shulman, 1971 and Mozak, Schneider & Mozak, 1980.

REFERENCES

Adler, A. (1927). Individual psychology. *Journal of Abnormal and Social Psychology, 22,* 116–122.

Adler, A. (1929). *The science of living.* London: Allen & Unwin.

Adler, A. (1970). Fundamentals of individual psychology. *Journal of Individual Psychology, 26*(1), 3–16. (Original work published in 1930.)

Adler, A. (1983). *The neurotic constitution.* Salem, NH: Ayer. (Über den nervösen Charakter. Wiesbaden: Bergmann. Original work published in 1911).

American Psychiatric Association. (2000). *Diagnostic and statistical manual of mental disorders* (4th ed., text revision). Washington, DC: Author.

Ansbacher, H., & Ansbacher, R. (1947). *Alfred Adler's place in psychology today.* International Zeitschrift fur Individualpsychologie. New York: Basic Books.

Ansbacher, H., & Ansbacher, R. (Eds.). (1956). *The individual psychology of Alfred Adler.* New York: Harper Torchbooks.

Ansbacher, H., & Ansbacher, R. (1978). *Cooperation between the sexes.* New York: Norton.

Beck, A. (1967). *Depression: Clinical, experimental and theoretical aspects.* New York: Harper & Row.

Beck, A., Rush, J., Shaw, B., & Liese, B. (1979). *Cognitive therapy of depression.* New York: Guilford Press.

Bugental, J., & Bugental, E. (1984). A fate worse than death: The fear of changing. *Psychotherapy, 21*(4), 535–549.

Eckstein, D., Baruth, L., & Mahrer, D. (1982). *Life style: What it is and how to do it.* Hendersonville, NC: Mother Earth News.

Ellis, A., & Harper, R. (1975). *A new guide to rational living.* Englewood Cliffs, NJ: Wilshire.

Fine, R. (1989). *Current and historical perspectives on the borderline patient.* New York: Brunner-Mazel.

Freud, A. (1965). *Normality and psychopathology in childhood: Collected Works VI.* New York: International Universities Press.

Garber, J., & Seligman, M. (Eds.). (1980). *Human helplessness: Theory and applications.* New York: Academic Press.

Glover, E. (1932). Psychoanalytic approach to the classification of mental disorders. *Journal of Mental Science, 78,* 819.

Hadas, M. (Ed.). (1961). *Essential works of stoicism.* New York: Bantam Books.

Kalischer, A. (1926). *Beethoven's letters.* New York: Dover.

Kant, I. (1964). *The classification of mental disorders.* Boylestown, PA: The Doylestown Foundation.

Kasanin, J. (1933). Acute schizoaffective psychoses. *American Journal of Psychiatry, 97,* 97–120.

Knight, R. (1953). Borderline states. *Bulletin of the Menninger Clinic, 17,* 94–97.

May, R. (1970). Tributes to Alfred Adler on his 100th birthday. *Journal of Individual Psychology, 26*(1), 39.

Moore, T. (1921). The empirical determination of certain syndromes underlying praecox and manic-depressive psychoses. *American Journal of Psychiatry, 86,* 719–738.

Morris, P. (1978). *Life style assessment process.* Arnold, MD: Adlerian Counseling Services.

Mozak, H., Schneider, S., & Mozak, L. (1980). *Life style: A workbook.* Chicago: Adler.

Mozak, H., & Shulman, B. (1971a). *Life style inventory.* Chicago: Adler.

Mozak, H., & Shulman, B. (1971b). *Manual of life style assessment.* Muncie, IN: Accelerated Development.

Munroe, R. (1955). *Schools of psychoanalytic thought.* New York: Dryden Press.

Oberndorf, C. (1930). The psychoanalysis of borderline cases. *New State Journal of Medicine, 30,* 648–651.

Reich, W. (1925). *Der Triebhafte Charakter.* Leipzig: Internationaler Psychoanalytischer Verlag.

Rogers, C. (1957). The necessary and sufficient conditions of therapeutic personality change. *Journal of Consulting Psychology, 21,* 95–103.

Shulman, B. (1982). An Adlerian interpretation of the borderline personality. *Modern Psychoanalysis, 7*(2), 136–153.

Stern, A. (1938). Psychoanalytic investigation and therapy in the borderline group of neuroses. *Psychoanalytic Quarterly, 7,* 467–489.

Stone, M. (1980). *The borderline syndromes: Constitution, personality and adaptation.* New York: McGraw-Hill.

Stone, M. (1997). Ibsen's life-lie and Adler's lifestyle. *Individual Psychology, 53*(3), 322–330.

Stone, M. (1999). Ibsen and his feelings of inferiority. *Canadian Journal of Individual Psychology, 27*(1), 73–84.

Stone, M. (2000). Dostoevsky. *Canadian Journal of Individual Psychology, 27*(1), 73–84.

Vaihinger, H. (1925). *The philosophy of as-if.* London: Routledge & Kagan Paul.

8

A Cognitive-Developmental Formulation of BPD

Mark A. Reinecke and Jill Ehrenreich

This chapter presents a cognitive-developmental model for understanding borderline personality disorder (BPD) and describes how it may be used in conceptualizing and treating this disorder. The model represents an extension of standard cognitive and schema-focused models. It is developmental in that it postulates that BPD stems from (1) biological and genetic propensities toward affect dysregulation, (2) deficits in the acquisition of affect regulation skills, and (3) the establishment of maladaptive tacit beliefs about oneself and relationships with others. The cognitive-developmental model is similar, in many respects, to traditional cognitive and schema-focused approaches for understanding and treating personality disorders in that it emphasizes the central role of cognitive and perceptual processes in the development and maintenance of clinical disorders. It differs from them in that it incorporates insights from the developmental psychopathology literature (Cicchetti, 1989, 1990; Garber & Dodge, 1992; Rutter & Garmezy, 1983; Sroufe, 1990) and postulates that personality disorders may usefully be understood from a developmental-systems perspective (Geiger & Crick, 2001).

Variations in symptom patterns over time and across settings can complicate both the diagnostic and treatment process. With this in mind, the cognitive-developmental model focuses upon commonly occurring features of the disorder and directs our attention toward factors associated with their development and maintenance. Borderline personality disorder is characterized by (1) intense and unstable emotions, (2) behavioral impulsivity, (3) a tendency to view others as uncaring and rejecting, (4) a pattern of intense interpersonal relationships characterized by extremes of idealization and devaluation, and (5) negative self-concept or a lack of a coherent sense of self (Adams, Bernat, & Luscher, 2001; Sperry, 1995). Each of these factors must be addressed in a comprehensive model of BPD and its treatment. Research on emotional and social development may prove useful in illuminating our understanding of BPD in that the biological and social foundations of personality are believed to be present from birth, and emotional characteristics associated with adult personality disorders have been described among children and adolescents (Kernberg, Weiner, & Bardenstein, 2000).

TOWARD AN INTEGRATED
COGNITIVE-DEVELOPMENTAL MODEL

The question, then, arises—how does this constellation of risk factors contribute to the emergence of symptoms of BPD? That is to say, what is the mechanism by which early trauma, familial psychopathology, genetic factors, and personality variables interact in contributing to risk? We propose the following:

1. Parents who do not provide a consistent, supportive, nurturant, and responsive home environment, and who do not model and support the development of affect regulation skills, place their children at risk for the development of BPD.
2. Temperamental vulnerabilities, impulsivity, and affective dysregulation interact with parenting style to contribute to the development of a disorganized attachment style.
3. Disorganized attachment style places the individual at risk for the development of maladaptive schema regarding self-worth, abandonment and rejection, and impaired self-efficacy.
4. Maladaptive schema regarding loss, abandonment, and personal worth, when activated by specific life events, serve as proximal risk factors for behavioral and emotional characteristics of this disorder.

Individuals may manifest a biological or genetic vulnerability in that they may be temperamentally impulsive, neurotic, or labile. Inconsistent parenting may exacerbate these difficulties by interfering with the normative development of affect regulation skills and may contribute to the establishment of maladaptive belief systems and problem-solving styles. Factors associated with vulnerability for BPD are summarized below.

- Behavioral impulsivity
- Neuroticism/negative affectivity
- Emotional lability
- Familial history of depression, impulse control disorder, substance abuse
- Chaotic home environment
- Disorganized attachment
- Severe or chronic abuse/neglect
- Separation/early loss

Cognitive Model

Although the cognitive-developmental model includes a number of concepts and approaches not typically found in standard cognitive behavioral models of psychopathology and psychotherapy, its theoretical assumptions are consistent with these approaches. It is, in a true sense, a cognitive theory. As with other cognitive models, the cognitive-developmental model of BPD assumes that cognitive activity affects behavior, that cognitive activity may be monitored and changed, and that behavioral and emotional change may be affected through modifications in cognitive processes. The model implicitly assumes that cognitive processes are ongoing, active, and adaptive and that emotional, behavioral, and cognitive factors interact in a transactional manner over time. We assume that relationships exist between cognitive contents (i.e., what the individual thinks), cognitive processes (i.e., how he or she uses this information) and the occurrence of specific behavioral and emotional symptoms. The cognitive-developmental model of BPD is mediational; that is, we assume that cognitive factors mediate human adaptation, and we focus on these factors in therapy. In practice, the treatment of patients with BPD involves active attempts to change cognitive contents and processes, to develop affect regulation skills, and to address social behaviors that may be contributing to the individual's distress. Our approach is, like other cognitive behavioral therapies, problem-oriented, active, strategic, and structured.

Developmental Model

The cognitive-developmental model is also, in a true sense, developmental. Its tenets are consistent with those of the developmental psychopathology framework for understanding clinical problems. The model assumes that deviations from normal developmental processes during childhood place individuals at risk for later psychopathology. From this perspective, an understanding of normative development can serve as a foundation for understanding emotional and behavioral disorders. The model also assumes that human development and adaptation are multiply determined. Cognitive, biological, social, behavioral, and environmental factors interact over time in contributing to vulnerability for psychopathology. To fully understand (and treat) a complex disorder, such as BPD, it is necessary to address the full range of etiological and maintaining factors.

Developmentally based models suggest that individuals must address a series of age-related tasks over the course of life (e.g., development of a secure attachment during infancy, language acquisition, affect regulation, development of social skills, autonomy from caregivers, development of self-identity), and that failure to effectively address one or more of these tasks will place an individual at risk for later adaptive difficulties. Three specific domains—attachment security, affect regulation, and self-identity—are implicated in the development of BPD. Finally, developmentally informed models acknowledge that there are "sensitive" or "critical" periods for the acquisition of specific skills. The cognitive-developmental model proposes that early experiences and the development of a disorganized attachment style serve as distal risk factors for adaptive difficulties, including the development of BPD (Carlson, 1998; Carlson & Sroufe, 1995; Dozier, Stovall, & Albus, 1999; Liotti, 2002). Infants who exhibit a disorganized attachment style demonstrate erratic, disorganized, and often conflicting behavioral responses to their caregivers. These behaviors are believed to stem from the lack of a coherent pattern of attachment that, as Carlson (1998) observed, "places the infant in an irresolvable paradox in which the infant can neither approach the caregiver nor flee or shift attention to the environment. The caregiver serves as a source of fear as well as . . . reassurance" (pp. 1107–1108).

In describing the infant with a disorganized attachment style, Liotti (2002) remarked that "the infant is both comforted and frightened by the traumatized attachment figure, either simultaneously or in quick sequence" (p. 351), leading the infant to turn to the caregiver for safety or to withdraw defensively. This fluctuating pattern of relationships—seeking and even demanding closeness while simultaneously recoiling out of fear—characterizes both youth with disorganized attachment style and the interpersonal relationships of patients with BPD.

This disorganized working model is believed to serve as a template for relationships that BPD patients have with important individuals in their lives and is postulated to serve as a foundation for the development of dysfunctional attitudes and schema that characterize BPD. The notion that early experiences and attachment styles may contribute to the development of dysfunctional attitudes is supported by recent research on cognitive vulnerability for depression (Reinecke & Rogers, 2001; Roberts, Gotlib, & Kassel, 1996; Whisman & McGarvey, 1995). Experiences during early childhood, as such, are presumed to play a critical role in the development of this disorder.

Like other developmentally based models, however, the cognitive-developmental model views adaptation as mutable. We do not presume, as do psychodynamic models of personality, that BPD stems from the activation of maladaptive defenses or dynamic structures (Roberts, 2000). Rather, an individual's functioning varies depending upon the nature of the situation and the specific adaptive competencies the individual has acquired. Patients are not, from this perspective, viewed as "flawed" or "impaired" so much as being on a maladaptive developmental trajectory or pathway.

Formulation of Borderline Personality Disorder

As noted, the cognitive-developmental model proposes that borderline personality disorder stems from two factors: a breakdown in the acquisition and use of adaptive emotion regulation skills, and the acquisition, consolidation, and activation of maladaptive schema and information-processing strategies. Maladaptive schema believed to be associated with BPD include (1) a view of the world as threatening or hostile; (2) a belief that others are potentially rejecting, uncaring, or malevolent; (3) and a view of the self as inherently unlovable and incapable of coping effectively with the tasks of day-to-day life. Because BPD patients view the world as fundamentally dangerous or overwhelming and see themselves as incapable, they look to others for support, guidance, and reassurance. They maintain an adaptive propositional belief that "if I can maintain a close relationship with someone, then I can feel secure in my life." Because they believe themselves to be inherently unlovable, and others as potentially rejecting, they are at risk for abandonment. Individuals with BPD tend, as a consequence, to be attentive to signs of potential separation or abandonment and respond to them with feelings of anger (reflecting their view of the potential separation as both malicious and threatening) and by making intense efforts to re-establish the relationship. Given their deficits in affect regulation, the accompanying feelings of anger, anxiety, dysphoria, and desperation rapidly escalate and become subjectively severe. Because these individuals lack effective cognitive, behavioral, and social skills for self-soothing, they come to engage in a range of maladaptive behaviors to alleviate their distress. Their angry outbursts, demands for support, and suicidal gestures may be viewed as attempts to reestablish a significant relationship.

The cognitive-developmental model proposes that these variables can, in conjunction, account for the clinical presentation of patients with BPD. These factors are seen as necessary (but not sufficient) distal risk factors for the development of BPD. Negative early experiences with caregivers likely contribute to the establishment of a disorganized attachment. These experiences, in turn, are associated with the development of *specific* maladaptive schema. Disorganized children come to view themselves as unworthy or unlovable and to view relationships as unstable, unpredictable, inconsistent, and potentially dangerous. This is not to say the emotional and social competence during adolescence and adulthood is a direct consequence of early attachment disorganization. Rather, attachment security is viewed as one of several interacting influences on socialization and adjustment. Consistent with cognitive models of psychopathology, it is postulated that these maladaptive beliefs about the self and others are consolidated over the course of development, and that individuals come to selectively attend to and remember events that are consistent with these beliefs. The cognitive-developmental model of BPD is presented in Figure 8.1.

Clinical Implications

The goals in cognitive-development therapy for BPD are threefold: (1) to develop affect regulation skills, (2) to identify and change specific maladaptive beliefs or schema that may be contributing to the individu-

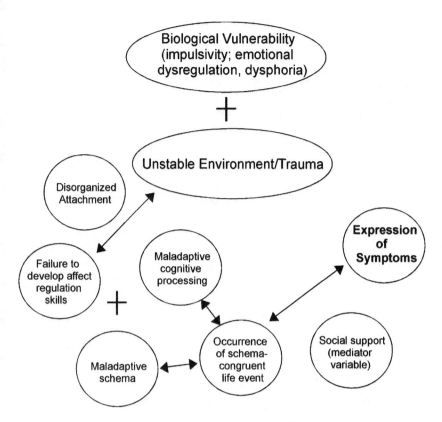

FIGURE 8.1   Cognitive-developmental model of BPD.

al's distress, and (3) to develop a more coherent, organized, and secure sense of self. This is accomplished through psychoeducation; the introduction of cognitive and behavioral techniques to alleviate feelings of depression, anxiety, and anger; and the use of developmentally informed interventions to address the lack of stable, coherent, and secure systems for understanding oneself and relationships with others.

Central to the cognitive-developmental model are the notions of "scaffolding" and "apprenticeship." Virtually all adaptive skills—including language, social problem-solving, academic, and social skills—are acquired over the course of development through guided modeling by individuals with a greater expertise than the child. A teacher, coach, or mentor, for example, guides the child in learning basic math, reading, or athletic skills by modeling skilled behavior and by challenging the child to perform actions that are just beyond his or her current abilities. The acquisition of adaptive skills, as such, is viewed as occurring within a zone of proximal development (Kaye, 1982; Vygotsky, 1962). The child may be viewed, in many ways, as an apprentice, acquiring adaptive skills though guided practice with a skilled instructor—a mentor. The mentor does not simply model and reinforce skilled action but also provides support and reassurance, maintains the child's motivation, and assists the child by facilitating component skills necessary for the completion of the action. As with the construction of a building, the acquisition of adaptive skills over the course of development is guided by the organizing framework. The scaffold provides a structure for the construction of the building, leading the area of construction. The scaffold bears the weight of the building and is essential for maintaining the form of the edifice during the construction process. A wall that is not supported by scaffolding is at risk of falling should a stressor occur (a gust of wind, for example) before the concrete has set. The development of affect regulation skills during childhood (and in the therapy session) can be viewed in these terms.

The Development of Affect Regulation

As noted, the cognitive-developmental model posits that change processes in psychotherapy are essentially similar to those in normative development. The cognitive-developmental therapist, as such, serves as the scaffold, guiding and supporting the patient's development of affect regulation skills by providing support, serving as a resource to "buffer" the patient from the effects of potentially traumatic life events, and guiding the development of more sophisticated emotion regulation skills through modeling and guided practice.

The unstable, intense, and volatile emotions that characterize individuals with BPD contribute to their risk for impulsive behavior (Eisenberg & Fabes, 1998) and may lead the individuals to view themselves as flawed, damaged, or unlovable. A reciprocal relationship may exist, as such, between deficits in affect regulation and the development of negative beliefs about the self. Strategic cognitive behavioral techniques, such as rational responding and a developmental review of evidence, are used to counter negative views about the self. It also can be helpful to use experiences within the therapeutic relationship to challenge negative beliefs about the self.

TREATMENT MODEL

Linda manifests many symptoms of BPD, including depression, anxiety, outbursts of anger, feelings of emptiness, unstable relationships, reactivity to perceived abandonment, dissociation, and impulsive suicidality. These difficulties are long-standing in nature and are subjectively quite severe. The cognitive-developmental treatment program for Linda would be designed to address cognitive, social, and behavioral variables that maintain these difficulties. Specifically, the therapist would attempt to help Linda (1) develop more effective emotion regulation skills; (2) change maladaptive schema that may contribute to feelings of depression, emptiness, anxiety, and anger; (3) improve her social skills; and (4) reduce suicidal and self-destructive behavior.

CLINICAL SKILLS OR ATTRIBUTES

An essential clinical skill is patience. It is quite likely that Linda will become suicidal, furiously angry, sexually promiscuous, or highly depressed over the course of therapy. Her difficulties are long-standing in nature and are firmly entrenched. The beliefs that maintain them are well learned, and the maladaptive coping strategies she uses in response to stressful life events are well rehearsed. It is not likely that she will change quickly. Given the severity of her difficulties, the therapist will likely feel compelled to quickly do something to rectify the situation. Short-term actions (e.g., providing support, encouraging expression of affect, and placing limits on specific behaviors) will provide only short-term relief. A more effective way of addressing concerns as they arise is to patiently, calmly, and objectively review the nature of the events that triggered her crisis, the thoughts and feelings she experienced at the time, how these thoughts and feelings are related to broader tacit beliefs or expectations, and how she can more effectively regulate her affect in this situation. As in standard cognitive behavioral therapy, teaching patients with BPD to reflect upon their experiences, to identify precipitants, to label emotions, and to identify specific upsetting thoughts will serve as a foundation for the introduction of techniques for developing affect regulation skills. Working with Linda to develop a clear and parsimonious formulation of what precipitated the crisis or outburst will allow her to see that these experiences are neither unpredictable nor inscrutable and will give her a clear sense of what might be done to prevent them from occurring again in the future.

A second therapeutic attribute is radical neutrality—the ability to maintain an even, calm, observant, and objective demeanor at all times. The therapist should not be drawn into becoming overly supportive, warm, or reassuring (lest this lead Linda to become dependent and to perceive that she will be abandoned when the therapist comes to know her flaws and imperfections) but also should not be cool, rigid, and formulaic. Patients with BPD can be exquisitely sensitive to others' behaviors. Note, for example, how Linda became enraged when her husband was 15 minutes late for dinner and interpreted this as evidence he was leaving her. Patients with BPD may react strongly to such subtle behaviors as the therapist leaning back in his or her chair or glancing away (indicating indifference or rejection) or leaning forward (which may be suggestive of emotional closeness or sexual interest). It is important, as a consequence, for the therapist to remain neutral and to be sensitive to the moment-to-moment fluctuations in the patient's mood.

THERAPEUTIC GOALS

Therapeutic goals should be collaboratively defined with the patient and should be explicitly stated. It may be helpful to have Linda write them out and note how she and the therapist will know when they have been accomplished. Reasonable primary goals would include (1) reducing the frequency and severity of Linda's suicidal gestures and self-destructive behavior; (2) reducing her feelings of depression, anxiety, and anger; (3) increasing the number and quality of her friendships; (4) reducing the frequency of her outbursts or mood swings; and (5) reducing the frequency of her dissociative episodes.

Secondary goals for treatment might be to develop Linda's affect regulation skills, identify and change maladaptive schema and interpersonal working models, develop social problem-solving skills, encourage cognitive flexibility, and increase adaptive interpersonal functioning. The primary goals include discrete behavioral and emotional targets, whereas secondary goals center on underlying mechanisms, mediating variables, and more diffuse behavioral objectives.

FURTHER INFORMATION NEEDED

Based on the cognitive-developmental model, the therapist will want to assess and rectify a number of factors that may contribute to Linda's distress. As noted in Figure 8.1, a range of factors may play a role in the etiology and maintenance of BPD, and the therapists will want to sensitively evaluate each of these domains. Both objective and subjective approaches may be used in assessing these factors. Therapeutically, the goal is to maintain an objective stance and to reliably evaluate each of these factors. The therapist should balance this with a phenomenological approach, seeking to understand each of these factors from Linda's perspective. Variables to be evaluated are listed below:

1. Biological vulnerability

   - Family history of psychiatric illness
   - Early temperament and social relatedness

2. Unstable environment/trauma

   - History of trauma, neglect, or physical or sexual abuse
   - Modeling of maladaptive coping and beliefs by caregivers
   - Parental availability, reliability, responsiveness, nurturance

3. Disorganized attachment

   - Relationships with parents
   - Current relationships (including romantic attachments)

4. Impulsivity
5. Emotional dysregulation
6. Maladaptive cognitive processes

   - Impaired social problem solving
   - Cognitive bias (dichotomized thinking)

7. Maladaptive schema

   - Negative self-concept; self-loathing (view of self as incapable, unlovable, fundamentally flawed, incompetent)
   - World as dangerous, threatening
   - Others as rejecting, uncaring, malicious
   - Low self-efficacy, perceptions of control
   - Heightened dependency, need for support

8. Life events

   - Schema-congruent negative life events (e.g., perceived abandonment, rejection, loss)
   - Social stressors

9. Moderator variables

    • Adaptive cognitive and behavioral coping skills
    • Social supports

10. Symptoms

    • Depression
    • Anxiety
    • Anger
    • Suicidality
    • Self-destructive behavior
    • Maladaptive social behavior

The goal in gathering additional information is to clarify the potential role of each of these variables and to develop strategies for addressing them. Those most amenable to change include security of attachment in current relationships, maladaptive beliefs (including negative automatic thoughts, attributions assumptions, expectations schema, and self-assessments), problematic information processing (including cognitive biases and social problem solving), affect regulation skills, and social supports.

Studies indicate that many individuals with BPD have a history of childhood sexual abuse (Bryer, Nelson, Miller, & Kroll, 1987; Paris, 1994, 1997). Although not reported in the case study, the possibility exists that Linda may have been physically or sexually abused. Fugue episodes can accompany both BPD and post-traumatic stress disorder (PTSD) and are often associated with more severe forms of early trauma. Linda was an attractive eldest daughter and was cast into an adult role as a caretaker when her mother was away at work. She grew up in a home with an impulsive father who abused alcohol and admonished her to "learn how to accept sex." It is not implausible, with this in mind, that there may have been an abusive relationship at home. Careful evaluation of this possibility is warranted.

Assessment Tools

Although Linda meets the diagnostic criteria for BPD, she also appears to manifest symptoms of other psychiatric disorders, including major depression, PTSD, and bulimia nervosa. Insofar as a significant percentage of patients with BPD also meet the criteria for a comorbid Axis I

(Farmer & Nelson-Gray, 1990; Widiger & Frances, 1989) or Axis II (Zittel & Westen, 1998) disorder, it may be helpful to complete a comprehensive, objective diagnostic evaluation. Structured and semistructured instruments, such as the Structured Clinical Interview for DSM-IV (SCID; First, Spitzer, Gibbon, & Williams, 1995) and the Personality Disorder Interview-IV (PDI-IV; Widiger, Mangine, Corbitt, Ellis, & Thomas, 1995) can be quite useful in this regard. The Structured Clinical Interview for DSM Personality Disorders (SCID-II; First, Gibbon, Spitzer, Williams, & Benjamin, 1997) and the Diagnostic Interview for Borderlines-Revised (DIB-R; Zanarini, Gunderson, Frankenburg, & Chauncey, 1989) are psychometrically strong instruments that can be used to clarify the diagnosis. Clinician interviews such as these can be augmented with patient self-report measures such as the Personality Diagnostic Questionnaire-IV (PDQ-IV; Hyler, 1994) or the Personality Assessment Inventory (PAI; Morey, 1991).

The cognitive-developmental model of BPD directs our attention to understanding Linda's early developmental history; the nature and quality of her early relationships with her parents, siblings, and peers; and whether she demonstrated a secure attachment to her caregivers. It is important, as well, to assess her temperamental style during her early childhood, for example, was she shy or inhibited as a toddler? Was she a withdrawn or angry child? Was she difficult to soothe, "slow to warm up," or a "difficult" temperament type? To be sure, it can be difficult to gather reliable and valid information on a patient's early developmental history. If available, however, such information can be quite helpful in developing a case formulation to guide treatment.

An objective assessment of mood can be important in beginning work with patients with BPD. In addition to understanding the patient's subjective experience of their difficulties, it can be helpful to have them complete brief, objective measures of their mood. Several excellent self-report measures are available, including the Beck Depression Inventory (BDI; Beck & Steer, 1987), Beck Anxiety Inventory (BAI; Beck, Epstein, Brown, & Steer, 1988), Hopelessness Scale (HS; Beck, Weissman, Lester, & Trexler, 1974), the Profile of Mood States (POMS; McNair, Lorr, & Droppleman, 1971), and the Center for Epidemiological Studies Depression Scale (CES-D; Radloff, 1977).

It is quite important when working with patients with BPD to attend to the occurrence of suicidal thoughts. Like a fast-moving thunderstorm, these often appear with furious intensity, wreaking damage, then pass as quickly. A number of measures, including the Scale for Suicide

Ideations (SSI; Beck, Kovacs, & Weissman, 1979) and the Suicide Ideations Questionnaire (SIQ; Reynolds, 1987) can be used to assess acute
risk of suicide. The therapist can augment questionnaires and interviews, such as these, with a careful discussion of Linda's motivations for
considering suicide. Is it because she views her problems as unsolvable?
She feels hopeless about her future? That she wants attention or revenge
because someone has abandoned or offended her? That she wants
others to pay attention to her, to recognize her distress, and come back
to her?

The cognitive-developmental model of BPD emphasizes understanding patients' maladaptive schema, affect regulation capacities, and the
attachment working models on which they are based. Information on
these factors can be gained both through clinical interviews and with the
aid of objective rating scales. The Young-Brown Schema Questionnaire
(YBSQ; Young, 1999) can be of assistance in identifying maladaptive
beliefs and attitudes that may contribute to Linda's distress. This can
be complemented with information provided by the Adult Attachment
Interview (AAI; George, Kaplan, & Main, 1996), a semi-structured, hour-
long research interview that provides information about relationships
with caregivers, early losses and separations, and experiences of rejection and abuse. The results of the AAI can be used to classify individuals
into one of four attachment types (secure-autonomous, dismissing, pre-
occupied, unresolved-disorganized). Given the length of this instrument
(as well as difficulties with scoring), it may not be practical to use the
AAI in clinical settings. However, several self-report scales are available
that can provide useful information about early experiences and attachment style.

The Parental Bonding Inventory (PBI; Parker, Tupling, & Brown,
1979) is a brief, objective self-report scale assessing recollections of
parenting on two dimensions—caring and protection—whereas the Attachment Questionnaire (AQ; West & Sheldon, 1988) can be used
to classify current attachment relationships into categories that are
consistent with Bowlby's formulation. The Adult Attachment Scale-
Revised (AAS-R; Collins & Read, 1990) is an 18-item self-report scale
developed to assess three dimensions of adult attachment—fears of
being rejected or abandoned (anxiety dimension), comfort with closeness to others (close dimension), and perceived dependability of others
(depend dimension). Although designed as research instruments to
assess representational working models of attachment, these scales can
be used clinically as a means of clarifying patients' thoughts and feelings

about relationships and their experiences with their parents during their childhood. They can be used both to provide a focus for therapeutic discussion and to monitor changes over time in variables believed to underlie their distress.

Controversy exists regarding the construct validity of measures of adult attachment style and their relationships to early experiences and attachment security during childhood. With this in mind, scores on scales, such as the AAS-R, might best be viewed as measures of current perceptions of attachment security. This said, the authors have found that information provided on this scale can provide a useful focus for discussions of feelings of insecurity, fears of abandonment, and views about the reliability of others in current relationships

CONCEPTUALIZATION OF PATIENT

A number of factors appear to contribute to Linda's current distress. Although we know little of Linda's early developmental or social history, it appears that biological (and perhaps temperamental) factors were present that served as a foundation for her current difficulties. Both of Linda's parents were affectively labile, and her father had a history of alcohol abuse. It is likely, then, that there is a familial history of undiagnosed psychopathology. Linda's mother was critical and perfectionistic, and her father demanding and explosive. It is not likely, then, that she experienced her parents as responsive, reliable, nurturant, and nonpunitive, or that she would have been able to develop a secure attachment to them. Rather, one can postulate that she developed an insecure-disorganized attachment style and that this served as a template or "working model" for relationships with others throughout her life. Research indicates that relations between attachment security and mood may be mediated by the establishment of maladaptive beliefs or schema (Roberts, Gotlib, & Kassel, 1996; Reinecke & Rogers, 2001).

For Linda, experiences during her childhood and her consequent disorganized attachment style may have led to the development of a range of negative beliefs, attitudes, attributions, and expectations. In Linda's case, it is hypothesized that she came to view herself as flawed, incapable, and unlovable, to anticipate that others would be abusive or rejecting, and to view herself as being unable to control important outcomes. Her lack of remorse regarding the auto accident and her offhand comment that it is "kind of like the lottery" are telling. Several pundits have recently noted that the growing popularity of lotteries and the legalization of casinos may reflect a fundamental change in American culture, in that success is now attributed more to chance than to diligent effort. The traditional American work ethic has been compromised. Linda's view that people "are just trying to get away with making money . . . like the lottery" may reflect a tacit belief that others are uncaring and malicious, and that important outcomes in life are due to happenstance.

Linda's affect regulation skills appear to be quite poorly developed. Her mood is labile and her behavior often self-destructive and impulsive. Like her mother, Linda appears to be critical and demanding, with high, rigidly held standards for performance. It does not appear that either of her parents served as models for adaptive coping or effective problem solving. The "explosive" home environment appears to have been characterized by high levels of expressed emotion.

In sum, it is hypothesized that genetic or biological factors and adverse early life experiences have contributed to Linda developing an insecure-disorganized attachment style that, in turn, has led to the establishment and consolidation of maladaptive tacit beliefs about the self and others. Effective problem-solving, social, and affect regulation skills were not modeled or reinforced. When confronted with schema-congruent life events, such as criticism or a separation, Linda becomes vulnerable to rapid mood swings and begins to use a range of dysfunctional coping strategies (including withdrawal, shopping, promiscuous sex, suicidal gestures) both to ameliorate her negative feelings and to reestablish a sense of connection or attachment with others.

POTENTIAL PITFALLS

Substantial evidence indicates that reciprocal relations exist between cognition and mood. Not only do the ways we think about things influence our emotional reactions, but our emotional state can influence perception, attention, memory, problem-solving, and appraisal processes. It is possible, as such, that Linda's rapidly fluctuating moods will influence her recollection of events and the ways in which she interprets her experiences. A potential pitfall exists in therapists' natural tendency to empathize with their patients' experiences. When working with patients with BPD, however, therapists do not want to be pulled into accepting the validity of their patients' perspectives. Care must be taken to validate the legitimacy of Linda's emotional experience, and so have her feel understood, while at the same time remaining agnostic as to the reliability of her reports of events and questioning of the adaptiveness of her ways of coping with them. Linda was referred for treatment, for example, after angrily rear-ending an elderly couple in traffic. The therapist can attempt to understand and validate her feelings of frustration, while at the same time challenging her way of coping with them (it really isn't acceptable to bump others with your car) and supporting the development of more effective ways of managing feelings of anger.

A second potential pitfall stems from therapists' natural tendency to attempt to address immediate concerns. As in standard cognitive therapy, cognitive-developmental psychotherapy focuses on current problems and would attempt to assist Linda to manage them more effectively. Many patients with BPD present their therapists with crises that must be addressed. As important, however, will be to identify how current behavioral and emotional reactions derive from past relationship working models (attachment insecurity and schema), how they may be seen as attempts to reestablish a relationship, and how they reflect deficits in affect regulation. It is important to maintain the long view and to attend to underlying mechanisms while addressing crises that Linda presents.

A final potential pitfall may be Linda's tendency to become dependent on the therapist. This is a natural reaction, in that the therapist will likely be more attentive, empathic, understanding, acceptant, consistent, and reliably supportive than others in her life. This dependency can be used, at least initially, to encourage Linda to actively complete therapeutic activities. In the long run, however, it can be problematic. Given her low feelings of efficacy, it is possible she will attribute improvement to the therapist or to changes in her environment. It will be important, from the outset, to encourage autonomy and to help her to see how her efforts are responsible for bringing about change in her life.

PROGNOSIS

It can be very difficult to predict long-term outcome, and the authors hesitate to make predictions about Linda's progress without knowing her better. To be sure, a good deal of sophisticated research in recent years has examined predictors of response to treatment. Characteristics of the clinician and the patient, nonspecific relationship factors (including warmth, empathy, positive regard, collaborative rapport, feeling understood), motivation and readiness to change, compliance, understanding and acceptance of the therapeutic rationale, therapeutic activity and problem focus, environmental variables (e.g., socioeconomic status and availability of social support), and technical factors in the therapy all appear to play a role. That said, it is challenging to predict the response of individual patients to a treatment program. Perhaps the best that can be done is to attend to each of these predictor variables and, whenever possible, work to maximize them.

Linda's long-term prognosis for adaptive change depends on how she and her therapist define "adaptive change." With regular attendance and diligent effort, the likelihood that Linda will make notable gains is reasonably good. It should be possible to provide her with techniques that will reduce her feelings of depression, anxiety, and anger, and that will reduce the frequency of suicidal gestures and attempts. The underlying factors that maintain her distress, however, are long-standing in nature and will likely prove difficult to change. Whereas it should be possible to provide Linda with techniques to more effectively regulate her mood, it may prove difficult to identify and change maladaptive schema. Linda appears to view herself as fundamentally flawed, unlovable, and incapable, and she views others as unreliable and rejecting. Transforming her into a confident, warm, and resilient woman who is tolerant of others' shortcomings and acceptant of the vagaries of close relationships is a tall order. Reconstruction of schema is difficult under the best of circumstances. If the goal, however, is more modest—to modify her most malignant beliefs and provide her with techniques for coping with emotional reactions that they elicit—progress might be made.

To paraphrase Sigmund Freud, the defining feature of clinically significant improvement is whether the individual is able to love and to work. Linda's functioning in both of these domains is quite poor. Moreover, it is not clear that she is motivated to develop close, empathic, and reciprocal romantic relationships or whether she views her work as problematic. She appears to attribute her difficulties to external factors (e.g., "I get overwhelmed a lot by the things that I do") rather than to personal characteristics. She is, in terms of her readiness to address these difficulties, in the "precontemplation stage" (Prochaska, DiClemente, & Norcross, 1992). She appears to be unaware of her social and work problems and may not yet be motivated to change. A first step, then, may be to discuss these problems with her and to encourage her to identify specific problems in these domains that can be addressed during therapy sessions.

TIMELINE

The time frame for therapy can vary depending on a number of factors, including Linda's motivation and readiness to change, specific goals, level of distress, psychological mindedness, comorbid conditions, and expectations for change. Cognitive-developmental psychotherapy, like standard cognitive behavior therapy, is problem oriented, active, and strategic. For patients with severe BPD, sessions are typically held once a week for approximately 12 months. Sessions are held more frequently if there is an emergency or if the patient is experiencing acute distress.

SPECIFIC TECHNIQUES

Many of the techniques used in cognitive-developmental psychotherapy are essentially similar to those used in standard cognitive therapy (A. Beck, Freeman, & Associates, 1990; J. Beck, 1995; Sperry, 1999) and in schema-focused cognitive therapy (Young, 1999). After the therapist develops a case formulation and shares it with her, a problem list would be prepared. Initial interventions would be directed toward improving Linda's support system and encouraging her to engage in activities that provide her with a sense of accomplishment. Linda noted that her "life is empty" and that "there is nothing in her life." It would be worthwhile to explore these statements with her and to determine if there have been activities she has enjoyed or gained a sense of accomplishment from in the past. Did she, for example, feel a sense of meaning or accomplishment when she completed her master's degree? How does she feel when she trims a bonsai tree to perfection? Does she have goals for the future?

Initial interventions might also be directed toward reducing Linda's self-destructive behavior (Reinecke, 2000). She might, for example, be encouraged to identify situations where she is likely to experience suicidal thoughts and to prepare a list of strategies she can use should these feelings arise. These strategies might include reminding herself that she has "been through this before" and that "these feelings don't last; they will be gone tomorrow." She might carry a list of supportive people (and emergency resources) she can call and a list of activities that would distract her from thoughts of self-injury. Particular attention should be paid to "releasing cognitions," which are beliefs that give the individual permission to engage in self-destructive behavior.

Linda's compulsive shopping is of interest in that research indicates that impulsive and excessive shopping is associated with two beliefs— that material possessions are a source of identity and success and that purchasing goods will bolster self-concept by reducing discrepancies between how the person views him- or herself (perceived or actual self) and how the person wishes to be (ideal self). Excessive buying can serve as a temporary means of coping with feelings of anxiety or depression. Linda's excessive purchasing may serve to provide social status (McCracken, 1990), help her to regulate her emotions (Elliott, 1994), and serve as an indicator of who she would like to be (Dittmar, 1992; Dittmar & Drury, 2000). With this in mind, it may be helpful to discuss her thoughts and feelings as she anticipates heading to the store to shop, the triggers for these emotions, the meanings attached to the objects she has selected (compulsive shoppers consistently select high-prestige items, such as clothes and jewelry, rather than functional items such as food or utensils), and how she would feel if she resisted making the purchase. A discussion of Linda's shopping, then, may provide access to a range of negative beliefs about the self, her desirability to others, and her ways of coping with negative moods.

The development of affect regulation skills plays a central role in cognitive-developmental psychotherapy. Affect regulation may be viewed as a skill and, like other adaptive skills, is influenced by both environmental and biological constraints. Affect regulation comprises an integrated set of component skills that allows an individual to maintain a level of affective arousal that is appropriate for effective coping with stressful situations. These component skills include mood monitoring, cue identification, and implementation of cognitive and behavioral regulation strategies. If an individual is able to maintain a stable level of arousal when confronted with a stressful event, he or she will be better able to use more sophisticated skills, such as rational problem solving, assertive communication, and the like, to resolve the problem.

The first step in assisting Linda to more effectively regulate her emotions is for her to recognize that affective lability is, in fact, a problem. Like many individuals, Linda will likely view her reactions to her coworkers, ex-husband, fellow motorists, and neighbors as reasonable and appropriate. The first task, as such, will be to encourage her to describe a recent event that elicited a strong emotional reaction and to ask about her "feelings about the feeling." The question is not "Was your reaction justified?" but "Was it proportionate to the event, or was it stronger than it needed to be?" Insofar as strong feelings of depression, anxiety, and anger are uncomfortable, the therapist would guide her to reflect upon these emotions and to explicitly acknowledge that a goal of therapy is to reduce them.

A second step is to teach Linda to monitor her moods. As Roth and Fonagy (1996) observed, the ability to reflect upon one's feelings and their relations to events is a strong predictor of therapeutic change. Teaching Linda this skill will be no small task. Although cognitive behavioral procedures (such as thought records, emotion rating scales, and mood diaries) can be quite helpful, they require that patients have the prerequisite ability to discriminate and label internal states and that they be motivated to do so. Given the strength of Linda's emotional "surges," it is not likely she will wish to reflect on them outside of therapy. These skills can, however, be developed during the therapy session. An empathic, tolerant therapeutic stance that encourages the development of perceptions of personal control or self-efficacy will facilitate the development of this skill. It is important for Linda to see that the therapist can tolerate (and even encourage) the expression and labeling of frighteningly strong emotions during the therapy session. When Linda becomes able to comfortably use mood monitoring techniques during the session, she can begin to practice them at home.

As Linda becomes better able to identify and monitor emotions during the week, she will be asked to rate their severity or strength on a 0–100 scale. Most individuals find this task fairly easy. Quite often, individuals with BPD will rate the majority of their experiences as having been extreme (i.e., in the 95–100 range). This is not problematic because the emphasis is not so much on the ratings of severity as on the identification of triggering events. Once Linda is able to identify situations that were associated with strong feelings of depression, anxiety, and anger, the therapist will ask her to identify physiological, cognitive, or behavioral cues that led her to realize her mood was escalating into the extreme range. She might note that she began, for example, to experience feelings of tension, to swear internally, or to speak more loudly or quickly. The activity teaches her to identify internal cues that she is about to lose control rather than external triggers or precipitating events. If available, family members and partners can be quite helpful in pointing out to patients when their moods are beginning to escalate.

Once Linda has learned to identify internal indicators that her mood is beginning to change, she will be asked to identify the "inflection point"—the point at which her feelings of depression, anxiety, or anger escalate such that she does not perceive that she can control them. The next goal will be to collaboratively develop a set of cognitive and behavioral strategies she can use before she reaches this inflection point. These may include leaving the situation or turning away, relaxing, reviewing a list of adaptive self-statements or counter-thoughts, completing a cognitive-behavioral thought record (see J. Beck, 1995), writing in a diary or journal, talking with a friend, distraction, guided imagery, or engaging in a pleasant activity.

Finally, Linda might be encouraged to identify scenarios that would lead her to experience a surge of negative affect and to develop plans for how she might manage them. It is likely, for example, that Linda will become frustrated by a parent or delayed in traffic at some time in the near future. As these events are predictable, fairly detailed plans for how she will manage them should be developed and practiced in session. The therapist can teach, model, and role-play these skills with Linda; offer recommendations to her; and reinforce her efforts to cope effectively with stressful events.

Attachment security is based on the belief that others will reliably and consistently support and nurture her. Given the nature of her relationships with her parents, siblings, former husband, and romantic partners, it is not surprising that she has come to view herself as defective and unlovable, to feel that she cannot count on others to reliably meet her emotional needs, and to believe that she is not capable of managing life's challenges effectively. Unfortunately, her behavior appears to contribute to these relationship difficulties. Her critical demandingness, emotional neediness, and affective lability lead others to withdraw from her. This, in turn, exacerbates her feelings of isolation and depression, leading to further demands for emotional closeness. Changing these beliefs, expectations, and social templates will require a patient, focused approach. Linda might be encouraged, for example, to recount experiences in her past when she did feel close to someone, when she was able to empathize with another's feelings, and when she felt nurtured, supported, and understood. She might then be asked to consider what she would, in the best of all worlds, want her current relationships to be like. The therapist would, in short, be attempting to identify memories of relationships where she felt a bit secure, and to use them as a possible template for future relationships. Feelings of security in current relationships (including the therapy relationship) are discussed, and the fact that she may be capable of developing a trusting rapport with some persons would be explored. This would be followed by a practical discussion of ways in which trusting relationships can be facilitated, and skills for accomplishing this would be practiced in session. As in schema-focused cognitive therapy (Young, 1999; Guidano & Liotti, 1983), a developmental analysis of experiences contributing to maladaptive schema regarding herself and her relationships with others would be completed.

SPECIAL CAUTIONS

Linda's behavior is frequently a provocative, in the sense that it stimulates, excites, and provokes others to take action. The question then becomes, what is the action she desires, and does her behavior accomplish its intended goal? When Linda sends inflammatory notes to parents, calls the wife of her colleague, or destroys her husband's diploma she is seeking (maladaptively) to express her feelings to them and to accomplish specific goals. It will be important to focus not only on controlling these behaviors but also on understanding what her unstated goals are and how these reflect her tacit beliefs and expectations.

Linda appears, for example, to hold rigid beliefs about how others should behave and feels threatened when these expectations are violated. She does not appear to tolerate well the shortcomings of her fellow man. It would be interesting to know her thoughts and feelings about the parents of the children in her class. What thoughts occur as she sees that they have not assisted them with their homework as she would like? Her strong reaction suggests that this resonates for her in an important way. She remarked, for example, that "the kids will suffer, but that's their choice." Does she feel that she suffered as a child? Does she believe that she was, in some way, damaged by her experiences growing up? Does she believe that her parents, like those of the children in her class, made choices that were not in her best interest? Particular caution should be exercised should Linda begin to show displeasure with her therapist. Her thoughts and feelings about therapy and how these concerns are related to tacit beliefs and feelings of insecurity in relationships should be actively explored and resolved lest she leave treatment prematurely.

Although the concepts of transference and countertransference do not play a central role in cognitive therapy, the cognitive-developmental model explicitly acknowledges the critical role of early experiences for forming working models of interpersonal relationships. The therapeutic relationship can be used as a means of understanding Linda's thoughts and behaviors outside of the therapy session and as a tool for therapeutic change. Moreover, the therapist's thoughts and feelings in response to Linda's actions can yield important information about her effects on others.

The cognitive-developmental model presumes that relationships with significant others in one's past have important, enduring effects on the nature and quality of current relationships. This simple notion—that past relationships may influence emotional and behavioral responses in current relationships—has important practical implications. Whereas transference is understood from a psychodynamic perspective as reflecting the expression of drives or the recapitulation of representations of subjective interactive experiences, cognitively based models conceptualize transference effects from a social learning perspective (Reinecke, 2002). Put simply, all of us draw inferences about new people based on past experiences with similar individuals. Transference, from a cognitive perspective, occurs not only in therapy but also in a wide range of social relationships. Inasmuch as relationships can be complex and require rapid assessment and evaluation of a great deal of nonverbal information, transference-based processing—using past experiences in similar situations to make sense of a novel social situation—can be both efficient and adaptive. When applied in a rigid or inappropriate manner, however, difficulties can arise. It will be important when working with Linda for the therapist to be attentive to his or her emotional reactions during therapy sessions and to encourage Linda to describe her thoughts and emotional reactions about the therapist. Her reactions to the therapy relationship may offer important insights into her beliefs about relationships, feelings of insecurity, fears of abandonment and rejection, and desires for support and understanding.

AREAS TO AVOID

There are no specific issues that, if raised by Linda, would not be appropriate for discussion. However, certain clinical difficulties may be better addressed through other forms of treatment. If, for example, Linda reported experiencing difficulties with alcohol or substance abuse, a referral for a consultation with a specialist in substance abuse and dependence would be appropriate. Similarly, if she met the criteria for an eating disorder (e.g., bulimia nervosa), a referral for an empirically supported treatment (LeGrange, 2003) would be in order. The ways in which difficulties with alcohol abuse or eating disorders may be related to her affect regulation deficits, disorganized attachment style, negative self-concept, maladaptive schema, and ineffective problem solving would, of course, be discussed.

MEDICATIONS

Medications can play an important role in treating of BPD (Silk, 1996). Antidepressant, anxiolytic, neuroleptic, and mood stabilizing medications have all been used (Dimeff, McDavid, & Linehan, 1999) and can be effective in reducing dysphoria, anxiety, anger, and affective lability. It is worth noting, however, that effect sizes in controlled outcome studies tend to be modest and that the long-term effectiveness of medications with patients seen in community settings is not known. Moreover, risk of overdose remains an important concern. Given Linda's history of suicidal gestures, it will be important to monitor her mood carefully and select an agent with a relatively low toxicity. Tricyclic antidepressants and monoamine oxidase inhibitors might not, then, be first-line treatments. Medications might best be viewed as complementing psychotherapy as part of a broad, multidimensional treatment program.

PATIENT STRENGTHS

Linda has a number of strengths and resources that may be used in developing a treatment plan. It can be useful to think of strengths and resources as existing both within the individual and within the environment. These would include adaptive coping strategies and skills, cognitive skills, social skills, social supports, and community resources. Linda appears to be reasonably intelligent and is able to function effectively in predictable, stable settings. She was able to work while completing her graduate studies, suggesting that she can be resourceful and may be able to organize herself to complete challenging tasks. The process of therapy will be arduous. It will be helpful for Linda to see that she is capable of mastering difficult tasks and of acquiring new skills. The case study describes a range of maladaptive cognitive and behavioral coping strategies. It would be helpful to identify adaptive coping strategies that Linda has developed. How does she cope with stressful events in her life? Are there things she does to calm or soothe herself? Does she, for example, find gardening or watching television relaxing? Is she able to approach problems in a thoughtful, rational manner? In a similar manner, it will be helpful to identify social and community supports. Does she have any friends or relatives she can turn to for support? Is she able to turn to her physicians and therapists when she is distressed? Has she ever participated in community activities or been a member of a group? It was noted that she was raised in the Lutheran tradition. Does she finding attending church services or talking with a minister helpful? Developing a network of social and community supports may be helpful to Linda in stabilizing her moods and in reducing the risk of self-destructive behavior.

SETTING LIMITS

All things in development appear on the stage of life twice—first in the interpsychic and then in the intrapsychic. The concept that skills are acquired in a social context has important implications for understanding processes of change over the course of development and in psychotherapy. As noted, failures to develop affect regulation skills play a central role in BPD. By setting limits and boundaries, the therapist serves as a model for how one can manage stressful situations. The rules, boundaries, strategies, and guidelines that the therapist places on the therapeutic relationship—limit setting—are openly discussed with the patient and, over time, internalized. If, for example, Linda was to become upset that her therapist would not allow their session to run long (perhaps demonstrating to her that the therapist was uncaring and rejecting), this would become an explicit focus of discussion during the following session. Her thoughts and feelings about the time limit, the relationship to beliefs she holds about other important relationships, and how she is able to manage the emotions that are triggered by these thoughts would all be examined. Linda might come to recognize, for example, that ending the session on time need not mean her therapist is uncaring. It would also serve to demonstrate how her demands that the session continue may be related to her "need to have contact" with her colleague at school. Both are based on her belief that she must have an emotionally close relationship in order to alleviate her feelings of depression and anxiety. Setting appropriate limits and boundaries makes the therapeutic relationship a venue for developing affect regulation skills and for changing maladaptive beliefs. As noted earlier, the therapeutic relationship and the structure of the therapy session can be viewed as framework that guides and directs the process of treatment. Therapeutic limits and boundaries are an important part of this framework that serves not only to develop cognitive-developmental skills but also to help Linda recognize internal motivations and experiences she reacts to by engaging in maladaptive behavior (Green, 1988).

INCLUSION OF SIGNIFICANT OTHERS

It can be quite helpful to include family members in the therapy process. Care must be taken, however, to determine the role that family members may have played in the development of disorder. A history of severe abuse or neglect can complicate the treatment process. If, for example, Linda had been sexually abused by her father, encouraging his participation in therapy sessions could exacerbate her feelings of depression, anxiety, and anger. Similarly, if Linda's relationship with her mother continues to be characterized by criticism and perfectionistic demands, including her in the therapy process could prove challenging. A considerable body of evidence indicates that families that are characterized by high levels of expressed emotion (i.e., conflictual, critical, and demanding and/or obsequiously caring and controlling) tend to exacerbate feelings of depression, anxiety, and agitation among chronically ill patients. It would be useful to include Linda's parents or siblings in therapy sessions only if it appears they could actively support the treatment process and if there was the possibility of improving the quality of their relationship with her. As noted in the case study, Linda is divorced and lives alone. If she had a significant other, he or she could, with her permission, be invited to participate in her treatment.

HOMEWORK

As in other forms of cognitive therapy, homework plays an important role in cognitive-developmental psychotherapy for BPD. Every session should conclude with the collaborative development of a homework task, typically based on a skill discussed during the session, which can be practiced during the week. Commonly used homework assignments include (1) preparing a list of specific treatment goals; (2) mood monitoring; (3) participation in social activities; (4) rational problem solving; (5) identifying maladaptive thoughts and cognitive distortions; (6) formulating adaptive counter-thoughts; (7) preparing a journal of experiences that are consistent and inconsistent with maladaptive expectations or schema; (8) affect regulation exercises; (9) attachment-based exercises; (10) assertive communication skills; (11) relaxation training; (12) preparing a journal of expectations for relationships, the positive and negative consequences of maintaining these expectations, and the probability that others will meet them; and (13) practicing negotiation and compromise. Whenever possible, homework assignments are practiced during the session, and factors that may interfere with successful completion are discussed. A wide range of cognitive factors (e.g., Linda doesn't believe the task will be helpful or believes she is being coerced into attempting it), behavioral (e.g., Linda lacks the skill to attempt it), and environmental (e.g., Linda won't have the opportunity to attempt the assignment during the week due to her work schedule), can arise that may subvert the treatment process. These should be carefully examined and resolved. If at all possible, Linda should leave the session with a clear sense of what the homework assignment is and how it may be helpful to her, and confident in her ability to accomplish it.

TERMINATION ISSUES

Because patients with BPD have problems with abandonment, loss, and rejection, their reactions to an impending termination may range from heightened dependency and helplessness to cool indifference to anger and dismissive scorn. Dependent neediness and a desire to please the therapist (often by bringing gifts or offering compliments) are quite common. These patients may view the therapist as an essential source of support and guidance and may doubt their own abilities to manage events as they arise. An approaching termination may, as such, activate schemas that play a central role in BPD. The patient's thoughts and feelings about termination, as such, become a critical component of the treatment itself and should be openly discussed.

Dependent, indifferent, and dismissive reactions by the patient can elicit a range of emotional reactions in the therapist, including anger, irritation, frustration, avoidance, guilt, feelings of inadequacy, or a desire to redouble efforts to help the patient. Once again, an attitude of "radical neutrality" may be beneficial. Therapists will want to carefully monitor their thoughts and feelings in reaction to the patient and inquire, "What is it about the patient's behavior that is eliciting this reaction in me? How might these behaviors be adaptive or maladaptive to the patient? Do these behaviors occur in other relationships? Is there anything I've said or done to elicit this reaction?" The therapist and the patient can then work together to understand the patient's thoughts and feelings about the impending termination, how this may be related to schema and early attachment experiences, and how affect regulation skills learned earlier in treatment can be used to reduce these feelings.

Contemporary psychodynamic and cognitive behavioral theories of BPD frequently emphasize the central importance of abandonment and object loss as dynamics in the condition. Less frequently noted, however, are the notions of responsiveness and reliability. Individuals with attachment-based disorders such as BPD frequently expect and need others to be entirely responsive, nurturant, and reliable. Given their underlying disorganized attachment style, they look to family members, romantic partners, and therapists to be completely responsive and reliable (100% of the time, 24/7), and they react strongly to violations of this expectation (note, for example, how individuals with BPD react to unexpected changes in the date or time of their therapy session). Perfect reliability, of course, is not possible. Family members, partners, and therapists are not automatons. An explicit goal of therapy is to assist the patient with BPD to accept the unreliability of their fellow man, and to recognize that changes occur in relationships as individuals develop. Losses and changes need not be viewed as abandonment or a rejection. With this in mind, the termination process can become an opportunity for important therapeutic growth.

That said, termination is often quite difficult for patients with BPD. It can be useful, then, to taper sessions slowly, to offer the patient booster sessions as needed, to reinforce the skills learned, and to recommend that medications be maintained after psychotherapy has been completed.

RELAPSE PREVENTION

It may, in some ways, be inappropriate to think about relapse prevention when working with patients suffering from BPD. Based on a medical model, relapse refers to reemergence of symptoms of a disorder that has been cured. Extant treatments for BPD, however, do not offer the possibility of cure, only of management. Given the possibility that Linda will experience episodes of depression, anxiety, and anger in the future, it is essential to help her to prepare for them. Linda might be encouraged to identify situations that are likely to trigger the reemergence of symptoms. If these situations can be predicted, Linda can prepare for them in therapy. Linda would then be assisted in developing a list of strategies and techniques that have been most effective for regulating her mood. The ways these might be used in coping with high-risk situations would then be practiced. It is important, as well, to distinguish a lapse from a relapse. Feelings of anxiety, depression, and anger are a normal part of the human experience. Their reappearance need not mean that therapy has been ineffective. Rather, they indicate that it may be helpful to seek support and to use those techniques that have been helpful in the past. The goal is to prepare Linda for the disappointments and losses of life by instilling a sense of efficacy and hope.

MECHANISMS OF CHANGE

Cognitive-developmental psychotherapy is believed to promote behavioral and emotional change by rectifying affect regulation deficits, changing maladaptive schema, improving social problem solving, and developing a more secure adult attachment style.

CONCLUSION

Treating patients with borderline personality disorder can be at the same time challenging and fulfilling. A well-considered, developmentally based formulation that attends to the full range of factors implicated in the etiology and maintenance of the disorder is important if therapists are to help these patients overcome the long-standing and very debilitating emotional and behavioral patterns that characterize this disorder. The cognitive-developmental model of psychotherapy emphasizes identifying and changing maladaptive schema and social interaction patterns. Therapists endeavor to help patients develop affect regulation skills, improve social problem-solving abilities, and develop a more secure adult attachment style. They build on patients' strengths and recognize that individuals function in social contexts. Developing social supports and understanding the ways in which adverse early experiences may have served as templates or models for current relationships become an important focus of treatment. Cognitive-developmental models are quite new and sit at the interface of the cognitive-behavior therapy and developmental psychopathology literatures. Although promising, a great deal of work remains to be done. Research is necessary to refine and test these models, and controlled outcome studies are needed before we can have confidence in the efficacy and effectiveness of the procedures proposed.

REFERENCES

Adams, H., Bernat, J., & Luscher, K. (2001). Borderline personality disorder: An overview. In H. Adams & P. Sutker (Eds.), *Comprehensive handbook of psychopathology* (3rd ed., pp. 491–507). New York: Kluwer Academic/Plenum Publishers.

Beck, A., Epstein, N., Brown, G., & Steer, R. (1988). An inventory for measuring clinical anxiety. *Journal of Consulting and Clinical Psychology, 56,* 893–897.

Beck, A., Freeman, A., & Associates (1990). *Cognitive therapy of personality disorders.* New York: Guilford Press.

Beck, A., Kovacs, M., & Weissman, A. (1979). Assessment of suicidal intent: The scale for suicide ideation. *Journal of Consulting and Clinical Psychology, 47,* 343–352.

Beck, A., & Steer, R. (1987). *Manual for the revised Beck Depression Inventory.* San Antonio, TX: Psychological Corporation.

Beck, A., Weissman, A., Lester, D., & Trexler, L. (1974). The measurement of pessimism: The hopelessness scale. *Journal of Consulting and Clinical Psychology, 42,* 861–865.

Beck, J. (1995). *Cognitive therapy: Basics and beyond.* New York: Guilford Press.

Bryer, J., Nelson, B., Miller, J., & Kroll, P. (1987). Childhood sexual abuse and physical abuse as factors in adult psychiatric illness. *American Journal of Psychiatry, 144,* 1426–1430.

Carlson, E. (1998). A prospective longitudinal study of attachment disorganization/disorientation. *Child Development, 69*(4), 1107–1128.

Carlson, E., & Sroufe, L. (1995). Contribution of attachment theory to developmental psychopathology. In D. Cicchetti & D. Cohen (Eds.), *Developmental psychopathology: Theory and methods* (Vol. 1, pp. 581–617). New York: Wiley.

Cicchetti, D. (1989). Developmental psychopathology: Past, present, and future. In D. Cicchetti (Ed.), *Emergence of a discipline: Rochester symposium on developmental psychopathology* (Vol. 1.). Hillsdale, NJ: Erlbaum.

Collins, N., & Read, S. (1990). Adult attachment, working models, and relationship quality in dating couples. *Journal of Personality and Social Psychology, 58,* 644–663.

Dimeff, L., McDavid, J., & Linehan, M. (1999). Pharmacotherapy for borderline personality disorder: A review of the literature and recommendations for treatment. *Journal of Clinical Psychology in Medical Settings, 6,* 113–138.

Dittmar, H. (1992). *The social psychology of material possessions: To have is to be.* New York: St. Martin's Press.

Dittmar, H., & Drury, J. (2000). Self-image—Is it in the bag? A qualitative comparison between "ordinary" and "excessive" consumers. *Journal of Economic Psychology, 21,* 109–142.

Dozier, M., Stovall, K., & Albus, K. (1999). Attachment and psychopathology in adulthood. In J. Cassidy & P. Shaver (Eds.), *Handbook of attachment* (pp. 497–519). New York: Guilford Press.

Eisenberg, N., & Fabes, R. (1998). Prosocial development. In W. Damon (Series Ed.) & N. Eisenberg (Ed.), *Handbook of child psychology: Vol. 3. Social, emotional, and personality development* (5th ed., pp. 701–778). New York: Wiley.

Elliott, R. (1994). Addictive consumption: Function and fragmentation in postmodernity. *Journal of Consumer Policy, 17,* 159–179.

Farmer, R., & Nelson-Gray, R. (1990). Personality disorders and depression: Hypothetical relations, empirical findings, and methodological considerations. *Clinical Psychology Review, 10,* 453–496.

First, M., Gibbon, M., Spitzer, R., Williams, J., & Benjamin, L. (1997). *Users guide for the structured clinical interview for the DSM-IV Axis II personality disorders.* Washington, DC: American Psychiatric Press.

First, M., Spitzer, L., Gibbon, M., & Williams, J. (1995). *Structured clinical interview for Axis I DSM-IV disorders* (SCID Version 2.0). Washington, DC: American Psychiatric Press.

Garber, J., & Dodge, K. (1992). *The development of emotional regulation and dysregulation.* Cambridge, UK: Cambridge University Press.

Geiger, T., & Crick, N. (2001). A developmental psychopathology perspective on vulnerability to personality disorders. In R. Ingram & J. Price (Eds.), *Vulnerability to psychopathology* (pp. 57–102). New York: Guilford Press.

George, C., Kaplan, N., & Main, M. (1996). *Adult Attachment Interview protocol* (3rd ed.). Unpublished manuscript, University of California at Berkeley.

Green, S. (1988). *Limit setting in clinical practice.* Washington, DC: American Psychiatric Press.

Guidano, V., & Liotti, G. (1983). *Cognitive processes and emotional disorders.* New York: Guilford Press.

Herman, J., Perry, J., & van der Kolk, B. (1989). Childhood trauma in borderline personality disorder. *American Journal of Psychiatry, 146,* 490–495.

Hyler, S. (1994). *Personality Diagnostic Questionnaire—4.* New York: New York State Psychiatric Institute.

Kaye, K. (1982). *The mental and social life of babies: How parents create persons.* Chicago: University of Chicago Press.

Kernberg, P., Weiner, A., & Bardenstein, K. (2000). *Personality disorders in children and adolescents.* New York: Basic Books.

LeGrange, D. (2003). The cognitive model of bulimia nervosa. In M. Reinecke & D. Clark (Eds.), *Cognitive therapy across the lifespan: Evidence and practice.* Cambridge, UK: Cambridge University Press.

Links, P. (1990). *Family environment and borderline personality disorder.* Washington, DC: American Psychiatric Press.

Liotti, G. (2002). The inner schema of borderline states and its correction during psychotherapy: A cognitive-evolutionary approach. *Journal of Cognitive Psychotherapy, 16*(3), 349–366.

Livesley, W., Jang, K., Schroeder, M., & Jackson, D. (1993). Genetic and environmental factors in personality dimensions. *American Journal of Psychiatry, 150,* 1826–1831.

McCracken, G. (1990). *Culture and consumption.* Indianapolis: Indiana University Press.

McNair, D., Lorr, M., & Droppleman, L. (1971). *Manual for the profile of mood states.* San Diego, CA: Educational Testing Service.

Morey, L. (1991). *Personality Assessment Inventory: Professional manual.* Odessa, FL: Psychological Assessment Resources.

Paris, J. (1993). *Borderline personality disorder: Etiology and treatment.* London: Taylor & Francis.

Paris, J. (1994). *Borderline personality disorder: A multidimensional approach.* Washington, DC: American Psychiatric Press.

Paris, J. (1997). Childhood trauma as an etiological factor in personality disorders. *Journal of Personality Disorders, 11,* 34–49.

Paris, J. (1999). Borderline personality disorder. In T. Millon, P. Blaney, & R. Davis (Eds.), *Oxford textbook of psychopathology* (pp. 625–652). New York: Oxford University Press.

Paris, J. (2000). *Myths of childhood.* Washington, DC: American Psychiatric Press.

Parker, G., Tupling, H., & Brown, L. (1979). A parental bonding instrument. *British Journal of Medical Psychology, 52,* 1–10.

Prochaska, J., DiClemente, C., & Norcross, J. (1992). In search of how people change: Application to addictive behaviors. *American Psychologist, 47,* 1102–1114.

Radloff, L. (1977). The CES-D scale: A self-report depression scale for research in the general population. *Applied Psychosocial Measurement, 1,* 385–401.

Reinecke, M. (2000). Suicide and depression. In F. Dattilio & A. Freeman (Eds.), *Cognitive-behavioral strategies in crisis intervention* (2nd ed., pp. 84–125). New York: Guilford Press.

Reinecke, M. (2002). Cognitive therapies of depression: A modularized treatment approach. In M. Reinecke & M. Davison (Eds.), *Comparative treatments of depression* (pp. 249–290). New York: Springer.

Reinecke, M., & Rogers, G. (2001). Dysfunctional attitudes and attachment style among clinically depressed adults. *Behavioural and Cognitive Psychotherapy, 29,* 129–141.

Reynolds, W. (1987). *The Suicide Ideation Questionnaire.* Odessa, FL: Psychological Assessment Resources.

Roberts, J., Gotlib, I., & Kassel, J. (1996). Adult attachment security and symptoms of depression: The mediating roles of dysfunctional attitudes and low self-esteem. *Journal of Personality and Social Psychology, 70,* 310–320.

Roth, A., & Fonagy, P. (1996). *What works for whom? A critical review of psychotherapy research.* New York: Guilford Press.

Rutter, M., & Garmezy, N. (1983). Developmental psychopathology. In E. Herrington (Ed.) and P. Mussen (Series Ed.), *Handbook of child psychology: Vol. 4. Socialization, personality and social development.* New York: Wiley.

Siever, L., & Davis, K. (1991). A Psychobiological perspective on the personality disorders. *Journal of Personality Disorders, 6,* 109–116.

Silk, K. (Ed.). (1994). *Biological and neurobiological studies of borderline personality disorder.* Washington, DC: American Psychiatric Press.

Silk, K. (1996). *The biology of personality disorders.* Washington, DC: American Psychiatric Press, Inc.

Silk, K. (1999). Rational pharmacotherapy for patients with personality disorders. In P. Links (Ed.), *Clinical assessment and management of severe personality disorders* (pp. 109–142). Washington, DC: American Psychiatric Press.

Sperry, L. (1995). *Handbook of diagnosis and treatment of the DSM-IV personality disorders.* New York: Brunner/Mazel.

Sperry, L. (1999). *Cognitive behavior therapy of DSM-IV personality disorders.* Philadelphia: Brunner/Mazel.

Sroufe, L. (1990). An organizational perspective on the self. In D. Cicchetti & M. Beeghly (Eds.), *The self in transition: Infancy to childhood.* Chicago: University of Chicago Press.

Vygotsky, L. (1962). *Thought and language.* Cambridge, MA: MIT Press.

West, M., & Sheldon, A. (1988). The classification of pathological attachment patterns in adults. *Journal of Personality Disorders, 2,* 153–160.

Whisman, M., & McGarvey, A. (1995). Attachment, depressogenic cognitions, and dysphoria. *Cognitive Therapy and Research, 19,* 633–650.

Widiger, T., & Frances, A. (1989). Epidemiology, diagnosis, and comorbidity of borderline personality disorders. In A. Tasman, R. Hale, & A. Frances (Eds.), *Review of psychiatry, Vol. 8* (pp. 8–24). Washington, DC: American Psychiatric Press.

Widiger, T., Mangine, S., Corbitt, E., Ellis, C. and Thomas, G. (1995). The Personality Interview IV.

Young, J. (1999). *Cognitive therapy for personality disorders: A schema-focused approach* (3rd ed., pp. 59–68). Sarasota, FL: Professional Resource Press.

Zanarini, M., Gunderson, J., Frankenburg, F., & Chauncey, D. (1989). The revised diagnostic interview for borderlines: Discriminating BPD from other Axis II disorders. *Journal of Personality Disorders, 3,* 10–18.

Zittel, C., & Westen, D. (1998). Conceptual issues and research findings on borderline personality disorder: What every clinician should know. *Psychotherapy in Practice, 4,* 5–20.

9

A Lacanian Approach

Liliana Rusansky-Drob

TREATMENT MODEL

My treatment approach is rooted in Jacques Lacan's understanding of psychoanalysis and in the work of Lacan's followers. Lacan's understanding of psychoanalysis blends aspects of both existential and structuralist thought and works with the tension that exists between the patient's freedom and responsibility and his or her determination by unconscious, familial, and linguistic structures (Fink, 1995).

Although the word *treatment* (and *therapy*) is used frequently in psychoanalysis, these terms have been inherited from the medical field to refer to a process that leads to the cure or improvement of a condition (Evans, 1996). Within Lacanian terms, it is noteworthy that there is no cure. For Lacan, cure is neither possible nor ethically desirable (Lacan, 1959). Cure is not possible because once an individual's basic psychic structure and libidinal model have been established, they cannot be altered. The inherent helplessness of the human infant places him or her completely at the mercy of an "other" (i.e., the parent), who interprets the infant's needs according to his or her own psychical structure, as well as at the mercy of a wider "other," an inherited language and culture that preconditions the structures of the individual's unconscious. For Lacan, the individual's psychic structure, as neurotic, psychotic, or perverse, is an unalterable aspect of his or her mental life that is conditioned by an other's desire, but even if it could be altered, it would be both un-psychoanalytic and unethical to do so because it would simply amount to a repositioning of the subject in terms of the other's desire and would in no way respect the subject's own desire and freedom. For Lacan, the subject is caught between a constant search for his or her personal truth while, at the same time, wishing to rely on the familiar structure that was imposed upon him or her in infancy and childhood. An individual's neurotic, psychotic, or perverse structure is incurable per se (Dor, 1997). What psychoanalysis can hope to achieve is to assist the individual in articulating the truth of his or her own desire. That would be the goal of treatment. However, such truth does not exist a priori in the individual who comes to analysis, nor is it a "knowledge" that the analyst holds and can impart. This truth is constructed in analysis, and it is the construction of this truth, and the articulation of the subject's desire, that constitutes the analytic work. If the analysis is successful, the individual is not cured of an illness but is, to a certain extent, liberated from the desire of the other, a desire that is represented in the subject's rigid and automatic adherence to the structural patterns that were imposed upon him or her by the other.

The beginning of an analysis consists of a series of preliminary interviews that are conducted face to face with no particular time limit (Lacan, 1991). In these interviews the potential analysand is encouraged to freely express thoughts and feelings, while the analyst listens for the possibility of an analysis. The question of diagnosis (structure), although important, is placed on hold because it can only be articulated over time, in the actual course of treatment. For Lacan, the clinical (e.g., symptomatic) presentation of a patient can be very deceiving, and no menu of symptoms and signs can enable the analyst to make a diagnosis that is relevant to the psychoanalytic work. Any "diagnosis" that is made early in the course of the analysis is a presumptive one that can be, and often is, altered as the analysis progresses. As the patient (Linda) begins to articulate her complaints, her speech also determines the production of a symptom, which repeats and represents her basic "position" vis-à-vis an other, in this case, the analyst. By coming to understand the basic position of the analysand with respect to the analyst, a diagnosis is eventually achieved. Such diagnosis articulates an understanding of the analysand's basic position in her relationship to an other, whether this position is neurotic, psychotic, or perverse, and if neurotic, whether hysteric, obsessive, or phobic.

As the analyst listens to Linda's speech, particularly in the initial interviews during which she attempts to say why she is seeking treatment, the analyst creates a series of clinical hypotheses regarding Linda's position as a subject and the connection between this position and the emergence of her symptoms. Symptoms, like dreams and other formations of the unconscious, are regarded as substitutions. Thus the symptom is not an index of pathology, nor does it have any psychological or psychiatric value per se; its significance is only defined by its value in the speech of the subject (Fink, 1995). For Lacan (1981), as for Freud, symptoms are overdetermined and are linked to the subject's primary process via condensation and displacement. Further, a symptom is a "message addressed to an Other" and is a means that the subject has for saying something about herself. Moreover, symptoms are a source of satisfaction for the patient, and this is a major reason why individuals do not readily relinquish them. For these reasons, defining a "disorder" through a symptom or a cluster of symptoms (as in the *Diagnostic and Statistical Manual of Mental Disorders, 4th Edition, Text Revision*) is not helpful to a psychoanalyst. The same symptom can have radically different significance for different subjects. The question of meaning is always at stake, and the meaning of a given symptom is unique for each patient because it is entirely a product of the subject's own fantasies. Further, the significance of a given symptom, like the meaning of a given word, can never be said to be fixed (Lemaire, 1977). This is an inherent feature of the symbolic relationship between words and objects. As linguists such as De Saussure have pointed out, the meaning of a given word or sign (or symptom) is continuously in motion and is determined by the context and the mechanisms of metaphor and metonymy. For this reason, it is difficult to pin down a particular signification of a patient's symptom, word, or act, and is why psychoanalysts place such importance on the technique of free association. The meaning of the patient's symptom slides through condensation and displacement from word to word, reminding us of the relationship between present conflicts and primary repression.

As the interviews take place, the transference with the analyst is also at work. The transference not only expresses something about the analysand's demand for an analysis but also helps create a hypothesis about the psychic structure of the patient. Once it is determined that analysis is indeed appropriate, a contract is established and the number of weekly sessions determined, according to how the analyst wants to direct the treatment. A patient may initially need "to speak" several times a week or twice in the same day just to get the treatment started. After the preliminary sessions, the analysis is conducted on the couch, unless it has been determined that the patient is psychotic. The patient, as in a classical psychoanalysis, is asked to adhere to the fundamental rule of free association. The analyst's sole task is to direct the process of free association (not the patient) and to get the process going again when it becomes stuck (Evans, 1996). It is this process, and not any "treatment" or "therapy" on the part of a "doctor" that enables the analysand to articulate his or her own desire and achieve the measure of liberation from the desire of the other that analytic treatment affords.

ESSENTIAL SKILLS OR ATTRIBUTES

As I have discussed, the neurotic analysands (patients) are the ones who do the work in analysis; they are the ones who analyse, and the task of the analyst is simply to help them in the process. In this process, the analyst is not passive but is an active listener who must be in tune with what the analysand is trying to communicate through words, symptoms, and actions, including acting-out behaviors. The analyst assists the patient by reflecting back those "words" that are essential to the patient's fundamental fantasy. While the analyst has no a priori knowledge of the patient's desire, the analyst must (paradoxically) become, for the patient, "the place of the supposed knowledge" and also "a place of desire." As long as the patient attributes knowledge to the analyst about his or her condition and suffering, this will promote the patient's desire to continue the analytic process. In order to achieve this, the analyst always must remain incognito for the patient. The analyst must be an enigma in order to keep the analytic process moving forward. It is an important effect of the analytical work and the transference when the patient keeps thinking, "What does my analyst know that I don't? What does she want from me? What is it that she sees that I cannot see?" It is important to point out that, contrary to the vogue in certain American psychoanalytic circles, the analyst is decidedly *not* a model for the patient, nor does the analyst point to the possibility of the patient's adaptation to the environment. Further, the real person of the analyst, that is, his or her own desire as a subject, is not pertinent to the work of the analysand. The notion of the analyst as a role model figure actually creates, in Lacanian terms, a new "imaginary identification" that perpetuates a failure of the analysand to articulate his or her own desire. It is noteworthy that for Lacan, identifications always occur at the imaginary level, and thus the ego is considered an imaginary formation rather than a symbolic one (Lacan, 1991). This position has important consequences in the conceptualization of the ego as the seat of good judgment and reality testing. On the contrary, it is the proper wish of the analyst (what Lacan called "the ethics of psychoanalysis") for his or her patients to arrive at their own truth, a truth that is completely different from that of the analyst. This is why the analyst should, to put it in simple terms, get out of the way of the patient's associations. Interpretations should be delivered only sparely, and when overdone or without a proper foundation, they serve only to produce resistance in the analysand and acting-out behavior. In order to achieve the appropriate position with respect to patients, it is absolutely imperative that the analyst undergo analytic treatment, not only for the analyst's own personal development but in order to explore the very desire to be an analyst.

It is important to underline that when working with psychosis, the position of the analyst is quite different. The analyst cannot be positioned as an enigma for the psychotic patient because this position would only encourage the development of paranoid ideation. Analysts working with such patients should not encourage free association or the use of the analytic couch. This is why an appropriate (psychoanalytic) diagnosis must be made with regard to all so-called borderline patients. For a Lacanian, such patients are fundamentally either psychotic or neurotic (hysteric), and an appropriate diagnosis will determine the very course of the analysis.

THERAPEUTIC GOALS

It should be noted that Linda's initial reason for seeing a psychologist, the so-called referral question, appears to be limited to obtaining a psychological evaluation to be used by her attorney in the service of a possible psychiatric defense to the legal problems she is facing in connection with a car accident. As such, we have no information, as of yet, that the patient is interested in an analytic treatment or even a treatment relationship. If and when the question of an analysis does arise, it will inevitably do so in the context of the initial forensic referral. This is important because it relates to the patient's motivation and insight regarding the possibility of analysis. If the relationship with the psychologist is (at least initially) governed by the desire of her lawyer to obtain evidence for a psychological defense (which may or may not be desired by the patient), then Linda's position at the start of analysis has been determined and must be carefully considered in assessing the possibility of analysis. Certain psychologists may be of the view that a psychological intervention in the legal process is therapeutic for the patient in and of itself, and in such cases a favorable resolution of the legal situation becomes the primary goal of any psychological intervention. However, this can hardly serve as the basis for a course of analytic treatment. If the sole desire of the patient is to obtain a forensic evaluation and nothing else, then there is little if any hope of establishing an adequate transference, and the process of speaking and discovery that characterizes a subject in analysis will never begin. However, one must not always take the patient at his or her word about motives for seeking a consultation. Clearly, most of us (not only Linda), when meeting an analyst for the first time, are unclear about whether we are ready to engage in analytic work and take the risk of structural change. Why bring a symptom into question when it is serving an important adaptive function and when it is such a source of (unconscious) pleasure? Therefore, the reasons that Linda might express for consulting an analyst ("getting rid of this legal problem") need not be of particular concern for the analyst, since each analysand enters analysis through another's desire disguised as his or her own. What is important is the way the analyst listens to the words of the patient and encourages the desire to speak. How does Linda relate the car incident? What words does Linda select in speaking to the other, the analyst? It is noteworthy that the initial encounter with the analyst in this case will be marked by a fantasy of the analyst representing or intervening with the law. The analyst must listen to how Linda thinks of herself in this encounter with authority and how she positions herself in this encounter because this will be prognostic regarding the very possibility of an analysis in her case. Linda's complaints have been characterized as a relinquishing of personal responsibility and a concomitant shift of responsibility onto the other. This understanding of Linda's desire in the "hands of the other" already tells us something about the position she has taken in relation to the world and how she might position herself for her analyst (the worthless person, the victim of the other's actions, the vanquished older daughter usurped by her younger siblings' more important lives). Linda describes her own state of being as "empty" and states that "there is nothing in my life." She further states that she is easily angered and feels jumpy and anxious. She describes herself as crying frequently and partaking in solitary activities such as reading, watching television, and taking care of her plants. Although her superficial motivation for therapy appears to be "to get this legal thing off my back," the main goal at the beginning of her treatment would be an initial exploration of what might be termed "the quest for the subject's desire," the careful listening for a place in her discourse that differs from what she had to be for the other. If the analyst can listen for something that belongs to Linda, then the establishment of the transference guarantees a "listening ear," one that the patient has likely never experienced from herself or anyone else. The absence of meaningful listening is not likely to be rooted in her everyday reality or the callousness of those who surround her; rather, it is a function of her own mode of speech, which closes off the other.

Some clinicians may call the careful listening I am describing "a supportive therapeutic environment." However, although it is indirectly supportive, such listening is not intended to foster the illusion that the patient is not responsible for her words and actions. Indeed, such analytic listening is a means of reflecting Linda's responsibilities back to her. The analyst does not pose a diagnosis, theorize, forecast, or prescribe a treatment when there is no desire for one. To conclude, the main goal for this patient is to "stir up her own desire," to make her speak, to allow her to say a lot more about her anxiety. The analyst should not be carried away with interpretations or explanations, which may only reinforce obsessive defenses; on the contrary, the analyst should allow Linda to express what is at the root of her fundamental fantasy.

FURTHER INFORMATION NEEDED

The structure of treatment is not based on a predetermined model that can be applied to each individual who presents with the symptoms of a severe personality disorder. The patient must determine the structure of the treatment discourse directed to "someone who listens" (the analyst). The first necessary step is the establishment of the transference, which occurs when the patient (Linda) knows or believes that she has been heard, in other words, that there is "an echo of her own words." This idea is the basis for what Lacan regards to be the basic goal and value of the transference: establishing the analyst's role as the place of the supposed knowledge (Lacan, 1953). Once the patient attributes knowledge to the Other (in this case, the analyst), the transference is under way and the patient's desire for treatment truly established. The analysand's belief that the analyst "knows" something that the analysand does not know is the motor of the treatment and results in the patient's desire to keep returning to what, for the patient, is an enigmatic situation. However, it is important for the analyst to deal with the transference in a particular way. The analysand's perception that the analyst is the site of knowledge must not be used by the analyst as a license to provide suggestions, modeling, or interpretations. Indeed, in Lacanian work, interpretations generally are rarely made and are hardly ever addressed to the feelings or thoughts that the patient has toward the analyst. Although Lacanians understand quite well that aspects of the patient's old and current relationships will be transferred onto the analysis, they need to let the patient work with and through these issues, rather than close the path of the patient's associations with interpretations. In place of interpretation, Lacanians typically utilize a technique known as "punctuation," repeating a certain word or phrase used by the patient or ending a session on a particular thought or affect. The overuse of interpretation runs the risk of sliding over into suggestion, which, again, only reinforces the patient's willingness to have the other retain responsibility for his or her desire.

The course of treatment, particularly in a case such as Linda's, will depend on the degree and frequency of her acting out and her initial response to the treatment itself. Certain interventions in the real life of the patient may be necessary. For example, Linda may need to contact the analyst frequently or may need two sessions in one day from time to time, according to her need to put in words what she is feeling and thinking. By providing Linda with these additional opportunities for speech, the analyst also ensures that Linda's tendency to act out may well diminish. Lacanians are quite flexible regarding the scheduling and length of treatment sessions. In Linda's case, the analyst might choose to schedule a 10-minute phone call or two short sessions. It is important to emphasize that while the patient must assume responsibility for verbalizing in sessions, the analyst never grants the patient license to structure the treatment. The analyst both controls the length and frequency of sessions and sets certain other parameters and limitations as necessary.

Most therapists who work with patients with acting-out behaviors and intense affect understand the burden and responsibility involved in such treatments. However, in working with such individuals, it is absolutely necessary that the analyst be committed to the process of analysis, to be there for the patient, and to be resolute in encouraging and strengthening the transference. In this regard, an approach that varies the number and length of sessions may appear quite unorthodox (at least to other psychoanalysts); however, it may be important to carry the patient for some time in this way in order to sustain the treatment and the possibility of the patient's psychic restructuring. For a Lacanian analysis, no other tools are necessary than the ones just described. The gathering of information, per se, and the collection of data may be useful methodologies in research, but in the psychoanalytic situation each moment is unique and defined by the established relationship between analyst and patient and the patient's choice of words at the time (Evans, 1996). While the analyst certainly learns much from experiences with various cases, he or she must remember that one cannot generalize from one case or type of case to another. The belief that one can do so only robs the analysand of his or her individuality, and responsibility and creates a further stumbling block to the realization of the patient's own desire.

Case studies like Linda's are most useful when the data from the sessions, or at least the initial sessions, are available for the analyst's study. The words of the patient, as I have emphasized, are really the only (most) valuable tool in psychoanalysis. The narrative of a case based on facts, symptoms, and already-interpreted material, although useful as an illustrative tool, is less helpful to the understanding and transmission of the psychoanalytic technique. While it is true that analysts have learned greatly from Freud's case studies and those of other theorists, when data are taken from the patient's speech and/or the sessions are recorded directly, the transmission of psychoanalysis can be more accurately achieved. The words of the analyst and analysand occur in that instantaneous moment, which is singular and specific for those two people at that time.

CONCEPTUALIZATION OF PATIENT

According to Lacanian theory, psychic causality cannot be unequivocally determined. This is not only due to the fact that symptoms and behavior are always overdetermined but also because of the lack of predictable, fixed psychological laws. As such, the conceptualization of an individual's dynamics and personality structure is always a risky and approximate enterprise, one that is continually subject to revision. Further, there is never a direct, airtight connection between behavior, affects, and symptoms on the one hand and dynamic and personality functioning on the other. For example, based on the case description, we might hypothesize that Linda is a psychopath. She takes no responsibility for the car accident, never empathizes with the feelings of the victims, and when asked about the accident states she "lightly bumped them to give them the message." Further, she states that "the old people were trying to get away with making money out of me." Yet it certainly would be rash, and in all likelihood an error, to conceptualize this case as a psychopathic personality. Many other personality traits appear to be present, including sadistic traits, obsessional traits, hysterical symptoms, as well as well-articulated phases of appropriate behavior. Further, Linda's expressed affects are not necessarily helpful from a diagnostic point of view. When Freud studied the process of repression in a neurotic, he came to the conclusion that repression does not apply to the affect but to the ideational representation of the symptom. Thus, affects, along with intellectual statements, are not particularly good indicators in the work of analysis (Freud, 1911). The tears of a patient may reflect different aspects of a particular problem than her verbalizations might suggest. In fact, Lacan understood affects (like intellectualization) as a resistance to analysis, specifically a resistance to articulating the symbolic dimension of the patient's suffering through language. This aspect of Lacanian thought provides further insight into the nature of psychoanalytic treatment itself, which is viewed by Lacan not as a place to ventilate feelings or to arrive at an intellectual understanding but as a place where the patient articulates his or her truth.

It is therefore difficult and risky to assess an individual's personality on the basis of her reported feelings, thoughts, and symptoms. A diagnostic picture will emerge primarily through a careful listening to the patient's choice of words and noting where he or she fails to verbalize, rather than through the content (thoughts, affects) of her discourse.

In Linda's case, it is clear from her educational background and the number of years that she has worked as a teacher that she has a fair understanding of how reality works. Yet her cognitions, her understanding of herself, and her belief systems are all colored by her internal experience of herself, as is demonstrated fully in her acting out, which is a way of speaking when words fail to reach the other.

In spite of the preceding caveats, I will present several hypotheses regarding the case that remain at a hypothetical or, at best, presumptive level. It is noteworthy that in her initial presentation, Linda gives the impression of someone who is always in "a state of urgency"—unable to wait, pushed by her anxiety into a confrontation with others—to the point where she is able to act out her aggressiveness if the "waiting period" becomes intolerable. Her inability to "make a pause," to delay the satisfaction of her needs, is not so much the reflection of a cognitive or emotional style but evidence of the presence of an infantile mode of functioning that characterizes her behavior. The implications of this hypothesis are, in a Lacanian view, directly related to the vicissitudes of her primary relationship with her mother and the role of the paternal function in the economy of the triangular relationship between the parents (or images of the parents) and child. Lacan follows Freud in holding that it is this Oedipal process that conditions the subject's fundamental fantasy, desire, and sexual identity. As thinking about the Oedipal situation is no longer fashionable even for those who regard themselves as psychoanalysts, the Lacanian position regarding this process should be reviewed and emphasized.

For Lacan, the first phase or "time" of the Oedipus complex occurs in the context of what he terms the *imaginary* level of existence. In this phase, the "other" is the mother, and the child is initially involved in a relationship with her in which the child comes to recognize himself "somewhere else," beyond himself: in the mirror or in the mother's gaze. If the child is someone, it is only because he is someone for his mother (Lacan, 1998a). This position of total dependence leads the child to believe that his satisfaction is tied to the place he occupies for his mother, and as such he wants to be everything for her, to be "that which she desires," her complement and fulfillment. This is the realm of primary narcissism, in which the child, having no representation of himself, is a blank slate for the mother to *have*. According to Lacan, any attitude of the mother that will favor her possession of the child will alienate the child from his own subjectivity.

Although it appears that there is a dyad functioning between mother and child, there is already a triangle between the mother, the child, and this third factor which is initially represented simply as *that which the mother lacks*, which Lacan terms the *phallus*. For Lacan, the phallus is not to be confused with the biological organ, but is rather simply a representation of what the mother lacks or desires. In identifying himself with the phallus, the child is simply trying to satisfy the mother's desire and, in effect, be everything for her. Lacan regards the presence of the imaginary phallus as the third term in this early stage of the Oedipus complex, indicating that even here the imaginary father is already functioning, representing that object which the mother desires beyond the child (unless the mother implies that the child is indeed occupying that place, which means she does not "lack anything"). Therefore, there is never a dual relationship per se. In this stage, the prohibition of the father already operates over both, mother and son/daughter. With the strong emergence of sexual impulses in the growing child (infantile masturbation), anxiety in the child increases. As a result, the child is filled with feelings of impotence and confusion.

In the second phase of Oedipus, there is an intervention by what Lacan refers to as the "symbolic father." According to Lacan, if the father is to be recognized by the child, the mother, who acts as a sort of gatekeeper to the child, must first recognize the father's speech (Lacan, 1977). It is speech alone that gives a privileged function to the father, not the recognition of his role in procreation. This is the function of the father, in Lacan's terms, the Name-of-the-Father. With the introduction of the Name-of-the-Father, the child has entered the symbolic order. Lacan refers to the power of heterogeneity, which is the basis of the symbolic order, as opposed to the power of homogeneity, the fusion with the mother that occurs in the imaginary order. The father's speech denies the mother access to the child as a phallic object and forbids the child complete access to the mother. This intervention, which is called "castration" in psychoanalytic theory, has an implication of privation. However, while the father is the apparent instrument of this privation, it can only operate via the mediation of the mother. The mother's acknowledgment of the father's presence enables the father to occupy the third position in the Oedipal triangle in which the child sees the father as a rival for the mother's desire. This is called the phase of separation (Lacan, 1998a).

The third phase or "time" of Oedipus is marked by the real intervention of the father who signals to the child what he can and cannot have. Lacan discusses that the father, in introducing to the child the law of the symbolic order, relieves the child of the anxiety associated with occupying the place of the phallus for the mother. He can thus identify with the father and transcend the aggresivity inherent in his imaginary identifications. This is what Lacan calls the "normative function of the Oedipus complex" because it introduces a Law and a difference regarding the child and his parents, as well as introducing the norm of sexual difference. If, the child does not accept the Law, or if the mother does not recognize the position and speech of the father, the child will remain identified with the phallus and continue to be subjected to his mother's desire. If, on the contrary, the child does accept this Law, he identifies with the father, who, in the child's mind, possesses the phallus. In this way, the father reinstates the phallus as the object of the mother's desire, but the child is no longer identified with it.

According to Lacan, this process allows the child to give and receive in a full sexual relationship and to also have a Name, which for Lacan constitutes a place in a family constellation that promotes the realization of the self through participation in the world of culture, language, and society.

Thus for Lacan, castration is understood in both a negative (limiting) and positive sense. The negative aspect enforces the prohibition of incest, and the positive aspect ensures the child's inscription in the generational order of a family and society. Castration is not the fear of losing the penis but the symbolic operation that cuts the imaginary bond between mother and child and grants the child (boy or girl) the ability to symbolize this loss in words. This Law is not proper to the father; it is actually inscribed in language that was already present before any of the participants in the Oedipal triangle were born. Obviously, the child's parents also had to experience the situation of loss with their own mothers. When Lacan discusses the "father," he does not generally refer to the real father but to the one who implements the paternal function, a function that could be carried out by an uncle, a friend, another female, or even an institution.

For Lacan, diagnosis and personality are a function of the position that the individual ultimately assumes within the Oedipal struggle. If the Name-of-the Father is operative and the child is inserted within the symbolic order, then psychosis will be averted and the individual will be defined largely by the neurotic (hysteric, obsessive, etc.) fundamental fantasy that he has with regard to his or her relationship to the other. If the Name-of-the Father does not operate, the child will never fully be inserted into the culture and symbolic order, language and law will not function, and the individual's psychic structure will remain at the psychotic level. On the other hand, should the mother lead the child into the belief that he can actually be the phallus for her, the child will think of himself as his own law, and a perverse structure will result. These diagnostic considerations evolve as treatment progresses and can only be fully explored through numerous analytic sessions.

Returning to the current case, the issue of aggressiveness in Linda's life, her rage, and the attached fantasies are suggestive of a less-than-adequate separation from the mother's desire (Oedipal phases one and two). We may hypothesize here that Linda was left at the mercy of a strong, controlling mother who did not find any desire in her husband but satisfied herself only in her role of a mother. The child who remains exclusively as an object of satisfaction for the mother experiences a constant tension as the child struggles to establish his or her own identity. If the child is unable to escape from a "devouring mother," as appears to be true for Linda, she remains trapped, horrified by the possibility of being devoured. This fear prompts an aggressive response and the sense that one must fight for one's very existence and identity. In order to be, Linda has to fight by using the language of aggression (the language of enmeshed, imaginary relations) rather than the true language of dialogue (communication between two actually separate subjects). She acts aggressively toward her husband, her colleagues, and her neighbors in order to establish herself. Consequently, people respond to her by avoiding, abandoning, or rejecting her. Linda's discourse generally appears to be characterized by mistrust and extreme dependence toward others (again characteristic of her primary relation with the mother), and this sets in motion a paranoid style of relations with the ones she loves and the world at large. People want to hurt her, nobody loves her, and the school where she works is "loading her with garbage."

Had Linda remained fixated in the desire of the mother with no intervention by the Name-of the-Father, she may well have developed a psychotic structure. However, in her case, the Name-of-the-Father appears to have operated, and while she remains trapped by issues of "separation/individuation," she indeed has a tenuous hold on the symbolic order. On this point, Lacanians may differ from the other psychoanalytic theorists in terms of the vicissitudes of the later Oedipal phase (time three). This process comes into play regardless of the resolution of the earlier phases, resignifying and at times altering the nature of the maternal attachment. The emphasis here is on the structural effect of the Oedipal moment and the effect of the Name-of-the-Father operating "retroactively" on the primary attachments and thus upon all imaginary relations, involving the formation of the child's separate identity. Therefore, any pre-Oedipal events are resignified by the Oedipal process and reinterpreted in the light of this new development.

POTENTIAL PITFALLS

The most difficult hurdle in Linda's case would involve the beginning of, and even the possibility of, analytic treatment, as discussed above. However, further difficulties are likely to evolve as the transferential relationship becomes established and projected primary relations are experienced toward the figure of the analyst. On the one hand, fantasies of being devoured by the analyst and a tendency to push the analyst away and constantly argue are likely to alternate with excessive demands upon the analyst and moments of desperation in which Linda may experience an instant need for the analyst. However, these challenges to the treatment process are also the very content of the treatment itself, and Linda's articulation of and curiosity about them will provide the impetus to restructuring her mode of relating both to herself and to the world. The analyst must remain constant, always present, encouraging the patient to talk, and sustaining her through the rough periods that will be frequent at the beginning of the analysis. Although it is very likely that Linda will complain that the analyst does not like her, or likes her less than other patients, and will even attempt to destroy the analytic relationship, the analyst must sustain her and quietly refuse to confirm the expectation of rejection that has characterized her life (her father, mother, husband, parents of students).

In order to sustain the analytic process, the analyst must ask Linda about her sense of urgency (which drives everyone away from her) to determine what makes her feel always in a hurry. The analyst must question Linda in order to elicit her fantasies surrounding this urgency rather than judge or even interpret this behavior. As long as Linda is able to speak about her fantasies, the possibility of acting out diminishes, and the analysis will progress.

Potential problems can arise because the patient's presentation is confusing, her affect is intense, her aggression is patent, and her demands are unreasonable. As such, the analyst may be thrown into a state of chaos regarding the treatment, bringing the whole topic of the "borderline" concept to the surface. Applying the "borderline" label to the patient may serve as a justification for the analyst to limit his or her expectations for the treatment, to determine that the therapy should involve modeling and "ego building techniques," or to reject this patient altogether.

One other potential pitfall in this analysis is likely to appear in working with Linda regarding her disorganized libidinal and aggressive cathexis. These are likely to manifest in sexual and aggressive fantasies that may be experienced as intolerable to both Linda and the analyst. It is important that the analyst, through careful but insistent questioning, elicit this material by providing an environment in which these fantasies can emerge and be tolerated rather than be avoided by either patient or analyst because of their primitive and uncomfortable qualities. It is important that these fantasies do not remain underground in the treatment. Typically, these mixed sexual and aggressive fantasies reflect the nature of the patient's Oedipal vicissitudes, which, although occurring subsequent to the phase of maternal attachment, come to resignify retrospectively the primary love object: the mother.

PROGNOSIS FOR ADAPTIVE CHANGE

As described above, Lacanians do not give credence to the concept of mental health or normality but, like Freud, hold that human beings exist in varying degrees of disease, not as a result of any organic malfunction but as a result of the very conditions of social life. "Strengthening of the ego," "adaptation to reality," and "happiness" are all, in the Lacanian view, misguided treatment goals that can interfere with the analytic process. *Adaptation* is a term from biology that refers to organisms that adapt to fit their environment (Evans, 1996). This concept was adopted by ego psychology and applied to psychoanalysis, which was inherited by American psychoanalysis after many European analysts immigrated to the United States. I want to elaborate on this concept, which represents a major difference between the most important current of psychoanalysis in America and Lacanian theorists.

As already indicated, the aim of psychoanalytic treatment is to lead Linda to articulate her "own truth" about her desire. To that end, during the course of treatment she will experience "a shedding of the identifications" with parental imagos through which she was functioning according to *their* desire. So-called ego building techniques, designed to facilitate adaptation, actually work in the opposite direction of the analytic treatments because they encourage new identifications, which again lead patients away from the truth of their own desires.

The method of analytic work is that of Socratic questioning, understood as a deep inquiry without foreknowledge of where that inquiry will lead. The analyst never answers either his own or his patient's questions, not because he or she wants to refuse the answer but because, in spite of the analysand's inevitable and even necessary belief that the analyst holds the truth, the analyst does not know the answer. Only Linda's unconscious would put in motion the sequence of words and meanings that will enable the question to be answered in a manner that will permit the analytic work to proceed.

Lacanian psychoanalysis regards as a myth the idea of an adapted and integrated personality where particular affects, cognitions, and behaviors are catalogued and labeled in a hierarchical order in terms of their health, adaptation, and level of severity. In part, I believe, this is a misconception of Kernberg's (1975) conceptualization of the border-line personality organization. Symptom presentation cannot guarantee a diagnosis. Further, the question of diagnosis should be postponed until much later, when the patient is well on her way in her analytic experience and the transference is fully established.

Lacan follows a tradition in French philosophy that regards the ego as an objectified phenomenon that is outside of and alienated from the human subject. For Lacan, the ego is, above all, a construct produced by "the gaze of the other," and is not in any way the seat of subjectivity, judgment, reality testing, or the like, that it has become in ego-psychology. It is, rather, a narcissistic construction utilized by the subject to provide him- or herself with a false and alienating sense of coherence and value (Lemaire, 1977).

Lacan's critique of ego-psychology is of significance for a "deconstruction" of the borderline concept as it appears within ego-psychology and object-relations theory. According to Lacan, the young child enters a "mirror stage," during which he acquires a sense of the totality of his own body. This is achieved, however, only by way of narcissistic identification with others' bodies, which the child sees as being like his own. This identificatory process establishes a fundamental alienation of the subject in the other and leads to the subject's chronic misrecognition of itself. In fact, the child identifies with an optical image of himself rather than his own subjectivity (Lacan, 1998a).

According to Lacan, it is because of this alienating identification with an image outside of oneself that misrecognition becomes the fundamental characteristic of the ego (Lacan, 1991). Far from being the governing agency of the subject or self as it is in ego-psychology, the ego, for Lacan, is a snare and an illusion. While ego-psychologists hold that by analyzing defenses they permit the ego to recover its discerning abilities and adapt to external reality, Lacan holds the opposite view, namely, that the ego is the psychic representative not of the reality principle but of an "imaginary reality" (Lacan, 1966). The ego is trapped in the fundamental division of an alienated subject, who is unable to understand why reality constantly disappoints him. This misrecognition also has profound implications in the realm of language and speech. We have a mistaken belief that we know what we are saying when we speak, but we speak about a self that is fundamentally alienated and displaced. As the ego is the "other," an identification with the ego leads to an acceptance of the desires of the other at the expense of the true desire of the subject or self. In elevating this misrecognition, ego-psychology furthers a program of identification with the analyst and "adaptation," which is at complete odds with the radical, liberating nature of psychoanalysis. Lacan recognizes that misrecognition serves an adaptive function as the instinct of survival does for the animal. However, this adaptive function is at the expense of the subject's own truth.

TIMELINE

Initially, the number of sessions will be determined by a contract between analyst and patient. However, the analyst must be flexible regarding the number and duration of sessions, based not on the demand of the patient but on serving the progress of the treatment. The issue of time in Lacanian theory is crucial. The following general account of the way Lacanian analysts work using the so-called short session should help clarify the atemporality of the analytic process.

According to Lacan, chronological time has no meaning in analytic work. The actual events in objective time are not analytically meaningful until they are signified, understood, and resignified by the patient. Further, the actual length of the analytic session is also unimportant. The words exchanged in 5 minutes may be enough for a patient to open a new chain of signifiers. An interruption or "punctuation" may be necessary at that moment so that the patient does not leave the session before he or she can close the chain, thereby avoiding the "homework" that a genuine opening to the unconscious would entail. After a well-timed and appropriately punctuated session, the analysand will continue to produce new associations and elaborations between sessions and return to treatment having worked on material that will be very productive for the following session. Indeed, it is often the case that when an analyst, by rule or habit, automatically extends a session to 45 minutes, an initially promising chain of associations can be lost in a torrent of words that confuse both patient and analyst to the point that neither retains any real grasp of what they were working on.

Lacan (1953) wrote that the "formations" of the unconscious (dreams, parapraxis, symptoms) follow a logical rather than a temporal sequence. This "logical time" of unconscious processes has nothing to do with objective time. Although words are articulated in a temporally ordered fashion, their significance is not temporally ordered in a literal sense.

In relating his or her history in treatment, the patient presents the facts and events that occurred during the patient's life, emphasizing what he or she believes to be important for the treatment (usually the suffering related to the symptom). This narrative constitutes the patient's psychic reality. Regardless of what occurred objectively (if such a concept ever makes sense), what matters is the analysand's psychic experience. At a certain moment in the session, the patient might say something that the analyst wants to question or have further elaborated. A new chain of words (or signifiers) is produced that resignify the former experience. When the patient comes in the next session, having done his "working through" outside of the session (the "moment" of understanding), he may return to the words he spoke, and the exchange with the analyst may shift to a different point of view. As a result of analysis, the patient has constructed a new logical discourse regarding something that at one point had a different meaning.

In the history of psychoanalysis, the duration of a 45-minute session had the goals of maintaining neutrality and of equalizing the relationship with the analyst with all patients. It also ensured that the analysand would have an allotted space and time for bringing material into treatment and receiving the analyst's undivided attention. Further, the strict timing and duration of sessions ensured that any deviation would become a potential topic for interpretation of the patient's conflicts, resistance to analysis, transference, and the like. In practical terms, the 45-minute session has also evolved into a convenient means for maintaining the analyst's schedule and, to a somewhat lesser degree, the patient's schedule. Lacanian analysts have challenged and reworked these assumptions about therapeutic time. In the Lacanian framework, sessions are as long as necessary, sometimes shorter and sometimes longer than 45 minutes' duration. As such, the chances are reduced that the patient will resist by burying important material with subsequent small talk or will avoid an important revelation by holding out until the (45-minute) session is over. The end of the session is neither arbitrary nor guided by real time. It is determined by logical or psychological time and by the workings of the analysand's speech. In this way, the analyst exerts a greater control over the analytic process than when analyst and analysand are limited by the artificial constraints of scheduled time (Lee, 1990).

SPECIFIC TECHNIQUES

I have already discussed the forms of listening, inquiry, punctuation, and management of the session used in Lacanian treatment. Beyond that, I would point out that Lacanian "technique" is, in large part, conditioned by a structuralist view of language and the unconscious. Lacanian theory borrows fundamental concepts about language functioning from the structural theory of linguistics that arose in the 20th century. Structuralism involves a novel manner of regarding objects and entities studied in the human sciences. Instead of defining such entities in terms of their inner or "essential" characteristics, structuralism situates them in the context of their relationships with other objects. It is the system of such relationships that defines a "structure" as a matter to be studied. Such structured relationships can be understood in terms of the laws or regularities implicit in the structure, which are initially difficult to grasp and articulate and most often go unnoticed by those individuals to whom the structure applies. For Lacan, the structures of the human psyche are linguistic in nature, and consist of metaphor and metonymy. Lacanian theory uses these concepts with the autobiographical narrative expressed by the patient, applying them to understand formations of the unconscious—dreams, slips of the tongue, and especially symptoms—in structural terms. Metaphor, according to Lacan, corresponds to the mechanism of "condensation" in the dreamwork and in symptom formation. Lacan (1953) also holds that psychological symptoms are, indeed, metaphors. According to Lacan, "identification" is also a metaphor, since identification always involves the substitution of oneself for the identified object (Lacan, Seminar XIII (1966)). Metonymy involves the chain of associations in language in accord with nonsemantic principles, such as sound or temporal association. For Lacan, the notions of metaphor and metonymy are the basic concepts for understanding the phenomena of the unconscious. Topics such as the primary process, dreams, the formation of the symptom, jokes, and all unconscious symptoms are understood in terms of these two axes of language. Even such psychotic phenomena as neologisms, glossolalia, and delusional language are metaphoric and metonymic formations (Dor, 1997). These notions of Lacanian technique have profound implications and explain why the patient's precise words are of such significance to the Lacanian analyst. Without necessarily delivering any interpretations, the Lacanian analyst listens for the metaphoric and metonymic discourse that underlies the patient's symptoms and other formations of the unconscious. Such listening permits the analyst to question and punctuate the patient's discourse in a manner that is productive for the patient's own reflective thought and understanding.

SPECIAL CAUTIONS

Apart from the necessity of providing additional sessions and phone contact in the early phases of treatment, I do not believe that any further "cautions" need be observed in working with Linda. The use of cautions itself requires questioning because it can lead to actions on the part of the therapist that, although they may at times be necessary, may undermine the patient's personal responsibility. Often analysts' own anxiety compels them to assume a greater sense of responsibility toward patients like Linda, who they perceive to be more fragile than others. At times, analysts feel they should be more careful in their interventions and, above all, be attentive to any kind of verbalization regarding self-injury or dangerous behavior toward others. In Linda's case, the analyst may feel particularly anxious because Linda's presenting problem involved an accident in which she appears to have deliberately caused injury. In addition, Linda's intensity may produce a wish on the part of the therapist to build a "wall" separating therapist from patient through the use of medication, hospital confinement, or the like. In Linda's case, two specific symptoms might be interpreted as requiring such special interventions, or at least a dramatic change in therapeutic technique. However, these behaviors, cognitions, and affects are common in many patients who are seen, with good results, in individual psychotherapy. One of Linda's symptoms that might indicate special attention involves the incidents of time loss that she experiences. She relates that she gets angry and then "spaces out." She describes being unable to account for several hours after listening to her mother talk about her sister and her sister's new baby. On other occasions, although without providing details, she acknowledges having the experience of spacing out after talking to her sister or mother on the phone. Immediately after these incidents, she finds herself smoking without memory of having gone to buy the cigarettes, and she cannot recall the number of cigarettes she smoked. From the descriptive point of view, the issue of a dissociative or even brief psychotic episode with a concomitant loss of reality testing may come to mind. The issue is what caution or change in techniques, if any, these symptoms should indicate. Should the symptoms be silenced through a medical or other intervention? Are we concerned that she may act out against herself or others during a dissociative episode? Or would we be of greater service to Linda by allowing her symptoms to speak, as it were, by questioning them instead of attempting to eliminate them. Rather than medicate, I would be inclined to follow a chain of associations. It is noteworthy that her symptom involves a repression of ideational content but is associated with maternal figures and with that which differentiates a man from a woman—the possibility of giving birth. These questions would be in my mind, if I were the analyst, since this patient has a history of a very demanding, suffocating mother who appears to have no desire for her husband. In fact, the question of frigidity is brought up by the father regarding his wife and the patient herself. The question of her sister's child not only brings to the surface an unresolved sibling rivalry but raises questions regarding Linda's own capacity to become a mother by having sex with a man. Another question comes to mind: What is the difference between a woman and a mother? In fact, they represent two distinct positions of a person. A woman claims her sexual desire and finds it satisfying. Yet, if the woman's desire is not directed toward her partner, then when she becomes a mother, there is a high risk that the child will occupy her whole world. Linda's solution to her conflict is first to repress and then to find an "oral solution": the smoking of the cigarettes. This oral response may point to the lack of resolution in the realm of privation (second phase of Oedipal complex), the time when the father intervenes in the relationship between mother and child, depriving the mother from using the child as her object of satisfaction and thereby both liberating the child to follow her own desire and channeling the mother's desire back to him. If this moment fails, or is tentative but unsuccessful, then the child will be engulfed in the mother's unfulfilled, all-powerful love and will develop significant rage, which serves not only to rebel but to separate. In fact, about the question of Linda's impulsive sexuality, pursuing strange men in bars, we find again this pattern of "trying to separate," in that there is no attachment to a man (they are strangers), and that is where sexual satisfaction is possible to be fulfilled. In the attachments, there is rage. In the absence of a relationship, there is safety—following the mandate of the words of her father: "Either men attack you or you attack them."

MEDICATION

I am inclined to refer patients for a psychiatric consultation only under very specific circumstances. One of these is the presence of clear and active psychosis. The other is when there is a direct expression of a suicidal wish accompanied by a suicidal plan, especially in the context of a history of prior suicide attempts or serious impulsivity. Many patients make suicidal gestures or threats that are mostly messages to the therapist and others, and, as I have already made clear, I am disinclined to either limit the patient's autonomy and responsibility in such circumstances or to bring a halt, even if temporary, to the analytic work in such cases. My general rule is to let the symptom and, moreover, the analysand continue to "speak" wherever possible. It is important to remember that suicidal words when spoken in the analytic context do not occur in a vacuum. They are directed to the analyst-listener and are often an important clue to the position of the analysand in the relationship to the other. Further, it is my experience that once the patient can speak about the symptom, the need for acting it out is deferred or disappears.

PATIENT STRENGTHS

The question of "strengths and weaknesses" arises from an ego-psychological or adaptive point of view that is quite alien to Lacanian psychoanalysis. Looking at patients from this perspective raises ethical problems for the Lacanian analyst, because it suggests that individuals can somehow be rated in terms of certain adaptative "standards" and societal norms. If we engage in the exercise of reading Linda's case from a strengths/weakness perspective, we might well end up with a list of at least 20 negative qualifiers (i.e., weaknesses) and at most a few positive descriptors regarding this patient. One reason why therapists tend to pathologize such patients and see them as riddled with negative traits and weaknesses, relates to the therapists' feelings of helplessness from the very start of the patients' treatment. In a way, the so-called borderline patient turns the tables on therapists more than any other patient. With a neurotic or a psychotic patient, the diagnostic picture is clearer, and therapists feel more in control. A patient like Linda confuses and disempowers therapists, who feel that their "knowledge" and "technique" are beginning to falter. Therapists keep trying different therapeutic approaches but continue to feel they have failed because of the self-imposed demand to "do something." The more they try to do, the more the patient will prove them wrong. Who is on the border now?

Some aspects of the case may appear to be weaknesses, but I would regard them as the very starting point of therapeutic work. One of these, perhaps the most interesting symptom in her case, is Linda's "spacing-out" experience. Insofar as this symptom represents a "dilemma" for this patient, it is, quite importantly, an experience that she herself finds questionable. Indeed, because of Linda's questions regarding this phenomenon, the diagnosis of psychosis proper can likely be eliminated (psychotics are certain about their experience and unable to doubt or question its veracity). I understand this "symptom" of nonaction as the signal of a powerful unconscious formation breaking through the surface of all Linda's rush-to-action modus operandi. What Linda and others may regard as a weakness in her ego is, from the point of view of analysis, her greatest strength because it constitutes both the material and the doubt with which psychoanalysis can begin. It is an experience that furthers exploration because it generates a certain wonder in both the analyst and (potential) analysand.

From my perspective, another of Linda's strengths is that she is the one child in her family who rebels against the values of her parents. Each of her siblings followed the paths laid down by their parents: Her sister married and pursued a career in nursing like her mother, and Linda's younger brother, a military police officer, is following the path of his father, who was himself a member of the Chicago police force. On the other hand, Linda appears to have been able to break certain familial traditions and attempt to find her own way in life. While these attempts have not, even by Linda's own standards, been successful, her desire for independence and a certain rebellion against parental norms can be regarded as potential agents for therapeutic change.

LIMIT-SETTING

An important goal of Lacanian analysis is that the analysand takes responsibility for his or her symptoms and behaviors. However, this is not a condition that the analyst can assume at the start because a subject that already had assumed such responsibility would presumably not require treatment. As such, it can be anticipated that the patient will act out against the analyst and the treatment, for example, by arriving late for sessions, missing sessions, withholding payment, and conducting herself in a myriad of other ways that are designed to undermine the analytic work. The analyst must, of course, address these issues, but must do so in a way that is consonant with the patient's own position and progress in treatment. The guiding principle is that the analyst sets those limits that ensure the continuance of the analytic work. Of course, there are occasions in which limits must be set that (at least temporarily) break off the analytic work (e.g., the hospitalization of a suicidal patient), but in general the analyst is always interested in maintaining the patient's interest in and desire for analysis. In this regard, Lacanian analysts tend to be somewhat more flexible than other psychoanalysts, utilizing limit-setting not as a vehicle for combating resistance, but rather as a means of punctuating it and causing a certain anguish and wonder in the analysand. Thus a patient who arrives late to session will only have his or her session curtailed if this makes sense within the treatment, and the analyst may well instruct such a patient to return later in the day or twice on another occasion. A patient who fails to pay the analyst's fee might, depending on the analyst's estimate of the origin of this behavior, have his or her fee lowered or raised as a strategic, punctuating response, which would then be explored in the treatment. (One analyst I know insists that all of her patients pay her in cash as a condition for the start of sessions, both as a means of ensuring payment and as a means of underlining the financial nature and value of the transaction in relation to the symptom). At all times, the guiding principle in setting limits is the maintenance and furthering of the analytic work; it is not a vehicle for instructing or counseling the patient on time or money management.

INVOLVEMENT OF SIGNIFICANT OTHERS AND HOMEWORK

Because the work of analysis does not occur exclusively or even primarily on the conscious level, the idea of a Lacanian analyst assigning specific homework to a patient is not viable. Nevertheless, the notion of homework is not completely alien to Lacanian treatment and, in fact, can be said to play a pivotal role in the analytic work. The analyst, by punctuating the in-session material (e.g., by cutting the session short just as the analysand achieves an important insight, experiences a significant affect, or asks a psychologically meaningful question) ensures that the patient will not bury this material in an avalanche of in-session verbalizations. Rather, such punctuation is intended to increase the likelihood that this material will be thought about, experienced, and worked through unconsciously between sessions, thereby producing new associative chains for the next session. By cutting the session short at a pivotal psychological moment, the likelihood is greatly increased that the analysand will, in the following session, reflect on the analytic work rather than begin anew with his or her inter-session life events. In this way the so-called short-session not only ensures that "homework" will be attended to, but also increases the continuity of the analytic process.

Patients often experience a sense of shock or surprise when the analyst makes such an intervention because they feel interrupted in their communication and frustrated by an apparent lack of interest on the part of the analyst. However, the patient's anguish engenders a certain wonder on his or her part regarding both the analyst's and the patient's own words, a puzzlement that prompts analytically relevant ideas and fantasies to evolve. Indeed, when analysis is working, most of the analytic work is conducted by the patient outside of session because the analysand returns to the point of punctuation to question herself and her experience. When this change occurs, it alters the structure of the analysand's speech in dramatic ways. Viewed in the Lacanian perspective, change is not a subtle, step-by-step behavioral process but an unconscious transformation that alters the way the subject acts and speaks in his or her everyday life (Evans, 1996).

TERMINATION ISSUES

In point of fact, the vast majority of psychoanalytic treatments break off or terminate prior to what might be called the end of analysis per se. The end of analysis is a complex topic beyond the scope of this chapter. Suffice it to say that analyses break off or are interrupted for many different reasons that are not signals that analytic work has ended or that any further work can be accomplished by the analysand on his or her own. Nevertheless, a broken-off treatment is not an unsuccessful project. Rather, it is typically an incomplete project, one that may well have engendered certain changes in the analysand's life that are structural in nature; that is, the analysand has shed certain malevolent identifications, and consequently the position of his or her desire has been altered with respect to relationships, personal expectations, and life goals. Although much more progress might well occur were the analysis to continue, I would not consider any significant time of analysis a failed task.

In a Lacanian analysis, the analyst assumes a major role in the maintenance of the analysis. This is not only because the analyst is the driving force of the transference and the place of supposed knowledge (which engenders the analysand's interest) but also because the analyst sustains a role that opposes identification and "cure" and instead provides a space that allows all the patient's own fantasies to be articulated in language. It is often the case that the analyst's own resistance, or failure to listen, results in an interruption or termination of the analysis. (Lacan, 1953).

The termination of analysis cannot be judged in "integrative" terms. As I have emphasized, the question for the analyst is not how to relate to or represent a good object for the patient. Neither is the goal to strengthen the patient's ego. In fact, the opposite may be more desirable. The ego of a neurotic is quite strong, and it is not the goal of analysis to reinforce the narcissistic condition of a strong ego. Rather, analysis is about an examination of differences, a falling apart of the former associations, a *demontage* or deconstruction of the neurotic economy of desire. Under no circumstances does it have to do with a synthesis or integration of parts of the personality.

Relapse prevention is a particular terminology that refers to a plan that a therapist has and shares with the patient supposedly to avoid the patient's acting-out or self-injurious behavior. The only preventive measure that an analyst can provide that is consistent with the psychoanalytic endeavor is the continued possibility of speech. It is through the articulation of conflict, fantasy, and ultimately desire that the analysand can forestall acting out such conflicts and avoid the formation of new symptoms.

MECHANISMS OF CHANGE

Change in psychoanalysis is initially marked by a change in the analysand's discourse. By this I do not mean a superficial change in the analysand's speech, in which she anticipates and mimics the analyst's expectations, but rather a change in discourse that signals an alteration of the subject's position with respect to her symptoms, behaviors, and relationships. In short, such a change in discourse is a marker of change in behavior and attitudes. The general vehicle for such change is the analytic situation, which permits the subject, for the first time, to fully articulate his or her desire. In Linda's case, her intolerance, sense of urgency, and inability to delay gratification are all neurotic expressions of a truncated way of being that is not rooted in her own desire. She lives her life as a "reacting being" and is unable to produce and experience an "interval" within which her own desire can appear as distinct from that of an other who she can understand as having his or her own desires and faults. In order to produce such an interval, Linda must come to experience a certain anguish as she confronts her own "lack of being" in response to questions that arise for her in the context of (the punctuated) analytic sessions.

As a result of her increased self-reflection, and the consequent development of anguish as she hears herself speak, Linda will come to take responsibility for her own symptoms. This is an important step on the road to her acquiring a sense of freedom from enslaving identifications. It is always important that the analysand "picks up the tab" for her own actions and behaviors. Typically, this is initially evident in the context of the transference with the analyst, but it will later appear in the individual's external relationships as well. While it is impossible to fully anticipate the course of an individual's own freedom, in Linda's case it might be expected that among the important markers of analytic progress would be a change in her perception and attitude regarding her role in the car accident and a new understanding of her role in both the loss of her marriage and the position of dependence she demands in her relationships with her family. In addition, Linda would likely work through certain issues pertaining to her sibling rivalry and the conflictual (Oedipal) issues in connection with her parents. The depth exploration and working through of such issues can alter the general quality of an individual's relationships. At this point, mechanisms outside the analytic session will likely fall into place. For example, as Linda's expectations of others change, she will likely receive a more positive response from them, engendering a feedback loop that will enhance her interpersonal satisfaction.

A changed attitude toward others will naturally follow as Linda de-identifies with them. One example of an identification of this sort appears to be reflected in Linda's subjectivity "trapped" in the place that her mother had unconsciously chosen for her (e.g., the mother has a temper tantrum if her husband shows up 15 minutes late for dinner). Consequently, Linda's primitive rage can be understood both as a result of her wanting to fulfill her mother's desire and a reaction against this want because she unconsciously recognizes it as her mother's rather than her own. We might surmise that this dynamic permeates everything Linda does. If Linda can articulate her own choices, her own desires, she will gain the possibility of liberating herself from such identifications and will be able to see both her parents and the others in her life as separate individuals with desires, projects, and values that are distinct from her own. This is the modicum of freedom that psychoanalytic treatment can achieve.

REFERENCES

American Psychiatric Association (2000). Diagnostic and Statistical Manual, (4th ed., text revision). Washington, D.C.: Author.

Dor, J. (1997). *The clinical Lacan.* (Judith Gurewich, Ed.). Northvale, NJ: Jason Aronson.

Evans, D. (Ed.). (1996). *An introductory dictionary of Lacanian psychoanalysis.* London and New York: Routledge.

Feher, G. J., & Tort, M. (1999). *Lacan and the new wave in American psychoanalysis.* New York: The Other Press.

Fink, B. (1995). *The Lacanian subject: Between language and jouissance.* Princeton, NJ: Princeton University Press.

Fink, B. (1996). *Readings I and II. Lacan's return to Freud.* Albany: State University of New York Press.

Fink, B. (1997). *A clinical introduction to Lacanian psychoanalysis: Theory and practice.* Cambridge, MA: Harvard University Press.

Freud, S. (1911/1953). *Formulations on the two principles of mental functioning* (Vol. 12). London: Hogarth Press.

Kernberg, O. (1975). *Borderline conditions and pathological narcissism.* New York: Jason Aronson.

Lacan, J. (1953). *Ecrits. A selection.* New York: W. W. Norton.

Lacan, J. (1959). *The ethics of psychoanalysis.* (D. Porter, Trans.). New York: W.W. Norton & Company, 1992.

Lacan, J. (1977). "The mirror stage as formative of the function of the I," in *Ecrits. A. Section.* W. W. Norton. New York, London. (Original work published in 1966).

Lacan, J. (1981). *The four fundamental concepts of psychoanalysis.* (J.-A. Miller, Ed., A. Sheridan, Trans.). New York: W. W. Norton. (Original work published in 1973).

Lacan, J. (1991). *The ego in Freud's theory and in the technique of psychoanalysis* (J.-A. Lacan, J. (1994). *El seminario XIII: El objecto del psicoanalisis.* Editorial Paidos, Buenos Aires, Argentina: (Original work published in 1994).

Miller, Ed., S. Tomaselli, Trans.). New York: W. W. Norton. (Original work published in 1955).

Lacan, J. (1998a). *El seminario de Jacques Lacan, libro 4: La relacion de objeto 1956–1957.* Buenos Aires, Argentina: Editorial Paidos.

Lacan, J. (1998b). *El seminario de Jacques Lacan, libro 5: Las formaciones del inconciente 1957–1958.* Buenos Aires, Argentina: Editorial Paidos.

Laplanche, J., & Pontalis, J. (1987). *Diccionario de Psicoanalisis* [Dictionary of Psycho-analysis]. Buenos Aires, Argentina: Editorial Labor.

Lee, S. J. (1990). *Jacques Lacan.* Amherst, MA: The University of Massachusetts Press.

Lemaire, A. (1977). *Jacques Lacan.* New York and London: Routledge.

10

Imagery Rescripting and Reprocessing Therapy

Mervin R. Smucker and Anne Boos

TREATMENT MODEL

The clinical application of imagery as a primary therapeutic agent has it roots in late 19th-century Europe. In his work at the Salpêtrière in Paris, Pierre Janet (1898) used a clinical procedure called "imagery substitution" to help hysterical patients replace their distressing images with calming images. Before 1900, Freud's application of imagery interventions was quite extensive; he wrote about the imagined scenes and spontaneous images that his patients perceived "with all the vividness of reality" (Breuer & Freud, 1895/1955, p. 53). Jung (1960) viewed mental imagery as a creative process of the psyche to be employed for attaining greater individual, interpersonal, and spiritual integration. Much of Jung's own clinical work involved helping patients to focus on their images and creative imagination as a vehicle for addressing their neurotic conflicts. More recently, a number of cognitive behavioral clinicians have elaborated on the clinical application of imagery as a means of modifying maladaptive cognitions and reframing disturbing events and their meanings (Anderson, 1980; A. Beck, Emery, & Greenberg, 1985; A. Beck, Freeman, & Associates, 1990; J. Beck, 1995; Edwards, 1990; Peterson, Prout, & Schwartz, 1991; Smucker & Dancu, 1999; Staton, 1990; Weis, Smucker, & Dresser, 2002).

Developed as an extension of Beck's cognitive therapy model of anxiety disorders (A. Beck, Emery, & Greenberg, 1985), imagery rescripting and reprocessing therapy (IRRT) is an imagery-focused, cognitive behavioral treatment originally developed for treating adult survivors of childhood trauma suffering from posttraumatic stress disorder (Smucker, Dancu, Foa, Niederee, 1995, 2002; Smucker & Niederee, 1995; Smucker & Dancu, 1999). IRRT focuses on identifying, confronting, and modifying the patient's distressing "hot" cognitions, which may be visual or verbal in nature. Although best known for its use in alleviating Axis I symptomatology (e.g., recurring flashbacks, repetitive nightmares, intrusive upsetting images), IRRT has also been used to treat Axis II pathology with its focus on altering dysfunctional beliefs and maladaptive schemas (e.g., powerlessness, vulnerability, inherent badness, unlovability, abandonment), and on enhancing one's ability to self-calm and self-soothe, especially while in states of emotional distress.

The treatment components of IRRT include (1) imaginal exposure—activating upsetting imagery and its associated affect, (2) mastery imagery—replacing distressing imagery with mastery/coping imagery, (3) self-soothing/self-calming imagery—visualizing one's adult self today (or another compassionate adult) calming and soothing the traumatized or distressed self, and (4) emotional-linguistic processing—transforming distressing imagery and accompanying emotions into narrative language, while challenging and modifying the underlying maladaptive beliefs and schemas. Subjective unit of distress (SUD) ratings are used throughout an imagery session to give the clinician a reading on the patient's emotional state and to identify emotional "hot spots" that may require additional therapeutic intervention. An audiotape is made of each imagery session and given to the patient for daily listening. The patient is asked to record subjective reactions to the imagery tape in a journal. The patient also records three SUD levels on a homework sheet from each audiotape listening: (1) beginning SUDs, (2) ending SUDs, and (3) peak SUDs (i.e., the highest SUD levels noted during the tape-listening session). The SUD sheets are brought to each treatment session for review as a means of ascertaining homework compliance and progress (see Appendix 10A).

An additional feature that distinguishes the cognitive restructuring component of IRRT from other imagery-based interventions is its emphasis on Socratic imagery, which is essentially Socratic dialogue applied in the context of imagery modification. As such, patients are encouraged to develop their own mastery and self-calming/self-nurturing imagery as a means of both modifying the distressing imagery and challenging the associated underlying beliefs. Socratic imagery derives from the Beckian notion that it is healthier and more empowering for patients to come up with their own solutions, that is, to develop their own mastery/coping imagery, than to have solutions be directed, dictated, or suggested to them by the clinician.

Another critical component of IRRT is the interweave of primary and secondary cognitive processing, which is viewed as critical in the processing of emotionally upsetting material. In short, nonverbal, non-linguistic mental activity that is primarily visual and auditory in nature is viewed as a "primary cognitive process." By contrast, verbalizing one's thoughts and feelings about an event (e.g., through talking or writing) is viewed as a "secondary cognitive process" (Smucker, 1997). In IRRT, the cognitive processing of distressing material occurs simultaneously at both a primary level (reliving the traumatic imagery) and a secondary level (putting the images into words, talking about the imagery). During an IRRT session, the patient and therapist periodically "freeze" the upsetting imagery, especially during times of highly charged affect, to verbally discuss and process the patient's thoughts and feelings about the imagery and its symbolic meaning. Secondary cognitive processing not only examines the patient's immediate response to the imagery itself, but also addresses the underlying maladaptive schemas that reinforce and provide a cognitive template for the disturbing imagery. During an IRRT session, the patient will typically go back and forth from primary cognitive processing to secondary cognitive processing. At the end of an IRRT session, patients are encouraged to verbalize their thoughts and feelings about the imagery session, which further promotes the reprocessing of primary process material at a secondary level of linguistic/cognitive processing. This primary and secondary cognitive processing interweave is continued beyond the IRRT session as part of the patient's homework, which involves daily listening to an audiotape of the imagery session, documenting SUD levels, and recording other reactions in a journal.

ESSENTIAL SKILLS AND ATTRIBUTES

A number of general clinical skills and attributes would be essential to successful therapy with Linda. Establishing and maintaining a reliable and trusting therapist-patient alliance is a *sine qua non* to successful therapy with borderline patients. In order for Linda to feel a solid therapeutic connection with her therapist, she would need to feel accepted, understood, validated, and genuinely liked by the therapist. From a dialectic-behavioral perspective (Linehan, 1993; Bohus, 2002), the therapist would need to skillfully combine gentleness with firmness, flexibility with structure, emotional validation with behavioral limit-setting, schema understanding with schema challenges. A major challenge for the therapist would be to find the balance between validating Linda as an individual and confronting her dysfunctional behaviors, between understanding her intense emotional pain and how it relates to her urges to engage in self-injurious behaviors and establishing clear safety contracts, between conveying a sense of believing in her and challenging her maladaptive beliefs.

Conceptually, it would be crucial for the therapist to view Linda's disorder and style of interpersonal relating from a functional, positive perspective (Fiedler, 2000). Developing a strong therapeutic alliance with Linda could be significantly enhanced by collaboratively examining how her resistance, noncompliance, or other of her challenging behaviors might have been adaptive in her family of origin: What survival value might Linda's thoughts, feelings, or actions have had in other circumstances? What aversive interpersonal experiences could have led to the onset of her extreme behavioral patterns? What schematic templates might Linda have developed that make it difficult for her to behave in more socially acceptable ways?

Because IRRT involves the use of imagery to enhance the modification of upsetting images and thoughts, dysfunctional behaviors, and maladaptive schemas, the treating clinician should be able to offer a plausible rationale for the use of imagery and have some skill in the implementation of imagery as a vehicle for modifying distressing images and enhancing affective self-regulation. Since the activation of imagery tends to evoke highly charged affect, the therapist must be prepared to tolerate a high degree of emotional expression during an imagery session without stopping the imagery prematurely (e.g., to alleviate the therapist's own discomfort with the patient's emotional distress). The therapist must also be skilled in conveying a sense of empathy and safety to the patient while encouraging the patient to "stay with" the upsetting imagery, both as a means of emotionally processing the disturbing images and as a way to increase her threshold for emotional discomfort. Above all, the therapist must have a calm, soothing voice that conveys a sense of empathy, caring, trust, and understanding to the patient.

THERAPY GOALS

The two primary therapeutic goals would be for Linda to significantly improve her affective self-regulation and her interpersonal skills. Spe-

cific goals relating to affective self-regulation woul
following:

- Developing impulse control strategies that enable
  modulate her intense emotional reactions and pr⸱   ⸱⸱con-
  trolled emotional outbursts
- Learning self-calming, self-soothing techniques, especially for times
  of heightened emotional distress
- Learning appropriate strategies for managing conflict
- Developing effective anger-management strategies
- Improving her ability to cope with and process feelings of rejection

Specific goals relating to interpersonal skills would include the
following:

- Identifying, challenging, and modifying her interpersonal fears
  and maladaptive avoidance behaviors
- Improving her overall social skills
- Enhancing her understanding of her schemas (e.g., of abandonment, unlovability, mistrust, dependency), how they often clash
  and create intra-psychic conflict for her, and how they can ultimately be challenged, modified, and replaced with more adaptive schemas
- Improving her understanding of her interpersonal needs for closeness and devising strategies for developing the necessary skills to
  attain those goals

ADDITIONAL INFORMATION NEEDED

It would be useful to conduct a more extensive assessment of Linda's
clinical symptoms in order to glean additional information pertaining
to the possible comorbidity of additional clinical diagnoses (e.g., posttraumatic stress disorder, dissociative disorder, impulse control disorder), information that could be useful in developing Linda's treatment
plan. The Composite International Diagnostic Interview (CIDI) could
be used to diagnose Axis I disorders, while the Structured Clinical
Interview for DSM-IV Personality Disorders II could be used to assess
the presence of Axis II comorbid diagnoses. Using such assessment
tools could assist in (1) clarifying and prioritizing Linda's specific treatment needs and (2) increasing Linda's motivation to be in treatment

by identifying specific stressors in her life that therapy could assist her with, especially since she has identified "fear" as her chief complaint. A symptom-oriented approach addressing her Axis I symptoms could potentially help Linda to make progress toward her interpersonal treatment goals, and thereby serve to lay the groundwork for building a good therapeutic alliance.

CONCEPTUALIZATION OF PATIENT

Linda grew up in an extremely strict, rigid, and invalidating family environment, as reflected by her mother's strict, rigid perfectionism and her father's constant rejecting, aggressive, and violent behavior. While Linda's upbringing may not have been traumatic in the strictest sense, it appears to have been an emotionally abusive, deprived, and invalidating environment in which Linda felt emotionally abandoned by her parents, which significantly thwarted her emotional development and contributed significantly to Linda's difficulties with emotional self-regulation. It appears that neither parent was capable of being a calming, soothing presence to Linda during times of emotional upheaval and distress. As such, Linda has not internalized or developed effective self-calming, self-soothing strategies to help her cope effectively with her intense feelings during times of emotional upset (e.g., anger, rage, rejection). Her exposure to two extreme and highly dysfunctional parental role models for dealing with social and interpersonal tensions—her father's hostility and aggression and her mother's submissiveness—has also left her with huge interpersonal and social skill deficits. Need-based understanding and communication within the family was totally absent in Linda's upbringing. In addition, the expectation that she must be a perfect and "super-responsible" child (including "parenting" her younger siblings) no doubt further contributed to the emergence of her own rigid cognitive schemas that inhibited her emotional development and left her with huge social skill repertoire deficits.

With this background in mind, it is understandable how Linda came to develop her rigid "bipolar" style of dealing with interpersonal conflicts and intra-psychic tension by vacillating between extremes of aggressivity and submissive-dependency. At one extreme, in situations in which she feels taken advantage of or mistreated by others, or where others have broken rules she thinks need to be followed, Linda will exhibit hostile and aggressive behaviors toward the "offenders" without remorse or guilt (e.g., rear-ending a car in front of her for continuing to drive slowly in spite of her repeated horn-honking), or she will break off all contact with the "offending" parties without any regard for how her behavior might impact others (e.g., breaking off all communication with the principal's office and her pupils' parents after receiving a directive from the principal that she did not like). At the other extreme, Linda may exhibit submissive, dependent, and at times clingy behaviors in close interpersonal relationships (e.g., toward her new next-door neighbor in the apartment, toward a new "boyfriend," or toward her sister).

Ambiguous situations (e.g., congested traffic, new relationships) also tend to be triggers for Linda's exaggerated aggressive or submissive reactions because she appears unable to use good judgment or modulate her emotional reactions in such situations. She reacts to each perceived rejection or injustice with extreme sensitivity and intense emotions, which then propel her to engage in impulsive, primitive, and often reckless actions to try to make herself feel better (e.g., engaging in unprotected sex, going on spending sprees). It further appears that Linda gives little or no thought to the actions and rights of others (e.g., "all these old people want is money from my insurance company").

The roots of Linda's history of poor relationships with men may also be traced to her family of origin. Linda remembers being told time and again by her father that she had better learn how to accept sex with her husband and not be a "frigid bitch" like her mother. Yet she also received repeated negative messages from her father about men throughout her adolescence and youth and, as a teenager, was strictly forbidden to date because "boys want only one thing." This notion was reinforced by an actual near-rape experience she had while on her first date in college from which she escaped with a ripped blouse. Linda appears to have internalized this ambivalence toward men, as manifested by her tendency to either avoid intimate contact with men altogether or to engage in impulsive, unprotected sex.

However, Linda's difficulty in relationships is not limited to her intimate contacts with men. Rejection and abandonment fears appear to lie at the core of Linda's interpersonal difficulties with men and women, which in turn become triggers for her primitive, provocative, self-destructive acting-out behaviors (e.g., impulsive sex or food binges, suicidal threats/acts, aggressive actions toward others). As such, Linda appears to vacillate between a tendency to be obsessed with dominance and control, on the one hand, and, on the other hand, to manifest an eagerness for more closeness and intimacy combined with a heightened sensitivity for rejection. Her tendency to live alone and to have few, if any, social contacts could be viewed as an avoidance and a compensatory strategy vis-à-vis her fears of being rejected or abandoned. Thus, her approach-avoidance behaviors toward relationships reflect a schema conflict between her needs for closeness and belonging on the one hand and her deep fears of rejection and abandonment on the other. Indeed, her negative experiences with relationships, together with her negative self-image and low self-worth, appear to have led to the development of an unlovable schema and the belief that "Sooner or later anyone who gets to know me will see how unlovable and unworthy I am and will then reject and abandon me. Therefore, it's dangerous to get too close to anyone."

One might further conceptualize her hostile/aggressive outbursts toward others as a behavioral manifestation of a "perpetrator schema" (introject), which we may assume she has internalized from her father. These perpetrator-like impulses and behaviors, when emitted, no doubt serve to further reinforce her other negative schemas of low self-worth, defectiveness, and inherent badness. It is thus plausible that, in an attempt to ward off or avoid further impulsive, aggressive outbursts, Linda reverts to overly submissive behaviors, which her mother consistently modeled for her.

POTENTIAL PITFALLS

Linda's motivation to actively engage in therapy is potentially the most crucial pitfall from the outset. Since she was referred for therapy by her lawyer, it remains unclear how motivated she is to be in therapy, what her treatment goals really are, and whether she will remain in therapy once she has placated her lawyer or once the legal situation has been resolved. It is not unusual during such legal proceedings that the patient (under advice from legal counsel) will attempt to gain an advantage with the court by seeking psychological treatment (to appear to be working on the problems in good faith) but then abruptly end treatment once a verdict has been issued. To be sure, a good therapist-patient connection would need to be established early on in order for Linda to become, and remain, actively engaged in treatment.

Another potential therapy pitfall with Linda relates to her impulsive outbursts, which could propel her to abruptly end therapy (e.g., if she became upset with the therapist or the therapy itself). Until Linda learns to "stay with" and "talk through" her intense thoughts and feelings toward others, which at some point will need to be identified as a primary goal of therapy, the possibility of her dropping out of therapy on a whim will likely remain high.

PROGNOSIS

The most immediate focus of therapeutic interventions with Linda would be on significantly improving her affective self-regulation and her low tolerance for emotional distress and replacing her uncontrollable anger/rage outbursts and other self-destructive behaviors (e.g., unprotected sex, food binges) with more adaptive coping responses. The success of her efforts will be directly linked to how well Linda can learn to self-calm and self-soothe during times of heightened emotional distress, which should be an attainable goal in the early stages of therapy.

The specific IRRT intervention that addresses her difficulties with affective self-regulation is the therapist-facilitated adult-child imagery, in which Linda would be asked to visualize the calming presence of herself as an adult relating compassionately and empathically to the emotionally upset/angry child within. A primary goal of this imagery would be for Linda's "frightened self" (portrayed in the imagery as the child) to experience a sense of safety, calmness, and inner connectedness with her "competent/reassuring self" (portrayed by the adult in the imagery), such that by the end of the session she has experienced being able to calm, soothe, and "nurture" herself. These adult-child imagery sessions typically last for an entire session.

While the calm emotional state that Linda may experience via the adult-child imagery would be short-lived, an audiotape of the imagery session would be given to her as homework for daily listening as a tool for her to reexperience her calm emotional state on a daily basis. Repeated adult-child imagery sessions over a period of several months could further begin to lay the groundwork for the creation of a new self-calming/self-soothing schematic template that Linda could activate during times of emotional distress. These self-calming/self-nurturing imagery sessions could further provide Linda with an opportunity to "self-parent" (do "corrective parenting") by giving herself the emotional support and validation that she did not receive from her own parents.

Developing alternative behaviors (e.g., daily rigorous exercise) that provide a physical outlet and release of tension could also be helpful in diffusing Linda's intense emotional states. Having Linda keep a daily journal in which she records her thoughts and feelings about the day's events can be another useful technique in helping her to better communicate her emotions, gain more insight into her intense emotional states, and enhance linguistic processing of her emotions. Other between-session coping strategies that Linda might consider using as a means of controlling or reducing her impulsive outbursts during times of heightened emotional distress would be to take either a very hot or very cold shower, wet her lips with hot pepper sauce, or hold several ice cubes in her hands for 5 minutes.

An intermediate, attainable goal for Linda would be to significantly improve her interpersonal skills. Her years at college and her experience as a school teacher no doubt helped her to acquire social skills that she did not learn at home. Because Linda continues to be isolated socially, it would be important to increase her exposure first to relatively nonthreatening social situations. Taking part in well-defined, structured social activities (e.g., a female sports club, a nature club) could serve this purpose.

Long-term goals would include having Linda learn to recognize early danger or warning signs that could lead to maladaptive, impulsive behaviors or outbursts and then being able to control them via coping, self-calming imagery, and self-talk, for example, by activating an internal voice (her "observing ego," her adult self, her therapist "introject") that would self-instruct and visually guide her through the challenging situation, much as a good parent would talk to and coach a child.

Linda's prognosis for adaptive change depends, above all, on whether she remains in treatment and is able to form a good connection with her therapist. Linda will most definitely be confronted at times with intense feelings of transference vis-à-vis the therapist. If she is able to work through her positive and negative transference and develop a healthy, trusting therapeutic relationship, Linda might eventually be able to establish healthy and intimate relationships with "good" men.

TIMELINE

Linda suffers from a broad range of problems and basic psychological deficits, which makes it very likely that the therapy would last for several years with one or two sessions per week. Before significant process could be made with any of her Axis I or Axis II symptoms, Linda would need to develop a strong, positive connection with the therapist because the therapist-patient alliance would be a critical mechanism for therapeutic change.

While the therapeutic alliance with Linda is being developed, which itself may take a while, the initial Axis I skill-focused/crisis-management stage of therapy would target Linda's problems with affective self-regulation, self-injurious behaviors, uncontrolled emotional outbursts, low stress tolerance, and social skill repertoire deficits. With Linda, however, these goals will not be easily or quickly attained. Indeed, therapy with Linda (as is often the case with borderline patients) could initially be interrupted and threatened by numerous crises and session cancellations on the one hand and relapses and unpredictable challenges on the other (e.g., contacts with a perpetrator, new victimization experiences). To be sure, any significant Axis II schema modification work would likewise be a long-term process.

SPECIFIC TECHNIQUES

In Linda's case, the specific imagery techniques likely to be implemented would involve identifying, activating, and modifying her most distressing images and transforming the images and their meanings into narrative language so that a higher order cognitive processing can occur. The imagery activation and processing work with Linda could begin with Linda keeping an imagery journal in which she would write down specific images (baseline images) she experiences throughout the day and rate them on a 0–10 scale from least upsetting to most upsetting. (Typically, borderlines experience a myriad of upsetting, and often recurring, images every day, but they tend to report them only when asked). At each session, Linda could then choose which upsetting or traumatic image(s) she would like to target for that session.

The in-session imagery could begin by asking Linda to close her eyes while visualizing the beginning of the upsetting image or memory and verbalizing aloud, in the present tense, what is happening. If fear was the primary upsetting or trauma-related emotion, then the imaginal exposure phase (i.e., repeated exposure to the upsetting fear-based images) would likely be the primary focus of the imagery. However, if other nonfear emotions (e.g., guilt, shame, anger) appeared to be primary, which would likely be the case with Linda, then imaginal exposure would be used primarily to activate the upsetting imagery so that it could be challenged, modified, and processed (both within and outside of imagery) and its meaning could be explored.

Once the upsetting imagery was activated, therapy would proceed with imagery modification (self-calming imagery) facilitated by the therapist. Linda would be asked to visualize her adult self today entering into the upsetting image and engaging in direct dialogue with her "traumatized self" (represented in the imagery by the child). Throughout such imagery, it is important that the therapist remain nondirective and Socratic. This adult-child imagery could be facilitated by the therapist through questions such as the following:

What would you, the adult, like to do or say to the child?

Can you see yourself doing (or saying) that?

How does the child respond?

How do you, the adult, react to the child's response?

What do you, the adult, see when you look directly into the child's eyes?

If Linda's adult at this point began to hold or hug the child and offer reassurance, the therapist would continue to facilitate the adult-child interaction until Linda indicated that she was ready to bring the imagery to a close. With more severely disturbed patients, however, such intimate adult-child exchanges may activate hostile or perpetrator introjects, as well as an unlovable schema, during the imagery in which strong negative feelings are evoked toward the perceived bad, disgusting, evil, unlovable part of the patient (often represented by the child). Should this occur with Linda, it would provide a unique therapeutic opportunity to confront her unlovable schema and perpetrator introject via the adult-child directly. (See case examples in Smucker & Dancu (1999, pp. 159–179) for more on how to confront an unlovable schema during an adult-child imagery session.)

If Linda's adult had difficulty nurturing the child, blamed the child, or wanted to hurt or abandon the child, it would be important for the adult to express her anger (and any other negative feelings) toward the child directly and from close proximity. Such adult-child interactions could be facilitated by asking Linda:

How far away are you, the adult, from the child?

Can you go up close to the child and tell her why you are angry at her/why you want to hurt her?

Can you look directly into the child's eyes and tell her why she is to blame?

How does the child respond?

When you look directly into the child's eyes from up close, what do you see?

How do you, the adult, respond to what you see in the child's eyes?

What would you, the adult, now like to do or say to the child?

Can you visualize yourself doing/saying that?

Adult-child imagery with other borderline patients has shown that as the adult moves closer to the child in physical proximity, the adult becomes more affected by the child's pain and finds it more difficult to continue blaming, hurting, or abandoning the child. Such intense adult-child interactions generally increase the patient's overall level of affect and evoke strong feelings of compassion toward the child that are empathic, conciliatory, and apologetic in nature.

When it appeared that Linda was ready to bring the adult-child imaginal interactions to a close, the therapist would ask, "Is there anything more that you, the adult, would like to do or say to the child before bringing the imagery to a close?" Once Linda indicated a readiness to terminate the imagery session, the therapist would say, "You may now let the imagery fade away, and when you are ready you may open your eyes." Immediately following the imagery session, the meaning(s) of the upsetting imagery would be further examined and processed. This could be facilitated by questions such as the following:

How was that for you? How are you feeling now?

What thoughts and feelings do you have about the imagery session today?

What were you thinking and feeling when you, the adult, saw the pain in the child's eyes/began to feel the child's pain?

What was it like for you, the adult, to nurture the child?

What was it like for the child to be nurtured by you, the adult?

How did you feel when you began to inflict pain onto the child?

Why do you think you got so angry at the child?

What might the tension between your adult and child represent or mean?

Imagery sessions with Linda would be tape-recorded and given to her for daily listening as homework. Linda would be asked to record her general reactions to the tape in a journal and to record her SUD reactions (beginning, ending, peak) on a homework sheet (see Appendix 10A).

SPECIAL CAUTIONS

Several areas of special caution to be aware of while working with Linda would involve transference, countertransference, danger to self, and danger to others.

Transference

Linda's overgeneralized cognitive behavioral schema of control vs. submission are likely to emerge within the therapist-patient relationship and could become a real challenge for the therapist. Linda could be expected to initially idealize the therapist and want to build a close therapeutic relationship, while simultaneously testing the limits and boundaries of the relationship and engaging in behaviors designed to test the therapist's reliability, commitment, and availability. Linda's fear of being rejected by anyone to whom she gets too close will undoubtedly become an issue in the therapeutic relationship. One might also expect that as soon as she feels insecure or threatened in therapy (e.g., a perceived therapist rejection), Linda will respond with anger and hostility (e.g., blaming the therapist, accusing the therapist of "not caring") or withdrawal (e.g., cancellations, "no-shows," termination threats).

It would be critical for the therapist to attempt to respond to Linda's transference struggles in ways that weaken rather than reinforce her negative, maladaptive schema and that begin to lay the groundwork for a corrective emotional experience. Above all, any therapist working with Linda would need to be genuine and not hide behind the cloak of therapeutic neutrality. In addition, the therapist would need to be sensitive to Linda's needs for safety and control and invite her to actively collaborate in setting the agenda, goals, and focus of therapy. It would also be important to identify and reflect any ambivalence she might have about therapy and to validate her current emotional state. Any testing of limits, acting-out, or self-destructive behaviors would be addressed with a gentle but firm approach that emphasizes understanding and validation of Linda's feelings, life experiences, and her attempts to cope with pain and emotional distress, while simultaneously expressing concern about her self-injurious and self-destructive behaviors and insisting on the need for safety contracts to be negotiated and adhered to. Inviting Linda to verbalize her reactions to each session, as well as her thoughts and feelings about the therapist, could be a useful strategy to address her transference issues on an ongoing basis. Asking Linda at the end of each session what she found most productive and least productive, and then responding to Linda's session appraisal in a validating manner, would be another way to de-intensify her transference and directly challenge Linda's all-or-nothing thinking.

Countertransference

Borderline patients tend to engage in frequent and contradictory behavioral patterns that are more connected to previous life experiences than to current events. They also experience extreme and sudden mood swings, as well as regressive and acting-out behaviors, all of which can leave therapists feeling frustrated, impatient, angry, fed up, and wanting to "fire" the patient. In order for the therapist not to respond with countertransference acting-out behaviors toward Linda, it is imperative that the therapist understand conceptually that transference reactions and acting-out behaviors that invite limit-setting and "corrective parenting" are therapeutic opportunities. It is especially crucial that the therapist not personalize any of Linda's negative behaviors toward the therapist.

Self-Harm

Since Linda does have a suicidal history, it would be advisable to negotiate a safety contract within the first several sessions, as well as a specific plan of action to take if she has self-injurious or suicidal urges. It is indeed likely that Linda will continue to engage in self-injurious, self-destructive behaviors (e.g., unprotected sex) during the course of therapy. The therapist should refrain from making any moralistic, judgmental comments about such behaviors but should focus instead on understanding what Linda's unmet needs are that propel her to engage in such risky behaviors and whether these behaviors are working for her: "I sense that you have intimacy needs to be with a man but that you feel uncertain and fearful to be in a committed relationship. I can understand, especially given your past experiences with men, that you do not want to be hurt again. Could we take a look at whether your approach to getting your intimacy needs met without getting hurt is working for you?"

Harm to Others

Until now, Linda has referred to the ramming of her car into the back of another vehicle as a relatively minor traffic accident. Since there are no other known acts of aggression toward others, Linda is probably not a serious threat to others at the moment. However, the potential for this should be monitored throughout therapy.

AREAS TO AVOID

The one area that the therapist should not address with Linda (at least not in the early or middle stages of therapy) would be the therapist's own countertransference reactions to her. To do so would be detrimental to the therapist-patient alliance. To be sure, Linda would not be able to receive such feedback without feeling personally attacked and threatened, which, in turn, would likely activate her unlovable schema and result in regressive, decompensating, and possibly suicidal behaviors. The arena for sharing countertransference reactions would be with colleagues and in supervision.

MEDICATION

To date, there is little in the way of empirical guidelines or recommendations for the psychopharmacological treatment of borderline personality disorder (BPD). As such, the prevailing pharmacological treatments for BPD aim to reduce specific clusters of symptoms (e.g., relating to depression, anxiety, impulse control) rather than ameliorating the entire complex BPD symptomatology. According to recommendations from studies that do not yet fulfill the golden standard of empirical research, consideration could be given to treating Linda's depression and anxiety with selective serotonin reuptake inhibitors and to treating her problems of impulse control and extreme mood fluctuations with mood stabilizers. The taking of benzodiazepines or any other medications that, with prolonged usage, would increase the risk for developing a tolerance or dependency should be absolutely avoided (Bohus, 2002).

PATIENT STRENGTHS

Linda appears to have some psychological and social resources available to her that could be useful to her therapy and ultimate prognosis. She is able to hold down a job, live by herself, support herself financially, remove herself from harmful relationships (e.g., her ex-husband), and protect herself from environmental dangers (e.g., from a man who attempted to rape her). She also has the ability to initiate contact with others. Even though she has almost no experience with nonviolent or nonrepressive relationships, Linda is able to make a good first impression while presenting herself to others and is able to engage in close social contact in pursuit of her needs for contact and intimacy. This could be a useful resource in the initial establishing of the therapeutic alliance. The therapist might further use this behavior to initially explore, and later modify, her fear and avoidance behaviors that occur in the further development of the therapeutic relationship. She also appears able to make attentive observations of her environment (e.g., sending letters home from school to parents who were not involved enough with their children's homework, keeping tight records of neighbors who didn't clean up after their dogs). This attentiveness could be useful later in therapy when self-management and self-regulation techniques are taught and she will need to closely monitor and record her efforts.

LIMIT-SETTING

As a child, Linda did not learn about appropriate interpersonal boundaries, behavioral norms and limits, and acceptable emotional responses to social situations. As an adult, Linda continues to feel defenseless, confused, and uncertain about how to effectively interact with and respond to her environment, which she perceives as hostile, unpredictable, and threatening. Situations involving conflict, tension, or ambiguity are especially confusing for Linda. Her rigid, black-and-white cognitive coping style propels her to flip-flop between an aggressive, hostile response style at one extreme and an overly submissive response style at the other. Linda's long-standing difficulties with interpersonal boundaries and limits are sure to be manifested in the therapeutic relationship. The therapeutic relationship itself probably offers the best opportunity for Linda to learn that others' actions and reactions are quite predictable and interrelated with clear antecedents and consequences. Therefore, when Linda engages in behavior that tests the limits and boundaries of the therapeutic relationship, it provides the therapist with an opportunity to provide her with clear and consistent feedback about what is and is not appropriate behavior. From the outset, the therapist needs to be clear and consistent with Linda about the rules, limits, and boundaries and what she can expect the consequences will be when specific limits are not adhered to. This includes the handling of suicidal or other harmful behaviors as well as hospitalizations. Because of Linda's past struggles with suicidality, a safety contract would need to be negotiated early on in treatment, and clear guidelines for crisis management would need to be established. The therapist should also spell out clearly for Linda how session cancellations, between-session phone calls, and therapist vacations are handled. It is imperative that the therapist find a skillful balance between an overly rigid handling of boundaries and consequences on the one hand (which could potentially jeopardize Linda's actual needs and leave her feeling powerless) and too much flexibility with too little structure on the other (which could further reinforce her confusion vis-à-vis rules, limits, and interpersonal boundaries).

INVOLVEMENT OF SIGNIFICANT OTHERS AND HOMEWORK

Significant Others

Since much of the focus of therapy will be on improving the quality of Linda's interpersonal relationships and thus will likely involve schema work relating to her dysfunctional family of origin, involving additional family members (e.g., her sister or mother) at some point in her treatment might be considered, especially if improving her relationship with family members were a specific treatment goal. Indeed, it appears that Linda would like to have a closer relationship with her sister, even though Linda feels that her sister has no interest in her since the birth of her baby. Although the exact nature of Linda's relationship with her mother is unclear, they do apparently maintain some phone contact. Involving her mother in Linda's therapy (either in person, by phone, or by correspondence) may also be a consideration at some point. However, the therapist must also be aware that any contact with the family of origin could be a potential trigger for painful memories (implicit or explicit) and should be carefully planned. Contacts with her father should probably be avoided in the early and middle phases of treatment and for as long as Linda is unable to effectively regulate her intense cognitive and emotional reactions toward him. Imagery "encounters," as opposed to actual encounters, with her father and other family members may offer a safer and potentially more productive therapeutic forum for addressing her family-related anger and guilt.

Homework

One of the challenges of working with Linda involves the transfer of therapeutic progress to her day-to-day functioning. Because Linda's actual out-of-session life circumstances will play a critical role in the generalization of therapeutic change, homework assignments can become a useful vehicle for the transfer of such change as well as a measurable indicator of change. Homework with Linda would initially involve daily listening to the IRRT therapy session audiotapes, which could help to solidify the therapeutic alliance and teach Linda self-calming, self-nurturing skills. Homework assignments could also involve Linda documenting problematic situations and changes that occur between sessions, her emotional reactions to these events, and her attempts to cope with them. Linda could then bring her "data" into the next session for further discussion and processing. Homework assignments also offer Linda the opportunity to experiment with various behaviors in her day-to-day interpersonal contacts. Because a critical treatment goal for Linda would be to improve her ability to regulate her emotions and manage her behaviors, Linda would benefit from having a well-defined "therapeutic contract" regarding desired behavioral changes.

TERMINATION ISSUES

Linda, like most patients with borderline personality disorder, struggles with perceived unpredictable circumstances and uncontrollable interpersonal threats, which leave her feeling extremely sensitive to and fearful of change. As such, she may view positive therapeutic changes together with the end of treatment as a threat, since they represent significant changes in her life. Thus, one might expect the end of treatment to trigger an array of strong ambivalent thoughts and feelings about herself, about the therapy, and about relationships. In order to prevent an end-of-treatment crisis, discussions about termination should begin early in therapy as a way of ensuring that Linda will have ample time to express and process her related fears, concerns, and anxieties. A gradual phasing out of therapy would be advisable with Linda, and the time between sessions should be gradually increased (e.g., from weekly to biweekly to monthly to bimonthly to quarterly maintenance sessions), with the understanding that Linda may call the therapist between sessions if necessary. When and how Linda could contact the therapist, however, would need to be clearly specified, and she should be encouraged to handle crises on her own as much as possible. Before placing a call to the therapist, for example, Linda should try to have an imaginary conversation with the therapist, "listen" carefully to the therapist's "voice," and write in a journal what she heard the therapist "say." If after recording and processing this "conversation" with the therapist, Linda still felt the need to call, she would be encouraged to do so. For Linda, activating a positive image of the therapist and "hearing" the therapist's reassuring voice (during times of crisis as well as noncrisis) could continue to have a calming, soothing effect on Linda's mood long after treatment has ended and could eventually become part of her schematic internal representation of self.

Careful relapse prevention planning would also be a critical component of Linda's treatment. In order to minimize the threat of relapse, mechanisms will need to be in place for Linda to cope with future emotional or environmental crises. Reviewing together with the therapist interventions that have been successfully used throughout treatment and reflecting on how similar interventions might be used in the future could help Linda to feel better equipped to deal with future emotional and environmental challenges. Documenting these interventions in a concrete, step-by-step manner could further help to ensure their future accessibility and provides Linda a kind of "first-aid-kit" to help her transfer her therapeutic achievements to her post-therapy daily life.

Challenging Linda to identify her strengths and achievements would further serve as a reminder of the inner resources she has available to her during difficult times. Relapse prevention might also be aided by the therapist giving something tangible to Linda at the end of treatment that symbolized the therapist's optimism and belief in Linda.

MECHANISMS OF CHANGE

The complexity of Linda's difficulties with affective self-regulation, interpersonal skill deficits, and low stress tolerance underscores the notion that any lasting therapeutic changes will need to occur at a deep intrapsychic level. From a cognitive behavior therapy perspective, the hoped-for mechanisms of change can be described according to a schema-focused cognitive model. It would appear that the complex pattern of Linda's symptoms can be traced to the extreme affectively charged distortions that emanate from her underlying negative schemas. It follows, therefore, that until significant modifications occur at a schematic level, it will be difficult for Linda to manifest any persistent changes in her interpersonal behaviors, regulation of internal cognitive and emotional processes, and stress tolerance (including the experience and modulation of intense affect).

At an intermediate level, the hoped-for mechanisms of change would involve an increased awareness of her cognitive-emotional-behavior reactions to stimuli (i.e., the development of adaptive metacognitions), which should lead to an enhanced ability to regulate her affect and impulses. At that level, a more adaptive reformulation of rules, attitudes and norms (e.g., "other people have needs too," "just because others don't always comply with my wishes doesn't mean they don't like me") is the desired change that could lead to a modification of compensatory and avoidant strategies (e.g., replacing hostile and submissive behaviors with a more articulate, assertive expression of wishes and disappointments toward others). At a basic level, the careful use of the patient-therapist alliance can challenge the rigidity of Linda's cognitive behavioral patterns and begin to lay the groundwork for challenging and modifying her maladaptive schema.

REFERENCES

Anderson, M. (1980). Imaginal processes: Therapeutic applications and theoretical models. In J. Mahoney (Ed.), *Psychotherapy process: Current issues and future directions.* New York: Plenum.

Beck, A., Emery, G., & Greenberg, R. L. (1985). *Anxiety disorders and phobias: A cognitive perspective*. New York: Basic Books.

Beck, A., Freeman, A., & Associates (1990). *Cognitive therapy of personality disorders*. New York: Guilford Press.

Beck, J. S. (1995). *Cognitive therapy: Basics and beyond*. New York: Guilford Press.

Bohus, M. (2002). *Borderline-störung: Forschritte der psychotherapie—Manuale für die praxis* (Band 14). Göttingen, Germany: Hogrefe.

Breuer, J., & Freud, S. (1895/1955). Studies on hysteria. *Standard Edition, 2*, 1–305.

Edwards, D. (1990). Cognitive therapy and the restructuring of early memories through guided imagery. *Journal of Cognitive Psychotherapy: An International Quarterly, 4*, 33–51.

Fiedler, P. (2000). *Integrative psychotherapie bei persönlichkeitsstörungen*. Göttingen, Germany: Hogrefe.

Janet, P. (1898). *Nervoses et idees fixes*. Paris: Alcan.

Jung, C. (1960). *The structure and dynamics of the psyche* (R. Hull, Trans.). Princeton, NJ: Princeton University Press.

Linehan, M. (1993). *Cognitive-behavioral treatment of borderline personality disorder*. New York: Guilford Press.

Peterson, K., Prout, M., & Schwartz, R. (1991). *Posttraumatic stress disorder: A clinician's guide*. New York: Plenum Press.

Smucker, M. (1997). Posttraumatic stress disorder. In R. Leahy (Ed.), *Practicing cognitive therapy* (pp. 193–220). Northvale, NJ: Jason Aronson Publishers.

Smucker, M., & Dancu, C. (1999). *Cognitive-behavioral treatment for adult survivors of childhood trauma: Imagery rescripting and reprocessing*. Northvale, NJ: Jason Aronson Publishers.

Smucker, M., Dancu, C., Foa, E., & Niederee, J. (1995). Imagery rescripting: A new treatment for survivors of childhood sexual abuse suffering from posttraumatic stress. *Journal of Cognitive Psychotherapy: An International Quarterly, 9*(1), 3–17.

Smucker, M., Dancu, C., Foa, E., & Niederee, J. (2002). Imagery rescripting: A new treatment for survivors of childhood sexual abuse suffering from posttraumatic stress. In R. Leahy & E. Dowd (Eds.), *Clinical advances in clinical psychotherapy: Theory and application* (pp. 294–310). New York: Springer.

Smucker, M., & Niederee, J. (1995). Treating incest-related PTSD and pathogenic schemas through imaginal exposure and rescripting. *Cognitive and Behavioral Practice, 2*, 63–93.

Staton, J. (1990). Using nonverbal methods in the treatment of sexual abuse. In S. Stith, M. Williams, & K. Rosen (Eds.), *Violence hits home: Comprehensive treatment approaches to domestic violence* (pp. 210–228). New York: Springer.

Weis, J., Smucker, M., & Dresser, J. (2002). Imagery: Its history and use in the treatment of posttraumatic stress disorder. In A. Sheikh (Ed.), *Healing images: The role of imagination in the healing process* (pp. 377–391). Amityville, NY: Baywood.

APPENDIX 10A

Homework Record

Name of Client: _____   Date: _____

Name of Therapist: _____   Imagery Session #: _____

Homework Assignment: Listen daily to audiotape of the entire imagery session. Record date and time of each audiotape listening session.

Record the **Subjective Units of Distress** (SUDs: 0–100) at the beginning and end of each tape-listening session, as well as the peak (highest) SUDs experienced.

DAY	1	2	3	4	5	6	7
Date and Time							
SUDs Beginning							
SUDs Ending							
SUDs Peak							

DAY	8	9	10	11	12	13	14
Date and Time							
SUDs Beginning							
SUDs Ending							
SUDs Peak							

11

Unified Therapy with BPD

David Mark Allen

TREATMENT MODEL

Unified therapy (Allen, 1988, 1993, 2003) is an individual psychotherapy based on an integration of psychodynamic, cognitive behavioral, and family systems theories and techniques. It is designed for adults aged 23 to 48 who exhibit personality dysfunction and who have at least one living parental figure. The theory predicts that family therapy would be necessary for younger individuals. Unified therapy (UT) is particularly useful for the treatment of borderline personality disorder (BPD).

The treatment is based on the idea that ambivalence over role functioning in parents within the patient's family of origin results in a situation in which family members are faced with contradictory demands. These contradictory demands reinforce (in a manner analogous to the concept of a variable intermittent reinforcement schedule) the patient's intrapsychic conflicts and the resultant dysfunctional behavior. The patient's conflictual behavior then simultaneously reinforces ambivalent, dysfunctional behavior in the rest of the family. Ambivalence about role behavior within the family is, in turn, created by homeostatic family rules that lag behind behavioral expectations resulting from the evolution of the ambient culture. In particular, individuals are torn between introjected family values and demands from the larger culture for increasingly less role-driven, more individuated behavior. The idiosyncratic experiences of individual families within their ethnic and cultural group over two to four generations create a milieu in which once-useful family roles and rules are maintained. Therapy is designed to interrupt this process so that family members validate new, adaptive behaviors for one another instead of working to reinforce old, maladaptive patterns.

Parents or other family system leaders are thought, for genetic reasons, to be the most potent of all environmental influences in both shaping and reinforcing role-relationship behavior in all human beings. UT predicts that any insights or behavioral changes within the transference relationship with the therapist will not generalize to other important outside relationships unless the usual way that the family of origin members respond to the patient also changes significantly. The therapist is usually no match for the family in directly altering, positively or negatively, the patient's patterns of interpersonal behavior in typical social or occupational settings

In dysfunctional families, members of a family usually meet changes in the role behavior of individual members with significant invalidating responses. The other family members powerfully relay the message "you are wrong—change back" to any individual who challenges the homeostatic rules. Invalidating responses include subtle challenges to the patient's sanity, heavy "guilt trips," and severe parental acting out. Particularly in the families of BPD patients, parents may act out destructively. They may threaten or attempt suicide, threaten divorce, decompensate, or become violent in response to the patient's new behavior.

Although such behavior often appears malicious, a hidden altruistic motive is usually present. Dysfunctional behavior by all family members is usually mutually reinforced by every other member of the family, often because of the mistaken idea that everyone *else* wants or needs the patterns to continue in their current form.

The central theme behind the creation of BPD is a severe psychodynamic conflict in the parents in the patient's family of origin over the parenting role. This conflict leads parents to give out double messages to one or more of their children. The message that the focused-upon child receives is a mixture of "I need you desperately" and "I hate you—go away." These conflicting messages create conflictual role-performance demands on the patient in regard to autonomy and independence from the parents. Although some families of BPD patients are consistently highly enmeshed with them or become consistently cut off from them, the usual clinical picture is that families oscillate between hostile over- and underinvolvement with the BPD patient. A push-pull is created in which the child becomes a sort of yo-yo, pulling away and then being drawn back into the family chaos. These mixed messages reinforce "spoiling" type responses in the children, no matter their age. The child may also be subjected to a variety of additional double messages over other issues, creating the wide variety of clinical presentations of patients with BPD.

In order to alter this process, UT therapy aims to achieve the following strategic goals:

1. Frame the patient's chief complaint and current difficulties as a response to family-of-origin issues.
2. Gather information identifying interpersonal relationship patterns that cue or reinforce self-destructive behavior.
3. Gather information about the patient's genogram to understand family misbehavior so that the patient can develop empathy for targeted family members.
4. Make a hypothesis about both the patient's current role in the family and the reasons the family seems to require this role.
5. Plan a metacommunicative strategy designed to help the patient confront the problem with his or her family so that the reinforcing behavior is diminished or extinguished.
6. Implement the strategy and obtain feedback about its effectiveness.

Ideally, the patient learns to get past the defenses of each primary family member in order to effectively discuss the context of problematic family interactions, discuss mixed messages and their effects, and request concrete behavioral changes in the relationship.

ESSENTIAL SKILLS OR ATTRIBUTES

Many of the attributes necessary to work with BPD patients from the UT perspective are the same as those in any other treatment school. In addition, however, UT requires some unique clinical skills as well as personal qualities.

I believe that working with this population from any perspective requires the following attributes:

1. An ability to be caring and empathic without becoming emotionally overinvolved.
2. A strong sense of self-confidence and optimism in one's abilities as a therapist, tempered by the realization that one is not going

to be able to help every patient, nor to quickly relieve the suffering of any given patient at many points during therapy.

3. The courage to tolerate the knowledge that the patient might damage him– or herself despite one's best efforts and the courage to take risks (e.g., refuse to hospitalize patients when it would be counterproductive).

4. The persistence to stick with the patient through the long process of treatment despite periods of interpersonal tension, stalemates, and regression in treatment.

The attributes unique to unified therapy include the following:

1. A willingness to do a little more work than with other treatment models. In order to keep complicated interpersonal patterns in mind and apply them to a cast of characters unique to each patient, most therapists must take extensive notes following sessions and review them prior to the next session. The therapist may also need to think about a specific problem between sessions in order to come up with creative strategies for resolving blocks to family metacommunication.

2. The ability to find something redeeming about individuals who exhibit reprehensible behavior, such as severe child abuse. An important factor in maintaining a constructive attitude in this type of therapy is the strong belief that there are no ultimate villains in the family drama. This does not mean, however, that the therapist condones destructive behavior. In role-playing exercises, the therapist uses his or her empathy with family members in order to portray them effectively. Some talent for method acting also helps in this regard.

3. A sense of humor about both oneself and the human condition. While patients must be taken seriously to avoid invalidating them, the judicious use of a sense of playfulness helps the therapist both to maintain a positive outlook and to make therapy less of a tribulation.

The UT therapist must, in addition to the above, develop the ability to think dialectically (Allen, 1991). This involves understanding several complex patterns of interpersonal influence that all go on simultaneously. The patient and each family member try to "read" and respond to the motives of one another in a situation in which both members of the relationship are giving off double messages. In addition, each attempts to involve other family members in interpersonal clashes. Therapists who have been raised in a culture that presumes that individuals operate primarily from selfish motives rather than altruistic ones may need to retrain their thinking.

THERAPEUTIC GOALS

The UT perspective tends to see all treatment goals as highly interrelated. Successful negotiation of family metacommunicative tasks tends to have a domino effect on a number of different problems. Ultimately, the primary goal of the therapy is to resolve the patient's chief complaints.

Linda complains of chronic anxiety and depression as well as a legal problem. She also describes repetitive patterns of self-defeating behavior and discord within her family of origin. Since resolution of her chief complaint also involves these other problems, their resolution also becomes a goal of therapy. She exhibits impatience and impulsive angry outbursts or acting-out, conflicts over sexuality that involve dangerous impulsivity, a tendency to oscillate between overinvolvement and distancing in her relationships with both men and women, a sense of emptiness, and parents who reportedly "want nothing to do" with her. She may be on a mission to correct or punish misbehaving parents and elderly individuals.

As to her legal problems, I would tell her that I would be happy to write a report stating that her problems with her temper are related to her psychiatric diagnosis if her lawyer thinks that useful. However, I would add that in my limited forensic experience, it would probably not alter the outcome of the proceedings. In addition, I would inform her that if she did make her mental state an issue in legal proceedings, she would have to waive her right to confidentiality, which might open her up to embarrassing public revelations.

As described above, UT predicts that Linda's problems, both affective and behavioral, stem from the same source, and that directly altering family-of-origin relationships will be the most powerful way to resolve the presenting complaints and to diminish self-destructive behavior. This will, of course, take quite some time. Short term, I would offer whatever symptomatic relief might be possible with medication, perhaps augmented with cognitive behavioral stress-management techniques.

Long term, the therapist helps patients give up dysfunctional behavior while maintaining contact with important family members who have, up until then, reinforced it. Intermediate goals useful to accomplish this include identification of core conflictual themes (Luborsky & Crits-Christoph, 1990) that are shared by the entire family, identification of repetitive interactional patterns that trigger acting out, and tracing the genesis of the family problems over at least three generations through the use of a genogram. Patients must learn how their conflicts play out and feed into their problematic affects and behaviors, and also must develop empathy toward the others. Patients will eventually discuss family dynamics with family members in a way that avoids blaming. Role-playing is employed to develop and then train the patients to use strategies for overcoming the family's often-formidable defenses against metacommunication. The patients then ask each parental figure to alter behavior that serves to trigger the patients' destructive role within the family.

FURTHER INFORMATION NEEDED

I would first want to know more details about the BPD traits Linda exhibits. Do her dissociative episodes always seem to follow conversations with her mother or sister as the history indicates? Is there any evidence of more severe dissociation? Does she have current suicidal ideation or a history of self-mutilation?

For evaluation for medication, I would need to know the following: Does her anxiety lead to full-blown panic attacks? How much of the time is her mood depressed, and how severely? Does she have episodes of sustained periods of more severe depression lasting at least two weeks? Do her moods affect her sleep, appetite, energy level, and concentration?

In order to identify core themes, I would eventually need to know a lot more about the patient's early and current family relationships and about her family's background. How do they interact over each problematic issue? What do her parents know about her various behavior and relationship problems, and what do they say or not say about them? Do they avoid her, as she seems to imply? Do they give advice or financial assistance? Do they criticize? If they invalidate her, in what ways and over what themes? How did identified conflicts play out in the relationship between her parents and grandparents?

Several clues in the case study (see next section) suggest that her parents have conflicts over the parenting role. What factors in the family's history may have led to these conflicts? The patient also has become overinvolved with and then alienated female friends. Are there any past or present parallels to this pattern in the patient's relationship with her mother?

The parents reportedly had conflicts over sex. Was this related to the procreative function? What was the attitude of their evangelical church toward birth control? What did her father mean when he said that she would attack a man if the man did not attack her? Did he ever clarify this strange attribution? What was the attitude of the rest of the family, including aunts, uncles, and grandparents, about sex and about children? In addition to what the father said, I would also like to know about conversations that went on or did not go on between the patient and her mother regarding men.

A vital question is what consequences would follow if the patient were to stop acting out or if she were able to have a truly successful relationship with a man in which both of them got their needs met. Who might be negatively affected? Would her mother be jealous? Get depressed? Start acting out more with her husband? How would her father react?

I do not use any specific questionnaires or assessment tools to obtain the answers to these kinds of questions; rather, I gradually obtain the information as patients discuss their thoughts, feelings, and relationships during the therapy session. I ask more pointed questions as we generate and refine hypotheses.

CONCEPTUALIZATION OF PATIENT

UT views personality as an admixture of a patient's true self and a persona. The persona is a role developed to help maintain homeostasis within the patient's family of origin, even if, outwardly, it appears oppositional. It is almost invariably self-destructive and represents a sacrifice of the self for the perceived good of the family. Although Linda is seemingly independent from her parents, she is probably acting out parental conflicts. UT assumes that this somehow leads to increased family stability.

Linda has succeeded at getting out of a bad relationship, but not at getting into a better one. She was overly demanding of her husband's time, yet pushed him away with provocative behavior. She almost became a stalker in a subsequent relationship, but she often chooses men who are married or otherwise unlikely to be ultimately available. Similarly, her mother demanded more of her husband's time but put up with his absences and did not leave him. A reasonable hypothesis is that the patient's behavior allows her mother to vicariously experience a repressed wish to get out of her bad marriage, while allowing the mother to avoid envy of her daughter and depression over her own inability to do the same.

The evidence that her family is conflicted about parenting is that the parents married late, and spaced their children far apart, yet still had three of them. The mother seemed to find them a bother and expected them to function without her: Linda had to be "perfect." The mother became irate if Linda's "mistakes" required more of the mother's time. Linda was also expected to look after the younger siblings, probably so that the mother could devote more time to nonparental aspects of her life. The father avoided the children, spending much time away from the house. He wanted the children to be "fed and quiet," presumably so they would not be a bother. Linda is a teacher but wants to live in a place with no children. She assumes her sister has no interest in her because the sister's life is, in the patient's estimation, consumed with her own child.

The father also gave the patient a double message about sex. She was supposed to be more sexual with her husband than her mother had been, but she was to avoid men who, he seemed to imply, only want sex.

Linda rationalizes both the reason why she hit another car and her administrators' objections to the notes she sent home with students. Such irrational cognitions are generally used to bolster a false self through slogans supporting the family mythology or self-mortifying thoughts designed to "kill off" aspects of the true self that conflict with the persona. They thus serve a defensive function.

Her dysregulated affect is presumed to be due to her chronically being in a confusing and conflictual position with respect to her behavior within the family system. Once she is no longer in this position, it would be expected that she would gradually achieve a more modulated state.

POTENTIAL PITFALLS

Most of the potential pitfalls that might present themselves with Linda involve transference traps that might trigger countertransference acting out, and the patient's likely resistance to performing the homework assignments involving metacommunication with important family members. These are discussed below under question Special Cautions.

PROGNOSIS

Linda would be most likely to gain some modulation in her affective storms and her impulsivity over the short run through the use of medication. UT presumes, however, than any significant lasting improvements in her coping, ability to function, and self-defeating behavior patterns would depend on alteration of family interactions that reinforce problematic behavior. She would have to develop insight into her position in the family system and the reasons for her parents' dysfunctional behavior, and make an at least partially successful effort to effect a change in the dysfunctional interactions.

Linda has a lot of strengths, and her family's dysfunction, although significant, is somewhat circumscribed to a manageable number of conflictual issues. There is apparently no history of family violence. Prognosis for significant changes in all aspects of her dysfunctional behavior therefore seems to be fair to good. The final outcome depends on a number of factors. The therapist would have to be able to develop a good working relationship with her. Linda would, of course, need to persist in working in therapy and would ultimately need to be willing to proceed with homework assignments despite the high degree of anxiety that they would engender.

It is possible, of course, that during the relatively long course of therapy the family situation could worsen, leading to a deterioration in Linda's behavior. For example, her ability to function at work, although problematic to some degree, seems to be an area of stability. Whether or not it continued to be so throughout therapy may depend on developments in the ongoing relationship between her parents in the present. Hostile underinvolvement and neglect seems to be the predominant pole of the parenting conflict in this family. This is further evidenced by the fact that the patient and both siblings are out of the parents' home and functional. Since Linda in the past was episodically triangulated into the parent's discordant relationship (e.g., when she had to listen to the father's complaints about the mother's "frigidity"), the couple's ability to remain stable in the absence of such "assistance" would determine whether or not the patient remained independent. If Linda needed to return to help out, we might see an increase in her provocative behavior at work. This would get her fired, and she might then go on to become financially dependent on the parents. She might even have to leave therapy due to financial factors or a move to her parents' hometown. Her new "dependence" on them would allow them to blame her for being the "reason" for their fights, rather than their own increasing dissatisfaction with one another. It would also serve as a cover for her efforts to covertly look after them.

TIMELINE

The usual UT guidelines would be recommended for this patient. UT is performed once weekly or once every other week. Seeing the patient more than once a week is generally counterproductive because it often leads to the more frequent development of transference reactions to the therapist. Such reactions may impede the family work, which is considered the curative factor. Patients also need time between sessions to process any insights into the family that may have been achieved and to perform any homework assignments. Meeting weekly is preferred, although the therapy can be done every other week if there are financial considerations or insurance restrictions. The therapy may take longer if done at the reduced frequency, but this is not always the case. Seeing a patient less often than every other week is generally not recommended because it is difficult to attain the needed level of continuity between sessions.

Sessions generally last 45 minutes and are not extended significantly. Because the level of concentration required by the therapist is high, and because the therapist needs time between patients to write notes and review them, longer sessions are discouraged even when major progress seems to be occurring. As with other therapy paradigms, self-destructive behavior by the patient or the development of new crises are not rewarded by extra time or sessions with the therapist. Phone calls by the patient are allowed but are generally kept short unless the patient is having unanticipated problems with a specific homework assignment. They are not used for ad hoc problem solving. Specific techniques for managing inappropriate phone calls are described elsewhere (Allen, 2003).

The duration of UT varies widely and is almost impossible to predict based on any given patient's initial presentation. Therapy is rarely shorter than 40 sessions, but it is generally far shorter than most analytically oriented therapy. The usual range is 70–120 sessions. Some patients who would seem to be ideal candidates and are not too disturbed end up taking a long time, while others who seem severely impaired take much less time than expected. The presence of significant obsessional traits such as a tendency to latch on to one assessment of relationship patterns and refusing to entertain alternative viewpoints tends to predict longer treatment duration. This case history does not suggest such traits. Sociopathic traits, which are also not described in this case material, are likely to lead to early dropout from treatment.

SPECIFIC TECHNIQUES

UT use a variety of techniques, which are described in detail elsewhere (Allen, 2003). Some are used throughout treatment, but many are specific to a stage of therapy. The most important "technique" is actually an attitude. The therapist doggedly maintains and communicates to the patient that the patient and his or her family members are not defective. They have good reasons for seemingly dysfunctional behavior; they are strong enough to withstand powerful emotions. In addition, there are no villains in the family drama, even though family behavior patterns are both problematic and have a powerful negative effect.

Specific techniques are employed to prevent patients from alienating the therapist. These include the use of treatment contracting, paradoxical predictions, discounting of "obvious" explanations for dysfunctional behavior, and disclaimers. Specific types of statements are recommended to counter such typical BPD patient provocations as wild accusations, hyperbole, use of a negative tone of voice, inappropriate or impossible demands, absurd arguments, "splitting," and vague or taunting suicide threats. In the latter case, the therapist employs a technique known as the paradoxical offer to hospitalize.

Techniques that minimize so-called distortions and allow the therapist to obtain relatively objective descriptions of dysfunctional family interactions include recognizing judgments masquerading as descriptions and descriptions masquerading as explanations and pursuing the description or explanation; the use of follow-up questions; asking the patient precisely who said what to whom in important interactions and tracing those conversations all the way to the end; accepting the patient's responses to the therapist's interpretations and interventions as valid; and fearlessly but tactfully confronting apparent holes or contradictions in the patient's story.

The Adlerian question, "What would be the downside if the patient's behavior problems were miraculously cured?" is used to ferret out negative reactions by other family members to behavioral improvements on the part of the patient. The therapist may also make use of conjoint sessions with other family members or spouses, individually, for one or two sessions.

Role-playing techniques are used for a variety of purposes including clarifying family interactions, teaching the patient how to obtain genogram information from reluctant relatives or how to detriangulate peripheral relatives who may interfere with metacommunication, and devising and practicing strategies for countering the patient's family's defenses against effective metacommunication. In each instance, therapists start with a role reversal in which they play the patient and the patient plays the significant other. This allows the therapist to see what the patient is up against, try out or model strategic interventions, and develop and impart to the patient empathy for the other. This empathy also helps the therapist later play that person in direct role-playing. Direct role-playing, in which patients play themselves, is then used so that the patient can practice the agreed-upon strategy prior to it being assigned as homework. In direct role-play, the therapist uses the technique of playing the others as being as difficult as possible consistent with their prior behavior, so that the patient is prepared for a worst-case scenario.

SPECIAL CAUTIONS

Although Linda has made one suicide attempt and threatened suicide on one occasion, she does not appear to pose a large suicide risk. Her parasuicidal episodes were infrequent, did not exhibit a high degree of lethality, and involved specific relationship crisis points that could probably be avoided in a relationship with a competent therapist. Although she has made threats, there is nothing in the history to suggest that she might become violent or that her family would become violent in response to her attempts at metacommunication.

The transference/countertransference pattern for which I would remain alert is that Linda will act out her persona with the therapist, and try to induce the therapist to act out with her. She might attempt to induce the therapist to become a sort of enabler or accomplice rather an agent for change. She might also attempt to induce the therapist to behave in ways that "prove" any family myths that guide her behavior. She might try very hard to effect these results, but I would expect her to be, in actuality, highly ambivalent about doing so and really hoping to fail.

With a male therapist, Linda might try to prove the family myth that she must attack or be attacked by any man with whom she is alone. She might do so by becoming very seductive or, alternatively, devaluing the therapist in a way designed to attack his vulnerabilities. Despite the BPD reputation for "splitting," I would assume that Linda is highly adept at quickly figuring out what people's vulnerabilities are. If the therapist does not respond to her seductive efforts or her attacks, she may then accuse him of not really caring for her or not being "there" for her.

I would expect that Linda might attempt to prove that she is nothing but a big bother to everyone, including the therapist. This is in keeping with the neglect polarity that predominates in her family dynamics. As she has done in her outside relationships, she might become more and more demanding of the therapist's time and then vindictive when the therapist tries to set limits. Any such acting out within the therapy relationship can usually be nipped in the bud by using transference-reducing techniques.

Resistances in UT are difficult to predict with any given patient. Some patients do not initially accept the focus on family dynamics, although many immediately agree that the family relationships are at the heart of their difficulties. Patients have a wide range of reactions to attempts by the therapist to find redeeming qualities in abusive parental figures. Almost all patients are afraid of attempts at family communication. In BPD patients, prior attempts to communicate have usually resulted in unmitigated disasters, so it takes a lot of convincing by the therapist that such efforts can turn out better even in the most dysfunctional of families.

AREAS TO AVOID

No major area of Linda's emotional and behavioral repetitive dysfunction would be considered off limits in unified therapy. BPD patients are viewed as cognitively intact patients and, in spite of their multiple problems, as strong, competent adults who are able to withstand the emotional rigors of a course of therapy. This patient does not appear to be an exception.

If a therapist avoids certain subjects, many BPD clients think one or both of two thoughts, neither of which is desirable: (1) "The 'expert' therapist thinks I am weak. What more evidence do I need than that?" This thought has the effect of feeding into the patient's already low sense of personal potency. (2) "The therapist must be skittish about the avoided subject. Since I am depending on the therapist's being strong in order to help me, I must protect the therapist from this potentially unnerving subject. I must do so without pointing out his own weakness." The patient will usually then pretend that it is really she who is the one who "can't take it."

MEDICATION

Linda complains of chronic depression, presumably without much vegetative symptomatology suggestive of major depressive disorder. She also complains of chronic anxiety, anger outbursts, and impulsivity with eating, sex, and spending. This pattern of symptoms, in my experience, responds best to a selective serotonin reuptake inhibitor (SSRI) antidepressant. The response is often augmented with the use of long-acting benzodiazepines such as clonazepam. I believe a trial of an SSRI and a long-acting benzodiazepine is warranted with this patient. A drug abuse history, which may give a physician pause about using a benzodiazepine, has apparently not been an issue for Linda. Some authors believe benzodiazepines may cause disinhibition, but I have not found this to be problem

While SSRIs may help directly with Linda's symptoms, they would be more likely to be useful in decreasing her emotional reactivity (Coccaro & Kavoussi, 1997). They may also help with compulsive behaviors such as binge eating.

The medication would not be expected to work consistently. The reduced reactivity is a relative effect; if the level of the patient's stress becomes high enough, symptoms of affect dysregulation will invariably break through. However, even a moderate and inconsistent effect is better than nothing at all. The medication would be expected to help the process of therapy by allowing the patient to partially avoid extreme emotional reactions to discussions of stressful topics.

PATIENT STRENGTHS

Linda has several notable strengths. First, she is clearly quite intelligent, as evidenced by the fact that she became a teacher and has had at least some graduate school. Second, her work and school history has been fairly stable. Her problems are relatively circumscribed to the relationship arena, which makes them somewhat more manageable. Her career success also affords her the financial resources necessary to pay for what may be an extended treatment. Third, the degree of her parents' ambivalence over the parenting role may be relatively mild compared to that of other families that produce a BPD offspring. This is evidenced by the fact that her siblings, given what we know from the history, seem to have escaped the family environment and become relatively functional. In my experience, the higher the degree of the family's ambivalence, the more likely it is that additional siblings will be adversely affected. The family history also indicates that the chaos in the family is not as pervasive as is often seen in families that produce a BPD offspring. The parents have stayed together, had stable jobs, and were apparently not physically or sexually abusive.

It is beneficial to the therapy that both parents are still living and cognitively intact. This allows the patient to revisit the source of her distress and renegotiate troublesome interactions that trigger or reinforce dysfunctional affects, beliefs, and behaviors. If one or both of the parents were deceased, this opportunity would be diminished. (The issue of chronic repetitive dysfunctional behavior that persists in the absence of continuing reinforcement from the family of origin is beyond the scope of this chapter and, in any event, does not apply to this particular patient.)

LIMIT-SETTING

Limit-setting is usually addressed in the same manner with all BPD patients in unified therapy. There is nothing in this patient's history that requires an alteration of the usual procedures. As with all psychotherapy, the therapist should maintain a professional demeanor and avoid any semblance of a dual relationship. I would avoid dressing casually, would address the patient as "Ms. P." unless she insisted on being called something else, and would appear somewhat oblivious to subtly seductive behavior unless it became repetitive. I would try to be warm but clearly "all business."

The transference-managing techniques and attitudes employed in unified therapy (listed under Specific Techniques) are often extremely effective in diminishing the need for the therapist to overtly set limits with a patient and in cutting short the patient's attempts to test limits. The therapist presumes that patients are almost invariably well aware of when they are stepping over the line. Patients do so in their ambivalent attempts to induce the therapist to respond to them with hostility, anxious guilt, or anxious helplessness, while covertly hoping that the therapist does not respond in this way. If the therapist does not, they tend to become more appropriate and appear more mature and objective.

There are no hard-and-fast rules when it comes to special requests by BPD patients, such as last-minute requests for changes in an appointment time. Generally I find there is no problem with being somewhat flexible as long as flexibility does not clearly lead to increased acting-out behavior by the patient. I have two guidelines. First, I try to accommodate the patient's requests no differently than I would if the patient did not have BPD. Second, my own convenience is paramount. If I am making an accommodation that I might resent for whatever reason, it is likely that I will be somewhat angry about it. An angry therapist is of little use to the patient. Thus, if I don't mind altering my schedule, I'll do it. If I do mind, I will not. I always return patient calls (my general policy toward telephone calls is described above), but I always do so at my own convenience, no matter how urgently the patient demands immediate attention.

If the patient is late for or misses an appointment, I inquire as to the reasons but do not spend much time exploring resistances unless they become repetitive, threaten the treatment, or adversely affect my own pocketbook. The reason for all of these policies is that the unified therapist does not use the analysis of transference as the primary mechanism of change. Thus, the therapist tries to minimize transference reactions but does not ignore them if they interfere with family-of-origin work.

INVOLVEMENT OF SIGNIFICANT OTHERS AND USE OF HOMEWORK

Since the active ingredient in the therapy is presumed to be alterations in the relationship between Linda and her family members, her significant others would, of necessity, be involved one way or another. The involvement may or may not directly include the use of conjoint sessions. Indirectly, however, Linda's relationships with significant others are invariably the focus of the primary homework assignments in the later stages of therapy.

Since Linda is unmarried and her parents and siblings live in another state, conjoint sessions would probably be impractical. If her parents were to come to visit, I would explore the pros and cons of inviting them—one at a time—to a conjoint therapy session. Possible reasons for scheduling such a session include getting further verification for a hypothesis about the family dynamics, allowing me to directly observe interactions for which a hypothesis has not been found, or helping the process by which the patient and the relative learn to metacommunicate. I do not directly mediate disputes, as patients must learn to do this for themselves when I am not around to provide assistance. A specific protocol for conjoint sessions in UT is described elsewhere (Allen, 2003).

Homework assignments are geared toward implementing the strategies, designed by the patient and therapist using role-playing, by which dysfunctional family patterns are altered. After Linda has practiced the strategies, she would be told to arrange a meeting with the targeted family member in order to proceed as planned. As in most behavioral homework assignments, patient and therapist would agree to a time and place for the interaction. Linda would need to devise a plan to get the parental figure alone in a place with an atmosphere conducive to intimate conversations. Discussing sensitive issues with more than one person creates the possibility that the other relatives may "gang up" against the patient. It is impossible for most people to stick to the strategy in the face of invalidation from several powerful family members all at once.

I would instruct Linda to continue with the strategy as planned until she reaches the goal of the conversation or becomes stymied, whichever comes first. If negative responses (Linda's or her relative's) begin to spiral out of control or if she cannot figure out where to go next, she would be instructed to withdraw from the conversation while indicating that she would like to resume the discussion at a later time.

Regardless of whether she had to abort the assignment, she would be instructed to write down the entire conversation as close to verbatim as possible, and as soon as possible after the encounter. The homework would be reviewed in detail at the next session. I would attempt to figure out what might have caused any negative interactions that took place and I then would redesign the homework to avoid the negative reactions the relative exhibited or to allow Linda to further practice earlier strategies to which she was unable to stick.

TERMINATION ISSUES

Three tasks for termination with Linda are encouraging experimentation with new types of relationships, dealing with "post-individuation depression," and instructing her about how to handle expected relapses in her own or in her family members' behavior. If she were still on medication, I would also wean her off. Once these tasks were accomplished, I would quickly suggest that we taper off treatment. I would praise her for having taken what we had talked about and putting it to good use. I would briefly discuss any feelings she might have about termination, but would expect an appropriate reaction to it.

After having altered dysfunctional family patterns, she might begin to spontaneously experiment with new behavior without input from me. If she did not, I would employ more typical cognitive behavioral techniques to get her to start. I would watch for evidence that she had started choosing and dating appropriate men and was no longer subjecting them to rages or unpredictability. I would verify that she was no longer engaging in impulsive or provocative behavior. If problematic behaviors were continuing on an ongoing basis, I would look for additional family patterns that I might have missed.

If the behaviors had stopped for a while but then recurred, or if Linda developed a recurrence of severe affective symptoms, this might indicate that she was experiencing post-individuation depression (Masterson, 1981). Should this occur, I would educate the patient about the phenomenon and reassure her that, although she may feel worse for a while, the feelings are a sign of progress and are likely to be temporary.

If Linda were avoiding men instead of acting out, I would encourage her to go out with at least three different types of appropriate men. If she were reluctant, I would ask about remaining automatic irrational thoughts that she might have, and dispute them. She might be subconsciously repeating to herself her father's prediction about attacking men. I might also encourage her to gradually increase the frequency of going out to places where she might meet new people.

I would explain that some degree of relapse into old patterns by patients and families is the rule rather than the exception, but would tell Linda that she now has enough skills to recognize such occurrences and put a stop to them. She would be instructed on how to do this by waiting until the family had calmed down and then discussing the occurrence as an example of what the family had talked about stopping. I would also warn her that family members might make requested changes in their behavior in an obnoxious way that invites criticism. For example, rather than acting as if he wants nothing to do with her, her father might start actively interfering with her life. Should this occur, she would be instructed to first praise her father for taking an interest in her before going on to quibble about the manner in which the attempt was made.

MECHANISMS OF CHANGE

As mentioned above, UT predicts that Linda's affective and behavioral problems stem ultimately from family relationship patterns that reinforce them, and that directly altering problematic relationships with important family-of-origin members will be far and away the most important mechanism of change. In order for Linda to be able to successfully challenge dysfunctional family rules and alter troublesome repetitive patterns of interaction, she must first learn to effectively metacommunicate with the leaders of her family about the family dynamics. She must let her parents know how their behavior is affecting her and request specific changes.

To help Linda accomplish this ultimate goal, the therapist must first help her to identify and accurately describe the patterns, and then to gain insight about the reasons why she and the family members behave the way they do. This latter step is necessary because she must remain empathic to get past the family's defenses against discussing family dynamics. If she is blaming or critical of family members instead, or if she does not acknowledge her own contribution to the troublesome interactions, she will induce a "fight or flight" response, and metacommunication will go nowhere.

While insights about family dynamics may themselves be powerful in inducing behavior change in patients with other disorders, in most cases of BPD, such as Linda's, these insights will not by themselves be effective in ultimately stopping self-destructive behavior. More functional families may initially react somewhat negatively to patient behavior changes but then adjust to them quickly. In such a case, a therapist who focuses only on the patient's "self" will be successful. In families that produce a BPD patient, however, the consequences of the patient changing his or her behavior without regard for the effects of such a change on others are almost invariably too grave for such patients to even contemplate.

REFERENCES

Allen, D. (1988). *A family systems approach to individual psychotherapy* (originally titled *Unifying individual and family therapies*). Northvale, NJ: Jason Aronson.

Allen, D. (1991). *Deciphering motivation in psychotherapy.* New York: Plenum.

Allen, D. (1993). Unified therapy. In G. Stricker & J. Gold (Eds.), *Comprehensive handbook of psychotherapy integration* (pp. 125–137). New York: Plenum.

Allen, D. (2003). *Psychotherapy with borderline patients: An integrated approach.* Mahwah, NJ: Lawrence Erlbaum and Associates.

Coccaro, E., & Kavoussi, R. (1997). Fluoxetine and impulsive aggressive behavior in personality-disordered subjects. *Archives of General Psychiatry, 54,* 1081–1088.

Luborsky, L., & Crits-Christoph, P. (1990). *Understanding transference: The CCRT method.* New York: Basic Books.

Masterson, J. (1981). *The narcissistic and borderline disorders: An integrated developmental approach.* New York: Brunner/Mazel.

12

Similarities and Differences in Treatment Modalities for Linda

Arthur Freeman, Mark H. Stone, and Donna Martin

Question 1. What would be your therapeutic goals for this patient?

M. David Liberman: A major goal of therapy would be to help Linda to restart the development of the self that was blocked. Ideally, by the end of therapy she would be able to feel gratified by her achievements and would develop the ability to self-soothe.

Andrea Bloomgarden: A general goal of the therapy would be for Linda to learn better interpersonal skills, reduce distress tolerance, increase her ability to self-soothe, and increase her emotional modulation. Finally, it would be essential at the outset of therapy to orient Linda to the type of therapy DBT is and to help her make a commitment to the treatment process.

Gina M. Fusco/Jack Apsche: A primary goal of treatment would be the elimination of Linda's self-destructive behaviors. This would emerge as Linda is helped to identify her tendency to engage in dichotomous thinking and generally modulate behavior. Linda would need to learn to be aware of her vulnerability factors and situations.

Windy Dryden: The therapist would initially work on (1) encouraging Linda to accept herself unconditionally for her problems so that she

Chapter compiled with the assistance of Rebecca Lynn Freeman.

could address her problems more effectively and (2) helping her to accept others as fallible beings that sometimes make egregious errors. A further goal would be for Linda to become better able to tolerate the frustration of having her wishes thwarted by others.

Mark H. Stone/Neide M. Hoffman: The therapist would make conscious Linda's hidden goals stemming from her feelings of inferiority, which are still hidden because they have excused Linda's action. The establishment of relationships would be a key component of the therapy. The therapy work would focus on helping to clarify Linda's hidden goals, whether adaptive or maladaptive.

Mark A. Reinecke/Jill Ehrenreich: An initial goal of therapy would be reducing the frequency and severity of Linda's self-destructive behavior; reducing her depression, anxiety, and anger; reducing her impulsive behavior; and increasing her affect-regulation skills. Finally, therapy would focus on increasing the number and quality of her friendships and social interactions.

Liliana Rusansky-Drob: The main goal at the onset of treatment would be to explore "the quest for the subject's desire" and to provide opportunities for expression that will decrease her need to act out.

Marvin R. Smucker/Anne Boos: Therapy would work on significantly improving Linda's affective self-regulation and interpersonal skills by developing impulse control strategies and by learning self-calming/self-soothing skills and conflict-management skills. Finally, to improve her ability to cope with and process and experiences of rejection.

David Mark Allen: The primary goals of treatment would be to resolve Linda's chief complaints—chronic anxiety and depression—and her legal problems and to alter her repetitive patterns of self-defeating behavior by identifying core conflictual themes. Finally, therapy would focus on reducing the discord within her family of origin by tracing the genesis of the family problems to their origins.

Summary for Question 1

It has been said that when one has a hammer, everything looks like a nail. Each of the contributing authors has a idiosyncratic view of what therapy with Linda would entail. Broad themes of helping her to self-soothe, cope more effectively with her life stressors, and overcome her self-defeating behavior seem common.

Only one author (Allen) would focus on Linda's family of origin and choose to include them in the therapy. Other authors would see Linda as an adult who would be treated on an individual basis. All therapists see the initial work of therapy as being to delineate the problems, identify therapeutic direction, and socialize the patient to the therapeutic experience.

Question 2. What further information would you want to have to assist you in structuring the patient's treatment? Are there specific assessment tools you would use? What would be the rationale for the use of those tools?

Liberman: Psychological testing that included projective testing should be included, with particular attention to Linda's ability to tolerate an emotionally taxing therapy.

Bloomgarden: The Dissociative Experiences Scale (DES) would be administered to address Linda's "blacking-out" experience. In-depth interviewing about her impulsive behavior would also be indicated.

Fusco/Apsche: Schema assessment would be important in terms of the activity/inactivity of the schema and how they influence her behavior.

Dryden: A UPCP Evaluation (Understanding the Person in the Context of their Problems) would be carried out. That identifies "A, B, and Cs" and the patient's compensatory strategies.

Stone/Hoffman: A full lifestyle assessment, an assessment of her early recollections, and Linda's perceptions of family demands would be elicited to derive her "Life-style."

Reinecke/Ehrenreich: Structured and semi-structured instruments such as the Structured Clinical Interview for DSM-IV (SCID), the Personality Disorder Interview—IV, the Diagnostic Interview for Borderlines—Revised, the Personality Disorder Interview, the Beck Depression Inventory, the Young-Brown Schema Questionnaire, and the Adult Attachment Interview may all be useful.

Rusansky-Drob: No specific assessment tools would be indicated.

Smucker/Boos: The SCID-II and the Composite International Diagnostic Interview could both be used to assess the presence of Axis II comorbid diagnoses.

Allen: No specific assessment tools would be used. Information would be gathered throughout the therapeutic process.

Summary of Question 2

With the exception of Rusansky-Drob and Allen, all of the authors would have Linda undergo some sort of assessment. While the assessment tools vary in complexity and focus, most of the authors would collect additional data. Both Rusansky-Drob and Allen see no need for the additional testing/assessment at any time in the therapy. Obviously, all therapists would continue to assess Linda's function throughout the therapy.

Question 3. What is your conceptualization of this patient's personality, behavior, affective state, and cognitions?

Liberman: Linda's self-development was interrupted at a very early level. She is looking for an intense mirroring relationship, probably at the level of the merger experience, which she missed out on early in life. She cannot tolerate being disappointed by her self-objects and is therefore prone to outbreaks of intense and inappropriate rage. Her use of denial and projection also speak to the early age of the damage.

Bloomgarden: Linda believes that there is something inherently wrong with her. She believes she is fundamentally bad or defective in some way. Her lifelong experience of invalidation directed her toward this position. She uses impulsive behaviors to soothe and distract herself from ongoing pain.

Fusco/Apsche: Linda exhibits a pervasive pattern of instability, reactivity, and impulsivity. Her schema include themes of abandonment, dependency, and vacillation regarding how she views "others." Her cognitive style is pervaded by dichotomous thinking, catastrophizing, labeling, jumping to conclusions, over-generalizing, mind-reading, fortune-telling, and emotional reasoning.

Dryden: Linda's behavior needs to be understood in terms of autonomy and sociotropy. She is impulsive and emotionally needy and can be capsuled as continually making overgeneralized, distorted inferences.

Stone/Hoffman: An important theme for Linda is her view that her problems are due to "everybody else." Caught in her either/or thinking that the fault is all hers or all others', Linda chooses others. It is Linda's fear that the problems she experiences could be all her fault, for this is what she was told early in life.

Reinecke/Ehrenreich: It appears that biological and perhaps temperamental factors were present that served as foundations for her present difficulties. Her disorganized attachment style may have led to a range of negative beliefs, attitudes, attributions, and expectations. She came to view herself as flawed, incapable, and unlovable; to anticipate that others would be abusive and rejecting; and to view herself as unable to control life outcomes.

Rusansky-Drob: Psychic causality cannot be unequivocally determined. She gives the impression of someone who is always in a state of urgency. Her inability to pause and delay her need for gratification is evidence of an infantile mode of functioning. This would be directly related to her primary relationship with her mother and the role of her father in the triangular relationship between the parents and the child. This would be capsuled in the Oedipus complex.

Smucker/Boos: Linda has no internalized self-calming or self-soothing strategies to deal with her strong feelings during times of emotional upset. She believes that she is unlovable and assumes that others will ultimately hurt her.

Allen: Linda's personality is an admixture of her true self and her persona. The persona is a self-destructive role that represents a sacrifice of herself for the perceived good of her family. She appears to be chronically confused and conflictual about her behavior with respect to her role within the family system.

Summary of Question 3

The consensus seems to be that Linda's behavior was somehow determined and "fixed" at an early level of psychological development. The exact nature of the fixation is debatable, but her present behavior is clearly reminiscent of the behavior of a child. She is demanding and impulsive, overgeneralizes, and lacks basic problem-solving skills or approaches.

Question 4. What potential pitfalls would you envision in this therapy? What would the difficulties be, and what would you envision as the source(s) of the difficulties?

Liberman: Acting out would be a potential problem. Linda may actually be suffering from a concealed psychosis that may emerge because of the intensity of the therapeutic relationship. While Linda may be hungry for such an intense relationship, she may also be unable to maintain a therapeutic alliance when she encounters the frustrations and disappointment that are inevitable. For example, she may be unable to except the limitations of the therapeutic relationship, and she may view the therapist as a "real" object rather than a transference object and make demands that the therapist cannot meet.

Bloomgarden: Pitfalls might occur throughout the therapeutic work. At the precommitment stage, she may have no desire to engage in therapy. She may fear allowing herself to become part of the therapy only to be later rejected and abandoned. At the commitment stage, she could be helped to see that she has the freedom to choose to continue with her life the way she currently lives it or to choose to be different.

Fusco/Apsche: Linda's conflicting schema could create a major therapeutic impediment. Given her dichotomous style, she may become intensely attached to her therapist and therefore perceive the slightest "rejection" as a reason for intense rage. Limit-setting will be difficult because Linda may perceive it as rejecting. A major pitfall can be the therapist's negative countertransference.

Dryden: At the outset of treatment, I would clarify that I could not, as her therapist, write a report to be used in court. This would have to be prepared by someone not concerned with her treatment. Linda's willingness and ability to do self-help assignments would be related to the therapist's ability to negotiate the assignments. Another possible pitfall may be Linda's reaction to the active-directive model of REBT.

Stone/Hoffman: Linda's response to the friendly, supportive environment of the therapy will be important. Will Linda see it for what it is, or will she be suspicious and constantly test the therapist, looking for a reason to avoid the therapy and the therapist?

Reinecke/Ehrenreich: The therapist must be careful to validate the legitimacy of Linda's emotional experience while remaining agnostic as to the reliability of her reports and questioning the adaptiveness of her coping. A second pitfall would be for the therapist to be focused on Linda's "crisis du jour." Finally, being aware of Linda's dependency would be important.

Rusansky-Drob: The major difficulties will likely evolve as the transference becomes established and projected primary relations are experienced toward the analyst. Another potential pitfall would be Linda's disorganized libidinal and aggressive fantasies, which may be experienced as intolerable to both Linda and the analyst.

Smucker/Boos: A key ingredient would be Linda's motivation for treatment. A second potential pitfall relates to her impulsive outbursts, which could propel her to abruptly end therapy if she became angry or upset with the therapist or with the therapy.

Allen: Most of the potential pitfalls involve transference traps that might trigger countertransference acting out. Further, Linda may be resistant to doing homework assignments involving dealing with important family members.

Summary of Question 4

The issue of potential pitfalls to therapy have all of the authors in agreement. They all predict a stormy and difficult therapy. Terms such as *resistance, acting-out, negative response, avoidance of therapy,* and *impulsivity* abound. How Linda will react to the therapist's personal style, therapeutic style, or interpersonal approach will be something that all of the therapists agree must be high on the therapeutic agenda. It will have to be carefully monitored and dealt with, as needed.

Question 5. What level of coping, adaptation, or function would you see this patient reaching as an immediate result of therapy? What result would be long term at the end of therapy?

Liberman: It is possible Linda might gain an immediate sense of relief. Linda is in desperate need of a continuing experience of feeling understood. The intensity and regularity of the treatment could meet that need and offer her that relief. Seeing an understanding therapist several times a week could help to provide a continuing source of understanding, acceptance, and soothing. Her ego strength is evident in her attainment of her education and maintaining a job. It might be possible for Linda to develop and maintain the ability to recognize, understand, and accept her own needs and those of others.

Bloomgarden: Linda's ability to cope would be motivated by her readiness to change. She would learn that she is not fundamentally bad but that there was a "poor fit" between her environment and her biology. It would probably take a few years for Linda to be fully functional, and she might resort to her old symptoms when under significant stress. Social relationships could be improved if she could learn to receive feedback and recognize her impact on others.

Fusco/Apsche: Linda's level of coping and adaptation will depend on the ability of the therapist to develop and maintain a collaborative relationship, despite Linda testing the relationship on a frequent basis. When she improves her ability to self-monitor for dichotomous thinking, suicidal and parasuicidal behavior, and mood changes, Linda's overall functioning is likely to improve. As she continues to examine her long-held beliefs, she can learn alternative means of coping and access her strengths.

Dryden: Predicting the outcome of therapy is notoriously difficult. The best way to know how well or poorly Linda will respond is to begin the therapy and observe Linda's response. She seems to thrive in a structured environment, and the structure of REBT may be extremely helpful. Successful therapy would mean that Linda would be able to tolerate her disturbed negative feelings, deal with them productively, reduce her impulsivity, think rationally, act appropriately when others act badly toward her, and respect the boundaries of others. Her maintenance of these gains would depend on the extent to which she practiced her REBT self-help skills.

Stone/Hoffman: Linda will challenge the therapist. The therapist must be aware of and in charge of his or her personal Life Style. A calm manner and firm and fair limits would be important to help Linda structure her experience. Linda's present coping strategies have served to safeguard her self-esteem. Trying other approaches may appear very threatening to her. But if the therapist is able to maintain a strong positive affirmation and support of Linda's capability to succeed, she can be helped to learn new ways of responding.

Reinecke/Ehrenreich: It would be very difficult to predict long-term outcome. Nonspecific relationship factors will play a major role. It should be possible to provide Linda with techniques that will reduce her feelings of depression, anxiety, and anger. These techniques will also likely reduce the frequency of suicidal gestures and attempts. Reconstruction of her schema will be difficult, and the goal of therapy will be to modify her most malignant beliefs and provide her with techniques for coping with the emotional reactions that they elicit. She may not be fully motivated to change and may even be unaware of her social and work problems because she maintains an other-blaming stance.

Rusansky-Drob: Lacanian psychoanalysis regards as a myth the idea of an adapted and integrated personality where particular emotions, cognitions, and behaviors are catalogued and labeled in a hierarchical order in terms of their health, adaptation, and level of severity.

Smucker/Boos: The success of efforts for improving affective self-regulation, increasing her low tolerance for emotional distress, and replacing her uncontrollable anger/rage outbursts will be directly linked to Linda's ability to self-calm and self-soothe. Taking part in well-defined, structured social activities could significantly improve her interpersonal skills. Her prognosis for adaptive change will be related to her ability to develop a healthy, trusting, therapeutic relationship.

Allen: In the short run, Linda might be helped to weather her affective storms and impulsivity through the use of medication. A strong working relationship, persistence in maintaining the therapeutic relationship and willingness to do the self-help assignments will be important to improve her overall function. It will be important to help Linda avoid her family dysfunction.

Summary of Question 5

There is broad disagreement over the course of therapy. The point on which several authors agree is that it is difficult to determine the outcome of therapy at the onset of the work. The nonspecific factors referred to by Reinecke and Ehrenreich will have a powerful impact on the therapy.

The consensus seems to be that Linda could be helped to gain some symptomatic relief of her depressive and anxious symptoms. The deeper, more pervasive issues of her personality style/disorder would be far more difficult to treat, as would be predicting the direction and success of treatment.

Question 6. What would be your timeline (duration) for therapy? What would be the frequency and duration of the sessions?

Liberman: Treatment would involve four or five sessions per week, with each session lasting 45–50 minutes. It would take at least 4–5 years for Linda to complete her analysis.

Bloomgarden: The skills training group would involve group and individual therapy, each on a once-weekly basis, for a year. She could re-contract for additional treatment. The length of treatment, therefore, would depend on her desire to continue to change or her satisfaction with her present status.

Fusco/Apsche: Linda would most likely benefit from psychotherapy for a minimum of 1 year, on a once-weekly basis. She may require additional sessions to support her through high-risk times or when she is experiencing intense anxiety. Sessions would be 50–60 minutes.

Dryden: If Linda can acknowledge the full extent of her difficulties, therapy should take 2–3 years, with weekly sessions lasting 50 minutes. She might also choose short term treatment when she thinks she needs further help. The short-term work would last approximately 2 years.

Stone/Hoffman: The time required for therapy will be based on the time required for Linda to develop better relationships. The work environment would be the best venue for this.

Reinecke/Ehrenreich: Therapy would be held once weekly for approximately 12 months. Additional sessions to deal with emergencies would be made available.

Rusansky-Drob: Within the Lacanian framework, sessions are as long as necessary (sometimes longer and sometimes shorter than 45 minutes). The end of the session is neither arbitrary nor guided by real time, but rather by logical or psychological time and by the workings of the analysand's speech. The sessions are not limited by the artificial constraints of scheduled time.

Smucker/Boos: It is very likely that Linda's therapy would last for several years with one or two weekly sessions of standard length.

Allen: Therapy would be once weekly or once every other week. More frequent sessions are counterproductive because they lead to transference reactions. Sessions last 45 minutes. Therapy is usually 70–120 sessions. New crises are not rewarded by extra time or sessions with the therapist.

Summary of Question 6

The expected time for Linda's therapy runs from 1 year to 10 or more years, therapy being an indefinite process. Agreement abounds that sessions would be "standard" at about 45–50 minutes and generally occurring on a weekly basis.

The open question for Rusansky-Drob is that therapy from the Lacanian perspective may involve a longer or shorter session depending on the session content and process.

Question 7. Are there specific or special techniques that you would implement in the therapy? What would they be?

Liberman: No modifications of the standard psychoanalytic treatment would be necessary.

Bloomgarden: Humor would be important in working with Linda. The use of paradoxical imagery (devil's advocate) could be used. Self-disclosure, if relevant, would be used.

Fusco/Apsche: "Standard" cognitive therapy techniques might be varied as needed. A major focus will be Linda's difficulty in trust. Linda's need for constant self-monitoring and improving her other monitoring skills will be essential.

Dryden: Standard REBT techniques would be varied as needed. Feedback would be important, so Linda would be offered behavioral parameters, which would be useful. The use of self-help workbooks could help Linda decide which techniques might be more or less useful. Building a sense of healthy boundaries would be important for Linda. Linda does not fully understand relationship rules, and she could be helped to develop these rules.

Stone/Hoffman: It will be essential to provide Linda with a great deal of support and encouragement. It will further be important to identify Linda's assets and capitalize on them. Even miniscule examples of productive change should be encouraged. Linda will need to learn how to express feelings and ideas to others without becoming fearful of what they think.

Reinecke/Ehrenreich: Many of the techniques are those used in standard cognitive therapy. Initial interventions would also be directed toward reducing Linda's self-destructive behavior. Developing affect-regulation skills will also be important. The development of fairly detailed plans to deal with frustration would be developed, wherein the therapist can teach, model, role play, offer recommendations, and reinforce Linda's efforts to successfully cope with stressful events.

Rusansky-Drob: The techniques of listening, inquiry, punctuation, and management of the session will be essential. Understanding dreams, slips of the tongue, and symptoms in structural terms can be accessed through the use of metaphor. Metonymy involves the chain of associations in language in accord with nonsemantic principles such as sound or temporal association.

Smucker/Boos: Specific imagery techniques would involve (1) identifying, activating, and modifying her most distressing images and (2) transforming these images and their meanings into narrative language so that a higher order, cognitive reprocessing, can occur. In-session imagery could begin by having Linda visualize the beginning of an upsetting image or memory. If the fear was trauma related, then imaginal exposure would be used and imagery modification would be facilitated by the therapist. It would be important that the therapist maintain the Socratic dialogue.

Allen: The most important technique is an attitude that the therapist maintains and communicates to the patient, i.e., that the patient and her family members are not defective. Other specific techniques include treatment contracting, paradoxical predictions, discounting of "obvious explanations" for behavior. Role-playing techniques would be useful for clarifying family interactions.

Summary of Question 7

The authors see their particular "standard" treatment as the basis for working with Linda. None of the therapists sees the need for reaching out beyond their specific school for help or additional treatment foci.

Question 8. Are there special cautions to be observed in working with this patient (e.g., danger to self or others, transference, countertransference)? Are there any particular resistances you would expect, and how would you deal with them?

Liberman: As the therapist allows the unfolding of an intense mirroring transference, Linda could misinterpret the stance of the therapist and begin to believe the therapist was there to gratify Linda's need for a "real" relationship. Linda would become unable or unwilling to accept the limitations of the therapeutic relationship and demand that the therapist meet her needs for praise and approval. It will be essential for the therapist to be aware of countertransference. Acting out is always a form of resistance, and the therapist would need to be alert to the possibility of Linda's acting out in response to both situational elements as well as to the ups and downs of the therapy.

Bloomgarden: Linda would be expected to have feelings, problems, and issues in the therapeutic relationship. This falls into the category of therapy-interfering behaviors. Linda would be encouraged to talk about her feelings regarding the therapy and the therapist. These reactions would be normalized early in the therapy, and Linda would be informed of the limits of the therapeutic relationship.

Fusco/Apsche: An ongoing assessment for potential self-harm, suicidality, and aggression toward others should occur throughout therapy. Many of Linda's resistances are likely to be products of dormant schema relating to trust and abandonment that become activated within the therapeutic relationship. The potential for powerful countertransference (both positive and negative) may impact on treatment, and the therapist must remember the nature and style of the patient's behavior. Further, the patient may try to manipulate the therapist by rage, expressions of mistrust, and statements regarding abandonment. It is essential that the therapist not internalize these manipulations but maintain the therapeutic collaboration.

Dryden: Linda may try to sexualize the therapeutic relationship because of a need for familiarity or the idea that this is the only way she can get attention from a male. This behavior would be identified and the above hypotheses put forward for her consideration. She would be helped to question her beliefs using empirical, logical, and pragmatic arguments. Similarly, Linda may show oversensitivity to rejection in the therapeutic relationship and would be helped to understand her core irrational beliefs about rejection.

Regarding countertransference, the therapist's feelings may be a reliable guide as to how others respond to Linda, in which case the reaction could be shared and discussed. If this is not the case, the therapist would need to identify, challenge, and change his or her irrational beliefs about Linda. Supervision might also be sought so that an objective view might be obtained.

Stone/Hoffman: Therapists might be aware of the transference issues, which are termed "social feeling." Essential to therapy will be a bond with the patient to facilitate movement. The relationship must always be addressed.

Reinecke/Ehrenreich: It will be important to focus on Linda's provocative style, which has the effect of stimulating, exciting, and provoking others to action. It will be important to focus not only on controlling these behaviors but also on understanding how these behaviors reflect her tacit beliefs, unstated goals, and expectations. The therapeutic relationship and the therapist's thoughts and feelings in response to Linda's actions can yield important information on her impact on others.

Rusansky-Drob: Apart from the necessity of providing additional sessions and phone contact in the early phases of treatment, no further cautions need to be observed.

Smucker/Boos: Areas of special caution would include transference, countertransference, danger to self, and danger to others. It would be critical for the therapist to identify and respond to Linda's transference struggles in ways that weaken rather than reinforce her negative, maladaptive schema, and to begin to lay the groundwork for "a corrective emotional experience." The therapist would need to be sensitive to Linda's needs for safety and control and may invite her to actively collaborate in setting the agenda goals and foci of therapy. It is crucial that the therapist not internalize any of Linda's reactions or behaviors. Given her suicide history, it would be advisable to negotiate a safety contract and a specific plan of action to take if she has self-injurious urges. Linda's potential for harm to others should be monitored throughout the therapy.

Allen: Linda might attempt to prove family myths that guide her behavior. That is, she must attack or be attacked by any man with whom she is alone. She might do so by becoming very seductive or alternatively devaluing the therapist and attacking his or her vulnerabilities. The therapist must be alert to Linda acting out her persona and trying to induce the therapist to act out with her.

Summary of Question 8

Most authors would gird themselves for problems that would emerge from the therapeutic relationship. Because the relationship would be microcosmic of Linda's world and experience, she might try to sexualize the relationship, and demand more of the therapist than the reasonable therapeutic boundaries and limits would allow, and possibly become frightened by the therapeutic relationship and try to run from it.

A second area where most authors would exhibit great care is in their reaction to Linda's evoking style. To be successful with Linda, the therapist must be able to weather the potential storminess without rejecting Linda. At the same time, the therapist must be able to reflect and make clear the consequences of her evocative style.

The issue of Linda's self-harming behavior is something with which all therapists would need to deal.

Question 9. Are there any areas that you would choose to avoid or not address with this patient? Why?

Liberman: Linda might come to a successful resolution to her therapy without having to transfer all of the painful and negative experiences of her life onto the analyst. She could finish her therapy without going through the rages and anguish that came from the failure of significant others to understand and appreciate the real "person" of the patient.

Bloomgarden: There is nothing that would be avoided. The therapist would help Linda prioritize the different symptoms so that Linda did not try to do everything at once or do more than she could handle.

Fusco/Apsche: It would be contraindicated to address "hot" cognitions too early in the therapy because they may overwhelm the patient. Therefore, emotionally laden experiences with her family should be initially avoided.

Dryden: There are no issues that would be avoided or not addressed with Linda. The therapist's response would be guided by two principles: (1) the primacy of the therapeutic alliance and (2) challenging but not overwhelming the patient.

Stone/Hoffman: The therapist would postpone moving Linda too quickly into issues regarding friends and the pursuit of intimacy. The work issue, which appears to be safer, would be a better goal.

Reinecke/Ehrenreich: There are no specific issues that, if raised by Linda, would not be appropriate for discussion. If, however, Linda were having substance abuse or eating disorder problems, a referral for an empirically supported treatment would be in order.

Rusansky-Drob: There are no issues that would not be addressed with this patient.

Smucker/Boos: Countertransference reactions would not be shared.

Allen: No major areas of the patient's emotional and behavioral dysfunction would be considered off limits.

Summary of Question 9

All authors agree that there are few, if any, areas that would be avoided in working with Linda. The key ingredient in the sharing would be the timing and the pacing of how various issues emerge in the therapy. The therapist must be in control as the issues unfold.

Question 10. Is medication warranted for this patient? What effect would you hope/expect the medication to have?

Liberman: Linda should be evaluated at the outset of therapy for antidepressants and mood stabilizers to help her with the emotional demands of the early stages of treatment.

Bloomgarden: Medication might be helpful for Linda's depressed or anxious feelings, and she would be supported in receiving a psychiatric evaluation.

Fusco/Apsche: Medication is often used as an adjunctive form of treatment with the aim of ameliorating key symptoms of BPD, which include affective instability, impulsivity, transient psychotic symptoms, and self-injurious behavior. It is important for the therapist to elicit Linda's automatic thoughts related to taking medications and maintaining compliance.

Dryden: Medication would be appropriate, given two concerns. First, would Linda use her medication to manage her feelings, thus interfering with the psychotherapy focused on raising her tolerance for negative feelings? Second, is there a risk that Linda could overdose on the medication? If yes, then medication would initially be withheld.

Stone/Hoffman: Individual psychology does not preclude other medical treatment. No evidence is seen at this point for Linda's need for medication.

Reinecke/Ehrenreich: Medications may best be viewed as part of a broad, multidimensional treatment program. Medication can be effective in reducing dysphoria, anxiety, anger, and affective lability. The risk of Linda overdosing on the medication remains an important concern.

Rusansky-Drob: Patients would be referred for psychiatric consultation only under very specific circumstances: i.e., the presence of a clear and active psychosis or the direct expression of a suicidal wish accompanied by a suicidal plan, especially in the context of a history of prior suicide attempts or serious impulsivity. Therefore, I would not recommend Linda for medication at this point.

Smucker/Boos: Pharmacological treatment would be aimed at reducing specific clusters of symptoms, such as depression, anxiety, and impulse control. The taking of any medication that, with prolonged usage, would increase the risk for developing a tolerance or dependency, should be avoided.

Allen: A trial of an SSRI and a long-acting benzodiazepine is warranted with this patient. The medication would be expected to help the process of therapy by allowing Linda to partially avoid extreme emotional reactions to discussions of stressful topics.

Summary of Question 10

All of the authors agree that medication is an important element in a comprehensive treatment plan. Whether they would refer Linda for medication or see medication as a key element in Linda's therapy is an issue upon which they disagree. Allen, speaking for one group, sees medication as a clear and important part of the overall treatment. Dryden cautions that, given Linda's suicidal danger, medication would need to be carefully monitored. Rusansky-Drob sees little reason to refer Linda for medication.

Question 11. What are the strengths of the patient that can be used in therapy?

Liberman: Linda has shown tenacity and determination in putting herself through school without financial or emotional support from her family. She has been able to hold on to her teaching position and work with her students over a number of years. These strengths would need to be identified, recognized, and mobilized in her therapy.

Bloomgarden: Linda's nuturance and cultivating of her bonsai plants would be something that could be built upon and possibly broadened to include other creatures. Linda's demonstrated competence to teach fourth grade is another strength, as well as is her ability to work well within a structured environment. Her completion of her graduate degree while working and her apparent intelligence and motivation to succeed are all strengths that could be used in the therapeutic endeavor.

Fusco/Apsche: Despite numerous challenges in her personal life, Linda has maintained steady employment. She has maintained a residence, suggesting a level of awareness of the basic requirements of independent living. She seems to respond well to direction from authority, which might suggest her responsiveness to limit-setting and adherence to emergency procedures and to external structure. Finally, Linda demonstrates an awareness of the basic struggles in her life; this insight may be used as a gateway into deeper and more complex schema.

Dryden: Linda did well in school and college, suggesting intelligence and persistence. This also shows that she can put a long-range plan into effect and carry it through. Linda is able to function in a well-defined job. Linda's interest in and caring for her bonsai trees suggests an others-focused caring ability. Therapy could focus on those constructive skills that Linda has that can be applied to her life circumstances.

Stone/Hoffman: Linda is intelligent and well educated. She can at times respond to reason and follow a line of discussion. In a supportive environment, Linda may even become comfortable enough to solicit additional information. She holds a responsible job in a highly sensitive area with impressionable children.

Reinecke/Ehrenreich: Linda appears to be reasonably intelligent and able to function effectively in predictable, structured, stable settings. Linda appears to be interested in developing a network of social contacts and support. This would be emphasized and reinforced along with helping Linda to develop insight regarding her present behavior and social skills where necessary.

Rusansky-Drob: Linda appears to have been able to break certain familiar traditions and to try to find her own way in life. While these attempts have not always been successful, her desire for independence and a certain rebellion against parental norms can be regarded as a potential agent for therapeutic change. Overall, however, the question of strengths and weaknesses is quite alien to Lacanian psychoanalysis.

Linda cannot be rated in terms of certain adaptive "standards" and societal norms.

Smucker/Boos: Linda is able to hold down a job, live by herself, support herself financially, remove herself from harmful relationships, and often protect herself from environmental dangers. She is able to make a good first impression when presenting herself to others, indicating a basic awareness of social skills. Finally, she appears able to make attentive observations of her environment, which could be useful later in therapy when self-management and self-regulation techniques are taught.

Allen: Linda is clearly quite intelligent, as evidenced by her work and her success in graduate school. Her work and school history have been fairly stable, and her problems in the relationship area are relatively circumscribed. It could be beneficial to the therapy that both parents are still living and cognitively intact. This will allow her to revisit the source of her distress and to renegotiate troublesome interactions that trigger or reinforce dysfunctional affects, beliefs, and behaviors.

Summary of Question 11

The authors agree that Linda's intelligence, her persistence, and her ability to achieve in school, maintain employment, care for her students, and maintain a hobby would all be important positive signs. This last, her hobby of bonsai, show that she can have patience, caring, nurturing, and a future orientation.

Question 12. How would you address limits, boundaries, and limit-setting with this patient?

Liberman: It would be explained to Linda that the analyst would sometimes have to forego the normal social conventions such as answering personal questions or saying things that one would normally expect another person to say. It would be acknowledged that these limitations might be frustrating and upsetting, but do have a use and purpose. Linda would also be urged to not act on her feelings of frustration and anger. She would be encouraged to note her feelings, to contain herself, and then to bring these feelings into her sessions so that the therapist could help her to understand the basis and context of her feelings, thereby making the feelings less disruptive and upsetting than they had been in the past.

Bloomgarden: Linda would be educated about the use of telephone consultation to help her in the moment of a problem. She would be taught that the therapist cannot always take a random phone call or call back immediately, which would be a natural limit and fact about the world. Her wanting or wishing to be called back immediately or to call at any time would not be wrong, nor would she be wishing for too much, but her wishes cannot always be met. She would be told when it would be most likely that the therapist could be reached. This could be used to help Linda learn to delay gratification and to work on things herself until she can reach her therapist. Another limit is that the therapist would not allow herself to be verbally abused. This information would be included in the informed consent form at the onset of therapy.

Fusco/Apsche: Because a major area of difficulty for Linda involves interpersonal and boundary issues, limit-setting would be essential. Boundary violations may include late-night calls, multiple intrusive interruptions, or requests/demands for additional time within therapy. In its extreme form, limit- and boundary-testing can also include threats of suicide or self-harm, or threats against another person. Clear, concrete, and ethical limits are discussed at the beginning of therapy and are a part of the therapy contract. Finally, Linda would be advised that the therapist's responsibility, at all times, is to ensure her safety.

Dryden: Clear boundaries and limits would be set out at the beginning of therapy. This helps the patient know what to expect, which may limit Linda's testing to see if the therapist is strong enough to cope with her. Second, limit-setting will help Linda understand that the therapist is a person and not some impersonal object without feelings who can be treated badly and who is expected to absorb the treatment. Third, limit-setting helps Linda to become more collaborative in the therapeutic work. The treatment contract would include statements regarding fees, session frequency and duration, extra therapy contact, and self-harming behavior. Continued boundary violations would lead to the termination of the therapy relationship.

Stone/Hoffman: Linda would need to keep regular appointments. The therapist needs to help her to see that the best tools for her are order and reason. Treatment goals would be worked out cooperatively, and additional goals can be developed as therapy progresses. Linda would need to be helped without the therapist solving her problems for her.

Reinecke/Ehrenreich: By setting limits and boundaries, the therapist serves as a model for how one can manage stressful situations. The rules, boundaries, strategies, and guidelines are openly discussed and, over time, would ideally be internalized. Setting and maintaining appropriate limits and boundaries allows the therapeutic relationship to become a venue for developing affect-regulation skills and for changing maladaptive beliefs.

Rusansky-Drob: The analyst sets those limit that ensure the continuance of the analytic work. Lacanian analysts use limit-setting not as a vehicle for combative resistance but as a means of punctuating it and causing a certain anguish and wonder in the patient. The boundaries, therefore, are very broad, and limits are mutable.

Smucker/Boos: Linda's longstanding difficulties with interpersonal boundaries and limits are likely to be manifested in the therapy, which makes the therapeutic relationship an excellent opportunity for her to learn that the actions and reactions of others are often quite predictable and interrelated with clear antecedents and consequences. From the outset, the therapist must be clear and consistent with Linda about the rules, limits, and boundaries of the therapy and what she can expect the consequences to be when the limits are not maintained. A safety contract would need to be negotiated early in treatment, and clear guidelines for crisis management would need to be established. It is imperative that the therapist find a skillful balance between an overly rigid handling of boundaries and consequences and too much flexibility with too little structure.

Allen: The therapist should maintain a professional demeanor and avoid any hint of a dual relationship. The therapist would avoid dressing casually, address the patient formally as Ms. P. (unless she insisted on being called something else), and appear somewhat oblivious to subtly seductive behavior, unless it became repetitive. Overall, the therapist would try to be warm but "all business." Patient calls would always be returned (at the therapist's convenience), and appointment times would be maintained flexibly so that patient requests for time changes could be accommodated, as long as the therapist's convenience is maintained.

Summary of Question 12

Dryden voices the response for all of the authors: "Clear boundaries and limits would be set out at the beginning of therapy." Through the explication of the boundaries and the maintenance of those boundaries throughout the therapy, the therapy can have a form and format that would protect both Linda and the therapist.

Question 13. Would you want to involve significant others in the treatment? Would you use out-of-session work (homework) with this patient? What homework would you use?

Liberman: Generally, significant others are not involved with the treatment of an adult patient. The only out-of-session work would be remembering dreams and attending to her feelings and bringing them into the sessions, rather than acting out.

Bloomgarden: If at all possible, the therapist would encourage the involvement of Linda's significant others, not necessarily in regular family therapy, but as an opportunity to observe Linda's relationship dynamics and interpersonal behaviors. It would allow the therapist to observe Linda's interpersonal skills and to guide her when she gets off track or provide positive reinforcement and encourage her when she is on track.

She would have weekly homework from her group, from the DBT workbook, as well as homework from the individual therapy, which would be developed collaboratively. Overall, the individual therapist can reinforce the group work.

Fusco/Apsche: Because Linda's parents have relocated at a distance from the therapist, it would be unlikely that they would come for sessions (except telephonically). Linda's siblings do not appear to be a major part of her life and would not be a part of the treatment. If, during treatment, Linda were to develop a romantic relationship, the treatment plan might be altered to include this individual.

Linda's out-of-session work would most likely include techniques and activities designed to help her identify and modify her dichotomous thinking. The DTR would help Linda learn to self-monitor her thinking. Linda would also benefit from homework assignments that address her mood changes and lability, such as the mood log.

Dryden: Given Linda's life and family situation, involving her significant others in therapy does not seem feasible. Homework would be used to encourage Linda to accept herself, overcome her feelings of unhealthy anger about the behavior of others, express healthy feelings of anger in an assertive and respectful manner, and contain her disturbed feelings long enough to deal with them in productive ways, rather than to impulsively strive to get rid of them quickly through self-harm.

Stone/Hoffman: It would be best to give Linda "center stage" and provide her the maximum attention; therefore, family involvement would not be a focus for treatment.

Reinecke/Ehrenreich: It can be quite helpful to include family members in the therapy process, if practical. It would be useful to include Linda's parents or siblings only if it appears they could actively support the treatment process, and if there was the possibility of improving the quality of their relationship with her. If she had a significant other, he or she could, with her permission, be invited to participate in the treatment.

Every session should conclude with the collaborative development of a homework task based on a skill discussed in the session, which can be practiced during the week. Commonly used homework assignments include preparing a list of specific treatment goals, mood monitoring, participation in social activities, rational problem solving, identifying maladaptive thought and cognitive distortions, formulating adaptive counterthoughts, preparing a journal of experiences that are consistent and inconsistent with Linda's maladaptive expectations or schema, affect-regulation exercises, attachment-based exercises, assertive communication skills, relaxation training, preparing a journal of expectations for relationships, and practicing negotiation and compromise.

Rusansky-Drob: Because the work of analysis does not occur exclusively or even primarily on the conscious level, the idea of assigning specific homework to a patient is not viable. Punctuating the in-session material—by cutting the session short just as the patient achieves an important insight, experiences a significant affect, or asks a psychologically meaningful question—ensures that the patient will not bury this material. From the Lacanian perspective, most of the analytic work is conducted by the patient outside of the session because the patient returns to the point of "punctuation" to question him- or herself and the experience.

Smucker/Boos: Involving the mother in Linda's therapy, in person, by phone, or by correspondence, may be a consideration at some point. Imagery encounters rather than actual encounters may offer a safer and more productive therapeutic forum for addressing her family-related anger and guilt.

Homework with Linda would initially involve daily listening to the therapy session audiotapes. Homework could also involve Linda documenting problematic situations and changes that occur between sessions, her emotional reactions to these events, and her attempts to cope with them. Linda could then bring her data into the next session for further discussion and processing.

Allen: Since the active ingredient in the therapy is presumed to be alterations in the relationship between the patient and family members, her significant others would, of necessity, be involved in some way. While conjoined sessions would be impractical for Linda, if her parents were to come to visit, the therapist would explore the pros and cons of inviting her parents, one at a time, to a conjoined therapy session.

Homework assignments are geared toward implementing the strategies, designed by the patient and therapist using role-playing, by which dysfunctional family patterns are altered.

Summary of Question 13

The term *homework* might be a source of disagreement for several authors. All agree that Linda will need to continue her therapy work outside of the consulting room. Whether that work involves structured exercises as suggest by Dryden, Fusco and Apsche, and Smucker and Boos, or more internal processing as suggested by Rusansky-Drob, Linda will need to do out-of-session work.

The availability of her family would make their involvement inconvenient at best and unlikely at worst. If they were more geographically accessible, it would still be questionable as to whether they would be actively sought to be involved in the therapy.

Question 14. What would be the issues to be addressed in termination? How would termination and relapse prevention be structured?

Liberman: The termination process would be a critical part of Linda's therapy. Linda may not have successfully negotiated the separation individuation process, and that would make Linda's process of separating with the therapist crucial. It would be quite conceivable that Linda would reenact and act out with her therapist the trauma of separation that she initially suffered in her family. It could be quite important to be in touch with Linda as she alternated between her wishes to be on her own and her wishes to be with her therapist. It would be quite common for all of the old issues to flare up again. This would represent a last desperate attempt on the part of the patient to stave off a healthy separation. As issues of separation and termination show up more frequently in the patient's associations and dreams, the therapist would begin to point out that leaving seems to be on the patient's mind. A timeline would be important for the ending of treatment. It is also important that patients know they can return to therapy if they feel it is necessary.

Regarding relapse, the therapist would point out to Linda that everyone stumbles and falls, which is a part of life. Stumbling is not viewed as relapse, and returning to therapy does not represent a failure in treatment.

Bloomgarden: Termination would occur when Linda felt ready to leave. When she felt satisfied with her life and wasn't in need of changing anything else, Linda and the therapist would deal with her feelings of loss in leaving this relationship. The termination plan would involve a slow tapering schedule, first every other week, then once a month to help her adjust to the change. At this point in therapy a review of what she had accomplished and changed in her life would be discussed.

With regard to relapse prevention, Linda would need to know what her early-warning symptoms would be. If Linda were ready to leave, she would ideally have some quality relationships in her life and thus would have people she could talk with to help her understand her life experience. She would need to use those relationships before seeking therapy again.

Fusco/Apsche: Linda's life themes of abandonment, dependency, trust, and unlovability will become activated and compelling when discussing the issue of termination. As a result, Linda may relapse to her long-held patterns of reactions, including acting out, to keep the therapist involved. The therapist would elicit automatic thoughts about the projected or pending termination so that distortions could be disputed or tested.

Relapse prevention would include careful self-monitoring and identification when Linda is beginning to experience an exacerbation of symptoms. Interventions to prevent relapse may include homework assignment, bibliotherapy, examples of healthy coping in high-stress situations, names and phone numbers of supportive individuals, reminders of the chain of events that led to impulsive behaviors, and a safety plan to deal with high-risk behavior.

Dryden: Termination with Linda will likely bring her issue of abandonment into sharp relief. As termination with such patients tends to discourage them from seeking further help from their terminating therapist, Linda might choose to see the therapist infrequently on a planned basis or for consultation when her attempts to help herself have failed. If therapy has not gone well, and Linda is one of those patients who will not help herself, then the clinical reality might involve ongoing therapy to prevent self-harm.

Relapse prevention would help Linda to distinguish between a lapse (a slight and temporary return to a problem state) and a relapse (a complete and more enduring return to a problem state). Linda would be encouraged to see that lapses are inevitable in the change process and provide her with the valuable opportunity to use her new–found self-help skills. Through the use of discussion, role-play, and imagery, Linda would be encouraged to practice coping responses to vulnerability factors that she responded to in the past with unhelpful behaviors, thoughts, and feelings.

Stone/Hoffman: The prognosis is for a long, slow course of treatment with periodic returns to her old ways of behaving. Change for Linda is probably more frightening than difficult and would need to be measured in small steps so that expectations do not get ahead of actions for client and therapist. Termination may be interpreted by Linda as abandonment. With the development of new skills over a relatively long treatment period, Linda may be helped to effectively cope with the broad range of life tasks.

Reinecke/Ehrenreich: Given Linda's style, her reactions to impending termination may range from increased dependency and expressions of helplessness to cool indifference, anger, and dismissive scorn. It would be useful to take recession slowly, offer the patient booster sessions as needed, reinforce the skills learned, and recommend that medication be maintained after psychotherapy has been completed.

Linda would be encouraged to identify situations that are likely to trigger the reemergence of symptoms. If she can predict these situations, she can be prepared for them and have a list of strategies and techniques that she has found to be effective for mood regulation. The goal would be to prepare Linda for the disappointments and losses of life by instilling a sense of efficacy and hope.

Rusansky-Drob: The vast majority of psychoanalytic treatments terminate prior to what might be called the end of analysis and are not signals that the analytic work has ended or that further work cannot be accomplished by the patient on her own.

The only relapse prevention that an analyst can provide is the continued possibility of speech. It is through the articulation of conflict, fantasy, and ultimately desire that the patient can forestall acting out such conflicts and avoid the formation of new symptoms.

Smucker/Boos: Linda struggles with perceived unpredictable circumstances and uncontrollable interpersonal threats that leave her feeling extremely sensitive to and fearful of change. The end of treatment may be viewed as a threat and may trigger an array of ambivalent thoughts and feelings about herself, the therapy, and relationships. Discussions about termination should begin early in therapy so that Linda will have ample time to express and process her fears, concerns, and anxieties. Therapy should be phased out slowly, with the time between sessions gradually increased from weekly to biweekly to monthly to bimonthly, to quarterly maintenance sessions. Linda may call the therapist between sessions if necessary. Before placing a call to the therapist, Linda would be encouraged to have an imaginary conversation with the therapist. She would listen carefully to the therapist's "voice" and write out in a journal what she heard the therapist say. If after recording and processing this "conversation," Linda still needed to call, she would be encouraged to do so.

Relapse prevention planning would include reviewing with the therapist the interventions that were successfully used throughout treatment and reflecting on how similar interventions might be used in the future. This list of interventions would be recorded in a concrete, step-by-step manner and would offer Linda a kind of psychological first-aid kit.

Allen: Four tasks for termination are encouraging experimentation with new types of relationships, dealing with post-individuation depression, instructing her on how to handle expected relapse in her own or in her family members' behavior, and weaning her off medication. Linda would be taught that after termination she may feel worse for a while but that those feelings are a sign of progress and are likely to be temporary. It would be explicitly explained to Linda that some degree of relapse into old patterns is the rule rather than the exception. Ideally, Linda would have enough insight and skill to recognize such occurrences and put a stop to them.

Summary of Question 14

Termination will likely bring with it an exacerbation of Linda's worst fears about abandonment, rejection, and isolation, resulting in an increase in her dependency. Weaning her from the frequency of the therapy is a tactic that most of the authors would endorse. The sessions would be tapered off over time. There would, of course, be relapse. Linda would be alerted to that eventuality and offered a review of the skills and insights that she has gained in the course of the therapy.

Question 15. What do you see as the hoped-for mechanisms of change for this patient, in order of relative importance?

Liberman: The mechanism of change is the remobilization of the self-object needs in the transference. Linda would develop compensatory structures as a replacement for the needed but unsatisfying defensive structures that were being replaced. A successful treatment outcome for Linda would be to develop a realistic appreciation of who she is, what she has missed out on, and what she has achieved. A crucial aspect of this treatment would be the development of insight. This includes the ability to understand what one is feeling and why one is feeling that way and the ability to understand the feelings of others. It would be hoped that Linda could develop a useful and effective insight into both herself and others.

Bloomgarden: Linda would learn about her temperament and become aware of her exquisite sensitivity. She would know how to ride the tide of a feeling and would have developed many skills to cope with possible uncomfortable experiences. She would learn about how her invalidating family environment left her with many skill deficits. Second, if she could learn to tolerate painful moments and grieve appropriately, she would no longer need to act in self-destructive and impulsive ways.

Fusco/Apsche: Because Linda's affective instability is seen as directly related to the distortions created by her all-or-nothing thinking, Linda would be helped to move toward a more moderate position. A second major mechanism of change would be to address and modify her impulsive style by self-monitoring, Linda can make choices out of awareness rather than out of a conditioned response set. Because therapy represents a microcosm of Linda's life, positive interactions with the therapist can be generalized to outside relationships.

Dryden: Linda would need to identify and tolerate her unhealthy negative feelings rather than act impulsively to get rid of them. By using her disturbed feelings, Linda could identify what she was most disturbed about in the specific situations under consideration. Linda would then identify the irrational belief that mediates between the situations and her consequential thoughts, feelings, and actions. She would challenge and change this irrational belief, formulate a rational alternative to it, and then act in ways consistent with this rational belief. She could then correct remaining cognitive distortions. Finally, Linda would be helped to generalize these skills more widely in her life.

Stone/Hoffman: To the three life tasks, a fourth task would be important, that of creative endeavor. Linda's creative energy that was used in the past to create self-delusions and misperceptions could be mobilized productively for her benefit.

Reinecke/Ehrenreich: The mechanisms of change would be to promote behavioral and emotional change by rectifying affect regulation deficits, changing maladaptive schema, improving social problem solving, and developing a more secure adult attachment style.

Rusansky-Drob: As a result of her increased self-reflection and the consequent development of anguish as she hears herself speak, Linda will come to take responsibility for her own symptoms. In Linda's case, it might be expected that there would be a change in her perception attitude regarding her role in the car accident, a new understanding of her role in the loss of her marriage, and the position of dependence she demands in her relationships with her family. Linda's primitive rage can be understood both as a result of her wanting to fulfill her mother's desire and a reaction against this want. If Linda can articulate her own choices and desires, she gains the possibility of liberating herself from such identifications. She will then be able to see her parents and the others in her life as separate individuals with desires, needs, and values that are distinct from her own.

Smucker/Boos: The mechanisms of change would include an increased awareness of her cognitive/emotional/behavioral reactions to stimuli, which should lead to an enhanced ability to regulate her affects and impulses. Further, she would have to reformulate many rules, attitudes, and norms and replace hostile and submissive behavior with a more articulate, assertive expression of wishes, needs, and disappointments toward others.

Allen: Linda's affective and behavioral problems stem ultimately from family relationship patterns that reinforce them. Directly altering problematic relationships with important family-of-origin members will be the most important mechanism of change. Linda must be able to let her parents know how their behavior is affecting her and assertively request specific changes. If, however, Linda remains blaming and critical of family members or does not acknowledge her own contribution to the troublesome interactions, she will induce a "fight or flight" response. In Linda's family the consequences of her changing her behavior without regard for the effects of such change on others are almost too grave for Linda to even contemplate.

Summary of Question 15

This review ends as it started. Each of the authors has a somewhat different view of what the hoped-for mechanism of change would be.

The most common themes are insight into her behavior, affect, and thinking patterns; ability to control her impulsive behavior; being able to assert her needs and not aggress against others; adopting a problem-solving style; and learning to tolerate her emotional discomfort.

Index